PRENTICE-HALL SERIES IN WORLD RELIGIONS

Robert S. Ellwood, Jr., Editor

CHINESE
RELIGIONS
a cultural
perspective

Christian Jochim

San Jose State University, San Jose, CA

CHINESE RELIGIONS
a cultural
perspective

Prentice-Hall, Inc., Englewood Cliffs, New Jersey 07632

Library of Congress Cataloging in Publication Data

Jochim, Christian, 1948–
   Chinese religions.

   (Prentice-Hall series in world religions)
   Bibliography: p.
   Includes index.
   1. China—Religion.   I. Title.   II. Series.
   BL1802.J63   1986   299'.51   85–9511

Interior/cover design: Maureen Olsen
Manufacturing buyer: Harry P. Baisley

Printed in the United States of America

10   9   8   7   6   5   4   3   2   1

ISBN   0-13-132994-4   01

Prentice-Hall International (UK) Limited, *London*
Prentice-Hall of Australia Pty. Limited, *Sydney*
Prentice-Hall Canada Inc., *Toronto*
Prentice-Hall Hispanoamericana, S.A., *Mexico*
Prentice-Hall of India Private Limited, *New Delhi*
Prentice-Hall of Japan, Inc., *Tokyo*
Prentice-Hall of Southeast Asia Pte. Ltd., *Singapore*
Editora Prentice-Hall do Brasil, Ltda., *Rio de Janeiro*
Whitehall Books Limited, *Wellington, New Zealand*

Contents

foreword *ix*

preface *xi*

part 1

AN OVERVIEW OF CHINESE RELIGIOUS TRADITIONS

part 2

AN ANALYSIS OF CHINESE RELIGIOUS TRADITIONS

6 *practical expression in chinese religion 135*

7 *sociological expression in chinese religion 157*

Foreword

The Prentice-Hall Series in World Religions is a new set of introductions to the major religious traditions of the world, which intends to be distinctive in two ways: (1) Each book follows the same outline, allowing a high level of consistency in content and approach. (2) Each book is oriented toward viewing religious traditions as "religious cultures" in which history, ideologies, practices, and sociologies all contribute toward constructing "deep structures" that govern peoples' world view and life-style. In order to achieve this level of communication about religion, these books are not chiefly devoted to dry recitations of chronological history or systematic exposition of ideology, though they present overviews of these topics. Instead the books give considerable space to "cameo" insights into particular personalities, movements, and historical moments that encourage an understanding of the world view, life-style, and deep dynamics of religious cultures in practice as they affect real people.

Religion is an important element within nearly all cultures, and itself has all the hallmarks of a full cultural system. "Religious culture" as an integrated complex includes features ranging from ideas and organization to dress and diet. Each of these details offers some insight into the meaning of the whole as a total experience and construction of a total "reality." To look at the religious life of a particular country or tradition in this way, then, is to give proportionate attention to all aspects of its manifestation: to thought, worship, and social organization; to philosophy and folk beliefs; to liturgy and pilgrimage; to family life, dress, diet, and the role of religious specialists like monks and shamans. This series hopes to instill in the minds of readers the ability to view religion in this way.

I hope you enjoy the journeys offered by these books to the great heartlands of the human spirit.

ROBERT S. ELLWOOD, JR., editor
University of Southern California

Preface

The Chinese intellectual heritage teaches us that the only constant in our universe is change. Acknowledging that this is true, and that the history of religion in China has itself been characterized by endless change and diversity, this book nonetheless aims to identify the most basic features of religious theory, practice, and social organization in China and to exemplify them with the most representative examples that Chinese history provides. In so doing, it seeks to offer a clear and practical "map" of the territory for all those who wish to venture into the world of Chinese religions, for whatever purpose.

This map covers Confucianism, Taoism, and Chinese Buddhism but is not structured around the division of Chinese religion into these Three Teachings, as they are often called. Rather, it focuses on the interaction between religion and other aspects of Chinese culture: the family, the community, the arts, philosophy, politics, etc. This is what is meant by a "cultural perspective," and nothing could be more suitable in the Chinese case. As the Chinese themselves have long proclaimed, "The Three Teachings form one whole." For apart from religious professionals such as Buddhist monks and Taoist priests, they have practiced religion primarily at local temples that represent all three traditions or have joined spiritual groups in which the teachings of these traditions are syncretically mixed. Necessarily, then, the purpose of this book is not to tell the history of particular religions in China. Instead, it is to make sense of the diverse, complex, and sometimes confusing world of Chinese religious life as a whole.

Chinese terms in the text will be spelled, primarily, according to the modified Wade-Giles Romanization System, because this is what one generally confronts in works on traditional Chinese culture. Chinese terms will also be spelled, secondarily, according to the Pin-yin Romanization System now used in the People's Republic of China because (1) it is generally adopted in works on contemporary mainland China and in international press reports and (2) it often provides one with a closer approximation of Chinese sounds, thus serving as a supplement to the Wade-Giles system in the matter of pronunciation. The Pin-yin spelling of a term will be given only when it differs from the Wade-Giles spelling and will follow only the *first* use of the Wade-Giles spelling.

Where contemporary Chinese culture is concerned, this book places a greater emphasis on developments in Taiwan, Republic of China, than those in the mainland People's Republic of China. This is because my opportunities for observation of Chinese religious life have been in Taiwan (where I resided during 1980–1983) rather than the mainland. Indeed, I feel obliged here to express my gratitude to many there who enhanced my understanding of Chinese religions, and especially to my host organization: the Pacific Cultural Foundation. For, in part, this work was completed with Pacific Cultural Foundation subsidy.

CHRISTIAN JOCHIM

CHINESE
RELIGIONS
a cultural
perspective

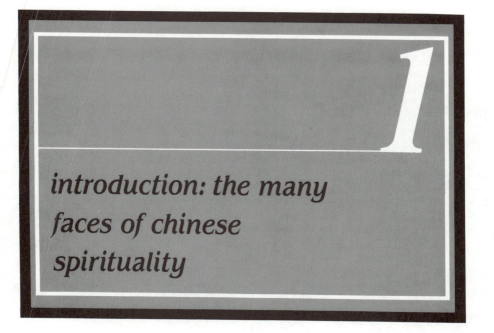

introduction: the many faces of chinese spirituality

A woman concerned with some personal matter enters a neighborhood temple to seek the god's advice. She offers incense to beseech the god's presence, picks up two cresent-shaped divination blocks from the altar and holds them together before her chest as she lets her mind focus on the question she wants to ask the god. She wears the same inward-looking, yet distant expression that one might see on the face of a religious believer anywhere. While one can thus intuit the nature of her feelings, only she and, in her view, the god know what particular matter occupies her mind. Is she concerned about a husband seeking health care, a daughter about to go overseas to study, a son entering military service, or perhaps some plan of her own? Whatever the matter, she will put it to the god in the form of a question: Will now acting on the plan lead to beneficial results? When she is convinced that the question has properly been put to the god, the divination blocks will be dropped to determine its response. Perhaps not immediately, but before too long, the blocks will indicate the agreement of the god with a particular formulation of her question, and she can then return to her ordinary state of mind to weigh the god's advice against other factors bearing on the matter at hand.[1]

---

[1] Chinese divination blocks are crescent-shaped blocks of wood that are slightly rounded on one side and, with some over-sized exceptions, usually about three inches long. A yes answer is indicated when a pair of them is dropped and one lands with the convex side up and the other with the flat side up (i.e., one "head" and one "tail"). Several yes answers in succession are frequently required to assure the god's agreement.

FIGURE 1.1. Activities in a Chinese temple courtyard. Palace of the Consort of Heaven, Lukang (Lu-gang), Taiwan.

The temple itself is nearly empty, yet it does not have the awesome silence of an empty Catholic cathedral or the austere solemnity of many a Protestant church. As the woman stands in the temple concentrating on her question, others drift in and out, offering incense and quickly bowing in reverence to the god. A few old men sit outside in the temple courtyard talking and smoking, while several young children chase one another around the stone columns on the porch. The sounds of the outside world easily penetrate the temple's interior through its large open doorways, breaking the silence within. However, there is still a feeling that one's surroundings are of another world: the smell of scented incense fills the air; sounds drift away into the temple's high interior and faintly echo back; the walls feature rich red and gold hues; intricate carvings of mythical creatures like dragons decorate the stone columns and woodwork; colorful murals depict the adventures of legendary heroes; beside the dimly lit altar stand guardian figures with faces fierce enough to drive off any unwelcome visitor; and nearly out of sight behind the altar one finds the richly decorated image of the main deity, aloofly seated like a high official or top executive forbidding easy access.

In such surroundings, one feels hints of otherworldliness but is not taken far from his or her ordinary sense of reality. But when a festival is held, such as on the god's birthday, the intensity of the sights, scents, and sounds increases tenfold. Extra tables set up near the altar become filled with colorful food offerings. The god will consume the spiritual essence and humans the actual substance, for those who give offerings will later take them home to feed family members and guests. The main deity and his spiritual subordinates are taken from the temple and paraded around the locality in large hand-held sedan chairs by men marching to the din of cymbals, drums, horns, and string upon string of firecrackers. The firecrackers and paper money burned for the god produce a pungent odor that competes with the perfumed scent of incense sticks set afire by the hundreds, all making clouds of smoke that transform an already fantastic scene into something nearly bizarre. Everyone present cannot help but sense something other than ordinary. Those most sensitive to this other dimension are likely to fall completely under its spell, becoming possessed by the god, thus giving further proof of its presence. These men and women, like shamans and spirit mediums the world over, often enter their trances shaking, then assume dancelike postures and speak in a voice that others recognize as the god's voice. Finally, they leave their state of trance, falling from exhaustion.

Of course, not all Chinese religion uses such spectacular means to direct the believer's attention toward the spiritual dimension. Were one to visit a secluded Buddhist monastery instead of a neighborhood temple, one might be drawn to the spiritual dimension by the tranquil mountain setting, the soothing effect of morning and evening chanting, and perhaps the solitude of deep meditation. Were the place a Confucian temple of the traditional state religion of the past, the spiritual dimension might be found in the solemn grandeur of its relatively unadorned exterior and the austere formality of its ceremonies. But while the setting and activities are different in each case, the function they serve for the religious believer may well be the same. But what is this function? And what is so important about it that religious activities of one kind or another have naturally become part of all human societies? These are questions that demand to be answered in any study of religion—controversial questions that can be answered in many ways. What follows is a brief digression concerning the particular perspective on religion chosen for this text. This digression should help to clarify the discussion that follows on the specific nature of Chinese religion.

RELIGION: A CULTURAL PERSPECTIVE

Whenever people enter the *sacred space* (temple, monastery, church) and *sacred time* (festival day, meditation session, ceremonial service) of a religious event, they usually experience something more than a vague sense of other-worldliness. They are bound to confront religious acts and symbols with very specific content. This means, in addition to being spiritually uplifted for a moment, they will also be exposed to certain messages about how to understand the world and act in it *all the time*. Such messages may be delivered directly through sermons, subtly through symbol-laden rituals, or even ineffably from the depths of meditation. These may be messages about the way the world was created, the nature of the true self, or simply what one should eat, wear, say, and do in daily life. This exposure, especially when it is deep and frequently repeated, leads people to regard the religious ideals thus communicated as right and true for themselves and perhaps for all humanity.

Another way of explaining this is simply to say that religion is part of *culture:* the sum of all the various influences on human behavior (beliefs, customs, knowledge, values, etc.) which are not simply biological, that is, not simply due to our genes or instinctual interactions with the natural world. Thus, becoming hungry and eating is a biological matter, whereas eating with forks and knives instead of chopsticks, for example, is a cultural one. Or, to give another example, the need for shelter is biological, whereas the knowledge about how to build a house, a tepee, an igloo, or a thatched-roof hut is cultural. Following this view, culture does not consist primarily of the concrete products of human endeavor (buildings, works of art, music, literature) but rather of the patterns of abstract knowledge and customary behavior that make their creation possible. To stress this point, the social anthropologist Clifford Geertz has described culture as a set of control mechanisms similar to what computer engineers call programs.[2] Taking the analogy further, without the "programs" culture provides, a human being would be helpless, just as unable to function as computer hardware into which no software had ever been programmed to tell it what to do.

Of course, if we want to consider all that culture entails, we must go beyond this analogy of human beings and computers. Culture does not exist to make people as blindly obedient as computers; nor is it limited in scope to passing on instructions about rudimentary tasks like building and eating. This is especially true in the case of religious culture, whose influence may lead *either* to obedience *or* disobedience toward recognized social authorities, and whose "programs" deal with life's ultimate problems: What is good and what is evil? What are the legitimate goals of life? What is the ideal way to treat other people? What is the origin and nature of the world?

This is why those seeking to distinguish religion from other dimensions of culture have frequently stressed the idea of *ultimacy.* Religion has been defined, for example, as a "belief in ultimate reality," a "state of ultimate concern," a "means of ultimate transformation," and a "set of symbolic forms and acts that relates us to the ultimate conditions of existence."[3] Here, in accordance with the idea that religious culture provides "programs" that govern world view and life style, religion is viewed as something that gives people a *context of ultimate meaning:* a system of

---

[2] Clifford Geertz, *The Interpretation of Cultures* (New York: Basic Books, Inc., Publishers, 1973), p. 44.

[3] The scholars responsible for these definitions, along with each one's most representative work in this regard, are as follows: (ultimate reality) Joachim Wach, *Sociology of Religion* (Chicago: University of Chicago Press, 1944); (ultimate concern) Paul Tillich, *Dynamics of Faith* (New York: Harper & Row, Publishers, Inc., 1957); (means of ultimate transformation) Frederick J. Streng, *Understanding Religious Life* (Belmont, Calif.: Wadsworth Publishing Co., Inc., 1976); and (relate to ultimate conditions of existence) Robert Bellah, *Beyond Belief: Essays on Religion in a Post-Traditional World* (New York: Harper & Row, Publishers, Inc., 1970).

beliefs, values, and behavioral guidelines with which they aim to understand their world and know how to act within it by reference to some spiritual dimension believed to impinge upon their world.

As we saw from the examples at the beginning of this chapter, the spiritual dimension is experienced quite differently from the ordinary world of common sense and everyday life. And within a typically religious point of view, precisely because this dimension is experienced as utterly different, it is believed to be the source of various miracles, visions, commandments, insights, and other "answers" to life's problems. Yet while religions tend to identify the spiritual dimension as the source of solutions to life's problems because of its "otherness," let us not forget how specific religions are in describing the particular nature of this dimension and the solutions that are said to emanate from it. Spirit is one; *or* it is many. It transcends the world; *or* it is found within the individual. One should withdraw from the world and spiritually perfect oneself; *or* one should stay there and work to change it.

Within Chinese culture alone there is nearly infinite religious variety, which makes the task of offering a coherent picture of Chinese religious life infinitely difficult. One way to confront this difficulty is to divide Chinese religious life into several different traditions and to describe their distinctive features. Taking this approach, one must mention at least four such traditions: Confucianism, Taoism, Buddhism, and so-called folk religion. Although this approach will familiarize the reader with certain basic themes, figures, and historical trends, it is ultimately unsatisfactory because it violates the wholeness of Chinese religion as a unified cultural system. Therefore, the expedient treatment of Chinese religion divided into four separate traditions will be followed by an analysis of it as one unified system. This latter approach will in fact anticipate the analytical treatment of Chinese religion to be undertaken in Part 2 of this book. There we will treat its theoretical expression (Chapter 5), practical expression (Chapter 6), and sociological expression (Chapter 7). What these categories mean and how they can be applied to the study of Chinese religion will be made clear later, following a general sketch of the four traditions just mentioned.

THE FOUR TRADITIONS

Of the four traditions to be described, three have the markings of organized religion: founders (real or legendary), professional leaders, institutional forms, written scriptures, liturgical traditions, etc. These have long been known in China as the Three Teachings: Confucianism, Taoism, and Buddhism. They represent what the anthropologist Robert Redfield referred to as a culture's "great tradition"; whereas the fourth tradition—Chinese folk religion—constitutes what he called the "little tradition."[4] The term *Chinese folk religion*, therefore, simply designates the unwritten religious

---

[4] Robert Redfield, *Peasant Society and Culture: An Anthropological Approach to Civilization* (Chicago: University of Chicago Press, 1956), pp. 67–104.

beliefs and practices of average people within traditional Chinese society. And since it was above all an eclectic mixture of the great tradition's Three Teachings, it can properly be discussed only after these teachings have been introduced.

Confucianism

A distinct tradition to which the label Confucianism can be applied did not exist until a time during the Former Han Dynasty (206 B.C.E.–8 C.E.) several hundred years after the life of K'ung Fu-tzu (Kong Fu-zi; "Master K'ung," 551–479 B.C.E.).[5] His name in its Latinized form, Confucius, has given the tradition its Western label. But its roots go back as far as history and legend take us into the Chinese world before Confucius. Thus, Confucius and his early followers looked back in admiration upon the exemplary figures of earliest Chinese antiquity. These included the legendary sage emperors Yao and Shun, as well as the founders of the Three Dynasties: Yü (Yu) the Great, founder of the Hsia (Xia) Dynasty (ca. 2200–1750 B.C.E.), King T'ang (Tang), founder of the Shang Dynasty (ca. 1750–1050 B.C.E.), and Kings Wen and Wu, father and son, who established the Chou (Zhou) Dynasty (ca. 1050–256 B.C.E.). And in connection with these figures, there already existed a long history of paradigmatic events, holding important moral lessons and believed to have been guided by T'ien (Tian), or "Heaven." (T'ien refers neither to a place to go after death nor to the equivalent of God as creator of the universe; instead, it indicates the deification of moral qualities that the ancient Chinese found inherent in the way the universe operates.)

Where, then, does the spiritual dimension lie for the Confucian tradition? One place it lies is in the distant past—in the golden age of antiquity. By the time the nominal "founder" of Confucianism lived, there was already belief in an ideal ancient era as a spiritual dimension against which contemporary realities could be judged. Moreover, early versions of key Confucian scriptures (to be identified in Chapter 2) were already in existence by then. These scriptures told of the deeds of early rulers and exemplified a basic Confucian principle according to which good rulers prospered while evil ones were punished. This principle, called the Mandate of Heaven (T'ien-ming), specified that a line of rulers received Heaven's support as long as they behaved virtuously but would lose it and be overthrown as soon as they did otherwise.

Despite what was already established before Confucius, who modestly called himself a transmitter rather than a creator, there is still a sense in which the true spirit of Confucianism can be traced to him. He took the reestablishment of ancient ideals as his Heavenly appointed mission and gathered a loyal group of disciples together to carry on his work. And at

---

[5] C.E. and B.C.E. stand, respectively, for "Common Era" and "Before the Common Era." They are used throughout this book in place of the more familiar A.D. and B.C., which we find too provincial for a contemporary book about a non-Western culture.

least according to the interpretation of later Confucians, he and his disciples first located the spiritual dimension *within* the human individual: the *hsin* (*xin*), or "mind-heart" (an intellectual as well as a moral "organ" represented by a Chinese character that originally designated the physical heart). This idea of an inner organ with the same moral qualities as Heaven, the moral guiding force of the universe, has given Confucianism its distinctively humanistic quality among religious traditions. For what became important for Confucians was not the worship of Heaven but the discovery of a Heavenly source of correct moral and social behavior existing within the individual. Thus, even when an explicit quest for spiritual sagehood developed among Confucians centuries later, imitating similar Taoist and Buddhist quests, Confucianism remained concerned with basic issues of moral and social life in this world. And for this Confucians rightfully owed gratitude and reverence to Master K'ung.

Yet if we wish to see Confucianism as an institution, we must turn to the Former Han era. It was during this era that a syncretic version of the Master's teachings (incorporating many elements from philosophical rivals of the early Confucians) became state orthodoxy, and his followers became the custodians of an increasingly fixed set of sacred scriptures and official ceremonies. It was the events of this era (described in detail in Chapter 2) that gave the religious dimension of the Chinese state the form it would have for nearly two thousand years. It is only from this point that one can speak of the Confucian religion, or the Literati Teaching (*ju-chiao; ru-jiao*), as the Chinese have referred to it.

Ultimately, knowledge of the Literati Teaching, demonstrated by passing state examinations on the classical scriptures, became the main avenue to Chinese government posts. And the performance of state ceremonies became an essential feature of government, for which a major branch of government—the Ministry of Rites—was established. By the time of the Ch'ing (Ching) Dynasty (1644–1911), at the end of China's imperial era, the complex of ritual sites and the calendar of annual ceremonies for which this board was responsible had grown to amazing proportions (see Chapter 6).

The Confucian quest for spiritual sagehood was also rooted in ancient traditions and also flowered in late imperial times. In fact, it first became a key aspect of Confucianism during the Sung (Song) Dynasty (960–1279), when such a major reformulation of the tradition occurred that it has been given the name Neo-Confucianism. Those involved in this reformulation of Confucianism often had a history of involvement with Buddhism or Taoism, practiced meditation, and sought spiritual enlightenment. But Confucian spiritual seekers did not leave society to become monks. They insisted on practicing sagehood-in-action, that is, on being social servants and spiritual seekers at the same time. They severely criticized Taoists and Buddhists for being escapists; and when one of them resigned from public service to become a recluse, it was usually as an act of political protest. This indicates probably the most fundamental difference between Confucianism and the other two of China's Three Teachings, to which we now turn.

Taoism

For Taoism, one locus of the spiritual dimension is also the ancient past. In contrast to Confucianism, however, it does not value the era of earliest human civilization but, instead, one which preceded even that. It imagines a state of primordial simplicity in which people existed close to nature and without the complicating problems of human moral, social, and political institutions. And just as it idealizes this "childhood" era of human evolution, it also envisions its spiritual goal as a life of childlike simplicity, using the "child" or "infant" as a symbol to represent the nature of sagehood. It can even be said that what it values most is the chaotic state that preceded all evolution, natural as well as human. This involves, of course, a positive interpretation of *chaos*. According to this interpretation, chaos is the primordial unity from which our world of complex "order" has arisen.

Compared to Confucians, then, the Taoists place more faith in nature than in humanity and, as a result, emphasize a path of sagehood quite unlike that of the politically involved and socially committed Confucian. The Taoist sage avoids political entanglements and shuns social conventions, following moral values considered to be implicit in nature and superior to anything ever invented by humanity. In accord with this, the Taoist concept of an ultimate reality in which these values are grounded is far less *anthropomorphic* ("having human form or qualities") than the Confucian Heaven. Called Tao (Dao; lit. "Way"), the Taoist ultimate is not conceived as an entity capable of favoring or punishing humanity, nor even as one that has any special relationship with humanity (as does Heaven according to Confucian theory). Showing no special concern or preference for humanity, Tao abides in all things that exist, imbuing each one with a unique manifestation of its "power" or "virtue," called Te (De). And it "rules" nature through "nonaction" (*wu-wei*), that is, without performing any acts or functions that would be characteristic of a human or superhuman "lord."

The relationship existing between Tao and each thing in existence reveals a key underlying principle of Taoism and, in fact, of Chinese religion as a whole: namely, that the universe is an organismic whole whose essential structure and energy abide in every constituent part. While, for Taoism at least, there is no essential difference in the way the ultimate (Tao) abides in human and nonhuman entities, it still places most of its emphasis on how the human individual, as microcosm, can realize its identity with the universe, as macrocosm. As a result, the microcosmic-macrocosmic relationship has been at the heart of every development in Taoism: religious or philosophical, mystical or liturgical.

Most of these ideas are contained in two seminal texts written during the latter part of the Chou Dynasty: the *Tao-te-ching* (*Dao-de-jing*, or "Scripture on Tao and Te") and *Chuang-tzu* (*Zhuang-zi*). The first is attributed to a possibly legendary figure named Lao Tzu (Lao Zi) and the second to the philosopher Chuang Tzu (fl. fourth century B.C.E. and traditionally considered to be a follower of Lao Tzu). These ideas constitute the heart of an intellectual tradition known as philosophical Taoism, which has fascinated all educated Chinese right up to modern times. They have also been part of the inspiration for various trends and movements within Chinese religion that have been categorized as religious Taoism, and which began to resemble organized religion only from the time of the Later Han Dynasty (25–220). Religious Taoism also has its roots, however, in other features of ancient Chinese culture, such as the practices of two kinds of religious figures called *wu* (shamans or spirit mediums) and *fang-shih* (ritual specialists who served as doctors and magicians). It bears the stamp of these two respective sources in what ultimately became its "mystical" and "liturgical" dimensions.

By way of clarifying these two terms, let it be said that *mystical* is used in a technical sense to refer to traditions that stress direct experience of a religious ultimate through specific psychological and/or physical techniques. *Liturgical,* on the other hand, is used to describe traditions that aim to effect their religious ends by means of outward ritual techniques. Both these dimensions were present as religious Taoism emerged during the Later Han period and the period immediately following. They coexisted within the rites that Taoism ultimately adopted for use by its village priests. And the villagers for whom the rites were used probably accepted the view that their efficacy depended just as much on a priest's mystical status as on his knowledge of rituals and sacred texts.

The mystical dimension of Taoism employed a full complement of psychological and physical techniques: hygienic, gymnastic, respiratory, meditative, sexual, and alchemical (the last being for the purpose of producing a pill of immortality). Its ultimate aim was to "nourish" certain life forces possessed by the body from birth, and its underlying principles are already known to us. In accord with the principle that childlike simplicity characterizes the desired spiritual state, Taoist adepts envisaged their quest as a matter of preserving those life forces with which they were born and which they would lose as they aged if nothing were done about it. The Taoist adept's key goal was, in fact, seen as the gestation of a new "embryo" within the adult individual so that he might, at least figuratively, be reborn as a primordial infant. A second principle underlying his quest concerned the "microcosmic-macrocosmic" nature of the relation between human individuals and the universe. In this connection, the adept sought to identify with the powers of the universe envisaged as particular Taoist deities. Success in this process of identification would engender spiritual prowess for the Taoist not only in his quest as a mystical adept but also in his possible role as village priest performing ritual services for the public.

Whether or not the liturgical dimension of Taoism depended in practice on the spiritual state of an individual Taoist priest, it surely depended on the connection made in theory between his "microcosmic" ritual performance and the "macrocosmic" universe. That is to say, the Taoist priest's ritual function was rooted in his purported ability to invoke the deities of the universe into the microcosmic realm of ritual, where their powers could be used on behalf of religious clients. In certain cases, this might have involved the efforts of several Taoist priests hired by the people of an entire village, for whom the most powerful dieties of the Taoist pantheon—the Jade Emperor and his court—would be called into service.

This group of deities was believed to rule the universe from their celestial abode in the region of the northern polestar. Their presence was, therefore, both very hard to come by and quite essential for communal rites, which typically involved invoking universal powers so as to consecrate community territory and make it safe from demons and disasters.

We see, then, that the liturgical dimension of Taoism was the one most closely involved with Chinese community or folk religion, its temples having served as the workplace of Taoist priests. More will be said of this matter when we come to Chinese folk religion.

Buddhism

One of the world's three major universal religions, along with Christianity and Islam, Buddhism was founded by Buddha Śākyamuni (ca. 560–480 B.C.E.) more than five centuries before it entered China. The universalistic tendencies of the faith were evident from the start. It was founded in northeast India as a religion opposed to distinctions of caste and class. Preaching the Dharma, the Buddhist "law" or "doctrine," it moved south into other parts of India and Southeast Asia, and north into Central Asia. From its Central Asian strongholds along the trade roots linking China with the Mediterranean world, it spread both east and west. But it was only in moving east that it ultimately found acceptance. For at the same time it was converting China, Christianity was converting the Roman Empire in the West, shortly to be followed in that part of the world by another stepchild of ancient Judaism: the Muslim faith.

Thus it was that the three major universal religions divided up much of the civilized world, and it was in China that Buddhism would find its largest if not most hospitable home. Buddhism did not end up replacing the religions already existing there, as, for example, Christianity had in converting the Roman Empire. Due partly to its own nature and partly to the nature of native Chinese religious attitudes, it was destined to become only one dimension of the overall framework of Chinese religion. And while China's indigenous world view would ultimately prove to be compatible with Buddhism, resistance to it never disappeared among China's staunch traditionalists.

For Buddhism, the spiritual dimension lies outside of time and history. Its quest to discover this dimension begins with inward meditation and ends with world transcendence. It paints the ordinary world in tones of false desire, illusory pleasure, and universal suffering; and it contends that ordinary life is played out within the great drama of *karma* and reincarnation: an endless chain of births, grievous lives, and deaths to which we remain bound by our ignorance. *Karma,* the seeds sewn by one's past actions, carries one through endless rebirths in this world of pain and misery—endless, that is, so long as one remains attached in ignorance to the habitual human desire for the ordinary world and its illusory pleasures. However, it further preaches, if one cultivates the wisdom and forbearance to extinguish the flame of desire, one can then gain salvation—the peaceful bliss of *nirvāna*.

Such doctrines were in many ways inimical to indigenous Chinese cultural norms. The rejection of life's pleasures, the metaphysical explanations of the illusory nature of the ordinary world, and the pursuit of salvation through asceticism were all rather foreign to Chinese soil. In fact, it was not so much doctrine as Buddhist ascetic practice that was hard to accept, for it required that one leave family life, shave one's head, and, observing sexual abstinence, have no progeny. To abandon one's duty to serve one's parents and, moreover, deny oneself the honor and pleasure of having descendants to honor and serve you in turn involved a radical departure from Chinese norms. But all this was the *sine qua non* of Buddhist monastic life. For Buddhism set itself up as an estate apart from the ordinary world, a refuge for those who dared to take seriously the quest for release from worldly miseries.

However, because of its new environment, Buddhism came to have a deeper involvement with ordinary social life in China than it ever had in India. In this regard, the key thing to realize is that Chinese Buddhism has been for the most part of the Mahāyāna type, not the Hinayāna. The former, the so-called Greater Vehicle of Buddhism, had already reinterpreted the world-rejecting quest for transcendence that characterized the earlier Lesser Vehicle (Hinayāna, or less disparagingly, Theravāda, the "Way of the Elders"). In contrast to the Hinayāna interpretation of spiritual quest as a matter of severing oneself from ordinary life and its concerns, the various Mahāyāna schools advocated the transformation of one's relation with the world and attitude toward life. Holding forth the dual virtues of wisdom and compassion, Mahāyānists stressed that one must rise above worldly ills and pleasures (wisdom), yet at the same time remain involved in the world to the extent necessary for also bringing others to salvation (compassion).

Further developing the "this-worldly" thrust of Mahāyāna Buddhism, China produced two uniquely East Asian forms of the religion: Pure Land and Ch'an (Chan; Zen in Japanese). The first of these was especially important for Buddhist laypeople, and the second for monks and nuns. Pure Land Buddhism gave laypeople an appropriately simplified way to gain salvation: calling upon the name of the Buddha Amitābha (an important Mahāyāna Buddha distinct from the historical Buddha Śākyamuni) in order to be reborn in his heavenly Pure Land. By contrast, Ch'an practice was identical, at least in spirit, to the method of ancient Theravāda Buddhism: an individual quest for spiritual insight through meditation. In fact, Ch'an claimed to represent a special "transmission of mind" (dating back to Śākyamuni himself) that was passed on from master to master outside the Buddhist scriptural and ritual traditions.

Nevertheless, Ch'an Buddhism developed a rather practical and "this-worldly" character. Its members engaged in gardening, not only begging for the food they ate but practicing various cultural pursuits (painting, sculpturing, making ceramics, writing poetry, etc.) as supplements to meditation. They looked *within the world* (especially the natural world) for inspiration, and they discovered that ordinary life situations could engender profound spiritual insights. Thus, it was not the wandering mendicant of

Indian religion that became the standard ideal for monks in China. Instead, it was a sedentary figure engaged in ordinary tasks—cooking, eating, digging, planting, or chopping wood—that became popular in Chinese monastic lore.

Further signs of the transformation experienced by Buddhism in China will emerge in the chapters that follow. Now, as we are about to turn to a discussion of Chinese folk religion, it is more apropos to mention a few key elements of Buddhist influence on native Chinese religious life.

Buddhas and Bodhisattvas ("enlightened beings") joined the ranks of divine beings for whom people made offerings, constructed images, and held birthday celebrations. Certain ones, such as the Buddha A-mi-t'o-fo (to use the Chinese name of Amitābha) and the Bodhisattva Kuan-yin (Guan-yin; Sanskrit: Avalokiteśvara), in fact assumed positions of supreme importance within Chinese folk religion. Likewise, the heavens and hells described in Buddhist scriptures greatly enriched Chinese conceptions of the hereafter, and the performance of Buddhist rituals became an accepted part of the ceremonies usually held for deceased Chinese. Even more important than this, however, was the fact that the originally Indian doctrine of *karma* and reincarnation added a new dimension to the way Chinese thought about ancestors and the afterlife.

The doctrine of *karma* and reincarnation was part of an Indian view of the universe as being infinite in both time and space. Within this view, not only were individual souls reborn countless times but so were the universe and its constituent "worlds" continually being destroyed and re-created. And while such a conception of the universe tended to dwarf the problems of particular individuals—and even dynasties—it still allowed for a complete accounting of the good and bad deeds of every existent being. These two factors taken together contributed to the view within Chinese religion that the universe extends well beyond our immediate world and is populated by a multiplicity of spiritual beings concerned above all with rewarding good deeds and punishing evil ones. Buddhism could take credit for some but certainly not all the essential features of this view, as we shall now see.

Chinese Folk Religion

Within the world view of Chinese folk religion, the spiritual dimension is another "world" coexisting alongside the world of immediate experience. And the striking thing about this other world is its similarity to this one. The *system of moral rewards and punishment* just mentioned permeates both alike; the beings who inhabit the other world are frequently quite *human in origin and temperament;* and its structure and mode of operation even mirror those of this world (with special reference to traditional China) in their *bureaucratic nature.*

Thus, the otherworldly realms inspired in part by Buddhism were operated by spiritual beings resembling earthly rulers and officials. Buddhist hells, for example, came to resemble those courts where justice was meted out here on earth, while Buddhas and Bodhisattvas were assumed

FIGURE 1.2. Ch'eng Huang image in his temple, Taipei (Tai-bei), Taiwan.

to have places alongside native deities in those celestial bureaus from which the universe was governed. Moreover, their concern with human fate was shared by the various deities of native origin. Beginning at the lowest level of authority, Tsao Chün (Zao Jun), the Lord of the Stove, watched over family members throughout the year and annually reported on their behavior to the Jade Emperor in Heaven. At the next level, T'u-ti Kung (Tu-di Gong), the Earth God, was responsible for the well-being of small local areas: neighborhoods, farm fields, mountainsides, etc. Above him was Ch'eng Huang (Cheng Huang), God of the City Wall and Moat, whose area of jurisdiction usually corresponded to that of the secular Prefect or District Magistrate. While there was nothing quite as specific corresponding to the national government, except for the gods of the official state cult itself, there were deities of nationwide significance. Confucius and Lao Tzu had been deified, as had many heroes of later periods. One such hero was Kuan Kung (Guan Gong), a loyal and brave general of the famous Three Kingdoms Period (which followed the Later Han Dynasty) who was ultimately incorporated into the state cult. Finally, of course, there were celestial Buddhas and Bodhisattvas, the Jade Emperor, and other deities of universal significance.

Although not so clearly arranged in a hierarchy as those just mentioned, there were other spiritual beings for at least as many aspects of life in the world as there are bureaus in any bureaucracy. A variety of earthly values that included wealth, loyalty, and happiness were represented by divinities. Aspects of nature, such as mountains and rivers, were revered for their spiritual powers. And actors, barbers, blacksmiths, carpenters, jewelers, papermakers, tea merchants, and even scholars were among the occupations that had patron deities.

Moreover, in addition to the fact that many of these gods were once historical figures, we must add that many Chinese thought there were spiritual beings among people still living in the world. The emperor and his officials had sacred status in the eyes of the populace. Certain Buddhist monks' spiritual accomplishments were considered to be so great that they were called living Buddhas. And Taoist recluses who had achieved their goal were considered to be Immortals—beings who could either remain invisible to ordinary human eyes or manifest themselves in mortal form to teach the virtuous and punish the wicked. The existence of such divine, or at least semidivine, beings within the world view of Chinese folk religion leads us to speak not simply of a "divine" but rather of a "divine-human" bureaucracy as one of its key features. And the thin line between human and divine that this implies can be seen even more clearly if we look at still another category of spiritual beings—ancestors.

Reverence for ancestors has been part of life for virtually all Chinese, regardless of their involvement with other forms of religion or their belief in gods and ghosts. Moreover, the set of concerns and obligations felt toward the souls of the deceased in China has provided the context within which other kinds of spiritual beings—namely, gods and ghosts—have been born. For reasons to be explained more fully later, whenever someone led an unusual life and/or met an unusual death, the concerns and obligations felt toward the person's soul were intensified, for the soul was believed to be in a restive, volatile state. Normally, ritual precautions were taken to pacify the soul, and extraordinary occurrences were thereby avoided. But sometimes a soul persisted in manifesting itself in ways that led to an unavoidable conclusion: A god or ghost had come into existence. Benevolent behavior meant a new god must exist, whereas malevolence revealed a ghost's intrusion into the world.

In practice, gods were worshiped, ancestors revered, and ghosts as well as demons propitiated. Yet the methods were very nearly the same in each case. Respect was a necessary ingredient in all dealings with spiritual beings, whether friends or enemies. Such dealings, therefore, usually began with a polite offering of incense and food, although when the aim was propitiation, the offering was made only to satiate and thereby pacify a malevolent being. But when the aim was worship or reverence, the offering was made out of hospitality and accompanied by ritual genuflections meant to show sincere devotion. Thus the simple rite of *pai-pai* (*bai-bai*)—a show of hospitality involving incense, food offerings, kneeling, and bowing— was the central ceremony of Chinese folk religion. It could be seen taking place on all ritual occasions, in front of every family and temple altar.

Now, while a simple *pai-pai* for one's ancestors or a god of the popular pantheon could be performed by anyone, there were many activities within

Chinese folk religion for which the services of religious professionals were needed. These religious professionals were first and foremost Taoist priests and Buddhist monks and nuns, but they also included a variety of others: astrologers, geomancers, spirit mediums, and so forth. They were generally employed on the basis of individual or family needs at a given time, not on the basis of permanent religious affiliation.

Before concluding, however, it must be added that sectarian groups demanding affiliation have existed in China, not only providing an outlet for religious needs transcending family and community but also offering an alternative to the three distinct great traditions. Syncretically combining elements from Confucianism, Taoism, and Buddhism, sectarian groups offered their members simplified rituals and scriptures as well as the opportunity to meet for congregational-style worship.

With the exception of these sects, there was no division of Chinese religion into mutually exclusive groups at the popular level. Only at the elite level of the Three Teachings was mutual exclusivity a major factor. That is to say, it was usually only a Confucian official, Taoist priest, or Buddhist monk or nun who was identifiably Confucian, Taoist, or Buddhist. And to understand Chinese religion as a whole, we should not focus on distinctions between the three elite traditions, nor between them and so-called Chinese folk religion. It is best to focus instead on the interrelations between these different dimensions of Chinese religious life as existing in the kind of elite-folk continuum depicted in Figure 1.3.

"ELITE" GREAT TRADITION	(1) The Three Teachings (Confucianism, Taoism, and Buddhism) are relatively distinct traditions. (2) Each of the Three Teachings has its own classical canon. (3) A relatively fixed system of thought and practice, based on a canon, provides a clear measure of orthodoxy. (4) The essential goals – sagehood, immortality, enlightenment – transcend ordinary life. (5) The means toward these goals are carefully specified, formalized, and controlled.	"FOLK" LITTLE TRADITION	(1) The Three Teachings are eclectically mixed together. (2) Nonwritten, oral traditions and semiclassical scriptures dominate. (3) Changing patterns of thought and practice exist, with no clear measure of orthodoxy. (4) Essential goals – health, happiness, long life, wealth, rank – are closely related to ordinary life. (5) The means toward these goals are fluid (defined by concrete needs), informal (defined by personal situations and resources), and often uncontrolled (ecstatic, gruesome, or even violent).

FORMS OF INTERACTION BETWEEN "ELITE" AND "FOLK"

(1) Great tradition officials, priests, and monks often come from among the common people.

(2) Great tradition canons are sources for popular rituals and semiclassical scriptures.

(3) Ancestral beliefs and practices are common to both levels.

(4) Folk deities often come from among sages who have attained great – tradition goals.

(5) Religious professionals of the Three Teachings perform key services within folk religion.

FIGURE 1.3. The elite-folk continuum in Chinese religion.

One reason we speak of an elite-folk continuum in Chinese religion is that traditional Chinese society was itself a continuum. Individuals from peasant families, although less frequently than their gentry counterparts, became Confucian scholar-officials through public examinations; and it was even more likely for them to enter the Buddhist or Taoist clergy. Moreover, with regard to certain basic moral and religious beliefs, such as those connected with Chinese ancestral practices, there was no significant gap between upper and lower classes or between great and little traditions.

Beyond this, there was an inevitable interaction between the two levels of society and tradition. Lower borrowed from upper because of the latter's prestige, and upper accommodated to lower out of the tendency of organized religions to adapt to their surrounding cultural environment. The prestige of China's great traditions lay, above all, in their classical scriptures and formal, time-honored rituals. Imitation of these by the little tradition, in predictably popularized forms, should not surprise us. Conversely, because all three great traditions had some role in serving popular religious needs, their beliefs and practices gradually succumbed to popular influence. This factor loomed largest in the case of Taoism, whose normal spheres of operation were the community temple and the common household. Thus, from its beginnings, Taoism has had difficulty maintaining canonical standards of orthodoxy.[6]

While these factors already yield sufficient reason to treat Chinese religion as a unified system, there is a further and more outstanding reason: the "unity of the Three Teachings" so often referred to by the Chinese themselves. As we shall see, moreover, this unity was rooted in beliefs and practices that were the spiritual common property of everyone—beliefs and practices whose origins predated Confucianism, Taoism, and Buddhism as organized religions in China.

THE THREE FORMS OF RELIGIOUS EXPRESSION IN CHINA

According to sociologist of religion Joachim Wach, the various ways in which religious believers relate to the spiritual dimension can all be grouped under three "forms of religious expression": theoretical, practical, and sociological.[7] In the first group, one finds doctrines, creeds, commandments, myths, and other statements of religious theory. In the second, one has ritual, prayer, meditation, charity, evangelism, and other religious activities. In the third, one sees churches, sects, monastic groups, primitive tribes, theocratic states, and even the *ad hoc* "congregation" that gathers at religious festivals like the one described earlier in this chapter. A thorough analysis of the religious system of China on the basis of Wach's

[6] See Rolf A. Stein, "Religious Taoism and Popular Religion from the Second to Seventh Centuries," in *Facets of Taoism: Essays in Chinese Religion,* Holmes Welch and Anna Seidel, eds. (New Haven: Yale University Press, 1979), pp. 53–81.

[7] Wach, pp. 17–34.

three categories will occupy three chapters in Part 2 of this book. Now we will present only a few of the most essential features of theory, practice, and social organization within this system.

Theoretical Expression

Looking at Chinese conceptions of the spiritual dimension, one is struck by a peculiar fact: While the universe is believed to be populated by a multiplicity of divine beings, in the final analysis, these beings are not responsible for the way the universe operates. This role is instead given to something—whether called Tao, Heaven, or something else—to which all these divine beings are, like human beings, subordinate. And this entity itself, unlike all beings, human or divine, is actually beyond name and form. However, to avoid confusing this conception of ultimate spiritual reality with the Western God, let it also be said that it is conceived of as the ultimate power or principle *within* the natural course of things, not as a Lord and Creator of the universe who is even greater than nature itself.

Of course, this almost naturalistic conception of divinity is not for popular consumption. Even when average people are aware of the divine so conceived, it does not play a large role in their religious practices. There is, however, a form of spiritual power that Chinese philosophers and peasants alike have seen as permeating the natural world and, also, as having very concrete uses in human society. Called *ch'i* (*qi*), this "spiritual" power is, in fact, a kind of raw physical energy ("matter-energy" or "material force," to cite two translations).[8] Our discussion of basic Chinese religious theory would be incomplete without a description of this power and its relationship to the all-important concepts of *yin, yang,* and the five elemental phases.

Ch'i is the life force of the human body and the natural world, of both the microcosm and the macrocosm. It is "raw" because, unlike a god or an ancestor, it must be located, captured, controlled, and sometimes cultivated before it can be used. Views about how to garner and maintain this life force underlie Chinese meditation, medical practice, martial arts, and *feng-shui*. *Feng-shui* (lit. "wind and water") designates a method that the Chinese traditionally have used in deciding where to build all government offices, palaces, temples, homes, graves, and so forth.

Of course, thorough knowledge of such views has been possessed mainly by religious, medical, and other relevant professionals in China, not by everyone there. For example, while most Chinese have some idea about what the ideal geomantic site for a home or grave should look like, only a *feng-shui* master can actually select one, for he knows the principles

---

[8] "Matter-energy" is the translation of Joseph Needham, *Science and Civilization in China*, Vol. 2: *History of Scientific Thought* (Cambridge: Cambridge University Press, 1956); and "material force" is that of W. T. Chan, *A Sourcebook in Chinese Philosophy* (Princeton: Princeton University Press, 1963). Both translations are offered with advanced philosophical concerns (especially of Neo-Confucianism) in mind. When considering *ch'i* in relation to popular religion, martial arts, geomancy, etc., as is the case here, it is preferable to speak of a physical/spiritual "life force."

underlying such a choice. To understand adequately the theoretical dimension of Chinese religion, we too must know something about these principles, or at least the most basic ones: *yin, yang,* and *wu-hsing* (*wu-xing:* the "five elemental phases").

In discussions of *feng-shui, ch'i* is often translated as "cosmic breath(s)." This accords with its use in modern Chinese word combinations referring to breath (in the human body) and the weather (in nature). The cosmic breaths thus indicated are of two kinds: *yin* and *yang.* To return to the example of the *feng-shui* master, he seeks to find a place where these two kinds of breath are in balance by locating the respective forms of the White Tiger (*yin*) and the Azure Dragon (*yang*) in the contour of the land to the west and east of the potential building site.

In addition to their connection with location, *yin* and *yang* have many other associations, for every natural phenomenon is conditioned by their interactions. Most fundamentally, the *yin* aspect of a phenomenon is passive, quiescent, settled, condensed, at rest, or even decaying; the *yang* aspect is active, incipient, unstable, transforming, developing, or even bursting forth. *Yin*'s original association was with shade, and *yang*'s with sunshine. Thus, all the terms listed in connection with the latter are like the effects of the sun's life-stimulating rays, while those listed in connection with the former are akin to the results of being shielded from these rays.

Similarly, those periods of nature's great annual cycle when the sun's influence is growing (spring and summer) are *yang,* while those during which its influence is declining (autumn and winter) are *yin.* On the basis of this kind of reasoning, one can perhaps understand why the following list of other basic associations has evolved:

> *Yin:* Earth, moon, dark, cold, female, wet, night
> *Yang:* Heaven, sun, light, heat, male, dry, day

Now, in the case of the four seasons and the four directions, further elaborations were made on the basis of the *five elemental phases,* which were termed *wood, fire, earth, metal,* and *water.* Sometimes translated as the "five elements," the five terms actually refer to cyclical phases, which we may still call elemental in the sense that they are fundamental in all natural processes. Their relationship to *yin* and *yang,* the seasonal cycle, and the four directions is shown in Figure 1.4.

The cycle shown in Figure 1.4 begins with *yang* in its growing phase, with spring, the east (where the sun rises), and wood (symbolizing potential activity). Then it moves toward *yang* at its extreme, with summer, the south, and fire (actual activity). Next it moves to *yin*'s phase of growth, with autumn, the west, and metal (potential rest). And, finally, it settles into *yin*'s extreme, with winter, the north, and water (actual rest). As for the elemental phase called earth, it is commonly connected with the center and the whole year in order to make the scheme complete.[9]

---

[9] Some of the usage in this discussion is from Manfred Porkert, *The Theoretical Foundations of Chinese Medicine* (Cambridge, Mass.: M.I.T. Press, 1978), Chap. 1, in which there is a detailed discussion of *yin, yang,* and the "five evolutive phases" (in Porkert's translation).

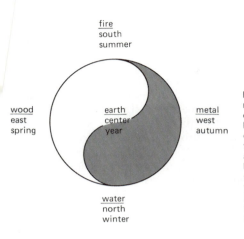

fire
south
summer

wood
east
spring

earth
center
year

metal
west
autumn

water
north
winter

FIGURE 1.4. Chinese diagram of the Supreme Ulti-mate. The Supreme Ultimate (T'ai-chi; Tai-ji) is the origin of *yin* and *yang,* which in turn constitute the basis of all natural processes. The light half of the diagram represents *yang,* the dark half *yin.* Also, for our special purposes, the five elemental phases and their associated directions and seasons have been added. The five phases follow their standard sequence: *wood, fire, earth, metal, water* (*earth* al-ways having third place in numerical order, despite its association with the whole year). And the sea-sonal cycle moves *clockwise* around the diagram—spring to summer, summer to autumn, and so forth.

The features of the annual cycle are thereby neatly defined, and various seasonal religious festivals occur in accord with them. Moreover, similar features are ascribed to all lesser units of time (months, weeks, days, etc.), determining what kinds of acts can be performed at a given time—journeys, marriages, funerals, construction, and so forth.

Practical Expression

We have just presented a set of assumptions about spiritual power in the universe that were accepted by the great majority of Chinese in premodern times. However, these assumptions were never formed into creeds to be catechistically disseminated to all believers, as were, for example, the teachings of those "religions of the book" (Judaism, Christianity, and Islam) that so dominated Western history. In the case of Chinese religion, then, one must concede the relative insignificance of belief in scripture as an end in itself. Certainly China has had sacred scriptures—especially Confucian scriptures—that were passed on for centuries as a kind of bible, without questioning their essential validity. And China has also produced religious groups—notably Pure Land Buddhism—in which simple faith, not acts, was advocated as the best means to salvation. However, because of the assumptions about spiritual power just described, the emphasis has been on practice over belief, methods over doctrine, and acts over faith.

This emphasis was expressed in both the great and little traditions in China, although somewhat differently in each case. For the great traditions, the ultimate truth was beyond words, and the way to realize that truth was to experience it directly for oneself. For the little tradition, with its concern for ordinary life and concrete goals, belief in a distinct and carefully defined creed was an unnecessary luxury. All that was necessary was the performance of good deeds and the avoidance of evil ones, the offering of appropriate items at appropriate times to gods, ghosts, and ancestors, and the observance of various other customary acts. This, rather than belief in an orthodox creed, would improve one's future and bring one's family the three great benefits of life in the present world: good fortune (*fu*), high status (*lu*), and longevity (*shou*).

Many of the religious acts that traditional Chinese considered to be obligatory in their search for such benefits were performed at their home altar or neighborhood temple, without the aid of religious professionals. The worship of ancestors, observance of basic seasonal rituals, and appeals to temple gods for good fortune did not require a religious professional's services. Of course, they were dependent upon the professionals of the three traditions for a variety of other services. Yet, as we have seen, they normally sought these services on the basis of concrete need rather than religious affiliation. And this is perhaps another result of the importance of practice over doctrine within the world of Chinese religion.

Nevertheless, it was largely due to the power of the written word—with the word of Confucius, Lao Tzu, or Buddha naturally carrying extra weight—that the professionals of China's Three Teachings could serve as mediators between average people and the powerful divinities who controlled their fate. Afterall, within the context of traditional Chinese society, middlemen were needed in the performance of numerous secular activities, from business deals to marriages. Their services inevitably required the skill of literacy, if not the actual preparation of written documents, in dealing with secular superiors. The mediating role of religious professionals was found, for example, in the state sacrifices offered to cosmic and agricultural deities by Confucian officials. It was found in the transfer of funds—in the form of spirit money—to the otherworldly account of someone's ancestor by a Taoist priest. And it was found in the transfer of merit—accrued by Buddhist monks reciting scriptures—from celestial Buddhas to the soul of an ancestor in order to expedite his or her rebirth into a better life.

It must be pointed out, however, that many religious professionals of China's Three Teachings had higher aspirations. They were more interested in individual spiritual cultivation than in making a living by performing ritual services. In fact, the emphasis on practice over doctrine in Chinese religion is perhaps best illustrated by a message delivered, in one way or another, by spiritual seekers in each of the Three Teachings: Trust experience over belief, and action over words. This was the message of the Confucian theory of the unity of knowledge and action, the Taoist quest to penetrate an ineffable ultimate, and the Buddhist commitment to meditation as the ultimate means of transformation. Moreover, as we are about to see, the emphasis on practice over doctrine also exerted its influence on the forms of sociological organization that obtained within Chinese religious life.

Sociological Expression

Although China has seen the existence of most forms of religious organization during its long history, it did not give a central role to those forms that are most obviously religious to Westerners: sects, churches, and denominations. The idea of belonging exclusively to one particular spiritual group never became widespread in China. As we have seen, people there generally went to a certain temple or religious professional according to situational need rather than permanent religious affiliation. A key reason for this lay in the emphasis on practice over doctrine. A second and stronger reason, however, lay in the fact that the family ever remained the *fundamental social unit* within Chinese religion, keeping other forms of religious organization from evolving to a high degree.

The traditional Chinese family was sure to have a home altar with ancestral tablets and, more often than not, images of gods and Buddhas; and it was there that the most basic religious obligations were carried out. Going to temples, participating in seasonal festivals, and employing the services of religious professionals were optional matters. Moreover, almost all religious units existing outside the family praised to some degree familial virtues, such as *hsiao* (*xiao*), which means "filial respect" toward parents and other elders. Stressing these virtues most strongly was the Confucian tradition, which argued that all of society, including government, could be run according to familial principles. Thus, the ideal Confucian state was headed by the emperor as Son of Heaven, who sought to preserve a father-son relationship with his officials, who were in turn expected to act like the father and mother of all the people.

This points to the importance of the state as another basic unit of religious organization in China and, therefore, to yet a third reason for the relatively minor role played there by specifically religious groups, such as churches, sects, and denominations. Now the primary sociological form of Confucianism was the state itself: a hierarchically ordered organization of noblemen and officials structured according to familial principles. And, as a religious organization, the Confucian state was not willing to allow the unrestricted development of any other form of religious organization, whether indigenous or foreign, whether of monastic elites or common folk.

While this inhibited the growth of nonfamilial forms of religion in China, it did not entirely prevent them. Just as Confucianism identified itself with life within the family, Buddhism defined itself as a faith primarily for those willing to abandon family life, remain celebate, and devote themselves to a way of life apart from the ordinary world, that is, to a monastic way of life. Taoism also came to imitate this way of life, but Buddhism must be given credit for its establishment in China. Of course, while the monastic way of life was a viable alternative only for those prepared to sever all attachments to the pleasures of ordinary family life, those unprepared to take this step could also find something in Buddhism, either as individual laypersons or as members of organized lay sects.

It was Buddhists of the latter type—those organized into sects—who had the most significant impact on the sociological dimension of Chinese religion. For, along with certain popular Taoist movements of the Later Han Dynasty (see Chapter 2), they became a model for the numerous religious lay groups that have emerged during the course of Chinese history. Regardless of their particular roots, they were commonly syncretic in nature, borrowing what they considered to be religiously relevant from all

China's Three Teachings. And they encouraged definitive, though not necessarily exclusive, religious affiliation and tried to distinguish themselves from society at large—sometimes radically. When they became too radically different, or achieved a degree of popularity that alarmed the Confucian state, they were likely to be suppressed as "heterodox teachings." There was thus a long history of conflict between the state and such groups, a number of which were involved in political rebellion from time to time.

Most Chinese stayed clear of involvement in rebellious sects, carefully observed their familial religious obligations, and, when occasion arose, participated in the system of local temples and popular festivals that made up China's little tradition. This system, if indeed it can be called a system, was characterized above all by its diffuseness. It had no sociological forms distinct from those of Chinese society as such (e.g., family, local community, and state). It had no central authority, distinct priesthood, well-defined creed, orthodox rituals, or rules of membership. What ultimately made it work was not the power and prestige of religious authority issuing down from above. Instead, it was the force of religious need surging up from below—ever in accord with the hope of attaining good fortune, high status, and longevity.

Whether we look at religious theory, practice, or social organization in China, we see expressions of a particular cultural environment at the same time that we see the expression—in its three characteristic forms—of a perpetual human concern with religious ultimacy. This means that two things can be observed in studying religion in China, or anywhere for that matter. On the one hand, one can see its various beliefs, practices, and social forms as yielding clues to the distinctive nature of a specific culture. On the other hand, one can see these beliefs, practices, and social forms as data relevant for understanding religion as a universal dimension of all human culture. Beginning with the next chapter, we will not again directly approach religion in its universal dimension. You are therefore encouraged to ponder on your own how the specific facts presented in the following chapters compare with your own experience of religion and contribute to your overall understanding of what it is.

history: the pattern of china's religious past

Many of the essential features of religion in China covered by Chapter 1 were present there from the beginning of recorded history. Nevertheless, internal developments and foreign influences, such as Buddhism, affected the evolution of religious thought in China. At the same time, popular cults continually grew up there around new divinities: gods from India and Tibet, heroes who died in national struggles and were deified, and figures from local cults whose reputation spread from one place to another within China. However, all this involved an *enrichment* of the basic structure of Chinese religion, not its eradication. Reverence for nature's divinity and human ancestors never lost its central role; the system of beliefs emphasizing human social relations and life in the present world was challenged but not fundamentally altered by Buddhist doctrines proclaiming the painful and illusory nature of existence; and Chinese religion developed along nonsectarian lines, producing one overarching pattern of diffuse but interrelated beliefs rather than several distinct "churches" with mutually incongruous dogmas.

Chinese religious history is often divided into three periods.[1] The

---

[1] See, for example, C. K. Yang, *Religion in Chinese Society* (Berkeley: University of California Press, 1970), p. 106; and Whalen Lai, "Toward a Periodization of Chinese Religions," *Bulletin: Society for the Study of Chinese Religions,* 8 (1980), pp. 79–90.

first of these saw the development of the classical tradition: the state rituals, canonical scriptures, exemplary sages, and moral ideals that would later become one more or less unified system to which the label Confucianism has been attached. This era began in prehistory and ended during the Han Dynasty (206 B.C.E.–220 C.E.), when Confucianism emerged as the state orthodoxy and official custodian of the classical tradition.

The second period dated from the end of the Han, when both Confucian ideology and the state supporting it fell out of grace; and it extended up to the Sung Dynasty (960–1279), when the classical tradition reasserted itself. However, the diminished influence of Confucian ideology was only a superficial feature of the second period, for at a deeper level this period was characterized by the emergence of organized religions independent of the state, both indigenous (Taoism) and foreign (Buddhism). These religions advocated that the ultimate solution to life's problems lay in rejecting the ordinary state of human existence for an infinitely superior state of liberation.

With the coming of the third period, which stretched from the Sung Dynasty to the twentieth century, the quest for world-transcending liberation gave way to the more humanistic and "this-worldly" thrust of a classical renaissance. On the one hand, the Confucian approach reemerged but gave more room within itself to individual spiritual cultivation; while, on the other hand, organized Buddhist and Taoist groups suffered a loss of formal elite-level influence, although their impact at the level of Chinese folk religion continued to grow. The next four sections of this chapter (and the time chart in Figure 2.1) cover the major trends of these three periods and, finally, the fate of religion in modern China.

DEVELOPMENT OF THE CLASSICAL TRADITION

According to China's own classical histories, the origins of Chinese civilization can be traced back to certain sages who lived during the third millenium B.C.E., even before the beginning of the Three Dynasties mentioned in Chapter 1. These figures represent the origin of various aspects of culture that archeologists in fact consider as having existed in China during that time—agriculture, cooking, houses, boats, carriages, and even writing— though no scholar today would associate their invention with any particular individuals. Nevertheless, because of the importance attached to these ancient sages by Chinese up into the twentieth century, they must at least be mentioned.

China's ancient sages have long been grouped as the Three Sovereigns and Five Emperors (although differing lists of both groups exist).[2] The

---

[2] This particular list of the Sovereigns and Emperors is based on a second-century stone relief mural as reproduced and discussed in K. C. Chang, *Art, Myth, and Ritual: The Path to Political Authority in Ancient China* (Cambridge, Mass.: Harvard University Press, 1983), pp. 2–3.

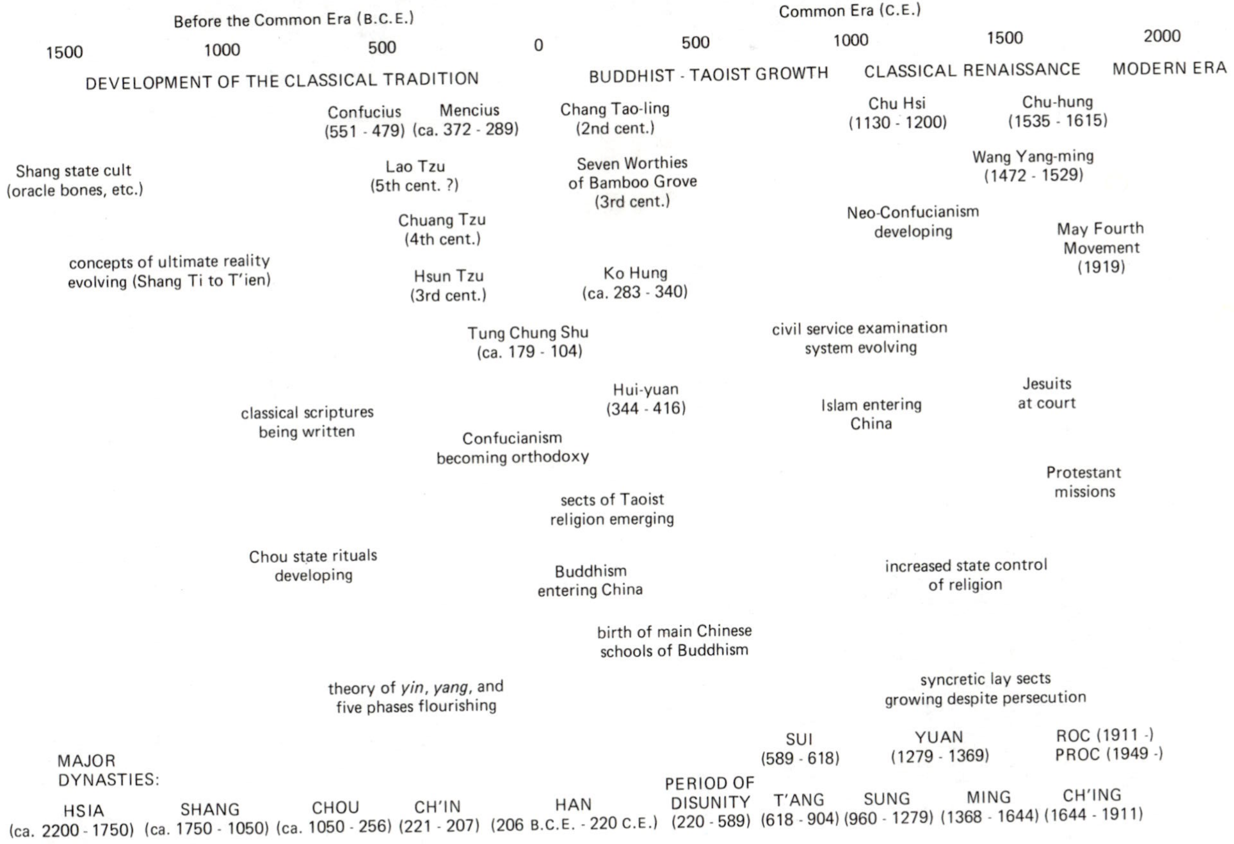

Before the Common Era (B.C.E.)

Common Era (C.E.)

| 1500 | 1000 | 500 | 0 | 500 | 1000 | 1500 | 2000 |

DEVELOPMENT OF THE CLASSICAL TRADITION

BUDDHIST - TAOIST GROWTH

CLASSICAL RENAISSANCE

MODERN ERA

Confucius (551 - 479)

Mencius (ca. 372 - 289)

Lao Tzu (5th cent. ?)

Chuang Tzu (4th cent.)

Hsun Tzu (3rd cent.)

Chang Tao-ling (2nd cent.)

Seven Worthies of Bamboo Grove (3rd cent.)

Ko Hung (ca. 283 - 340)

Chu Hsi (1130 - 1200)

Wang Yang-ming (1472 - 1529)

Chu-hung (1535 - 1615)

May Fourth Movement (1919)

Neo-Confucianism developing

Shang state cult (oracle bones, etc.)

concepts of ultimate reality evolving (Shang Ti to T'ien)

Tung Chung Shu (ca. 179 - 104)

Confucianism becoming orthodoxy

civil service examination system evolving

Islam entering China

Jesuits at court

Protestant missions

classical scriptures being written

Hui-yuan (344 - 416)

sects of Taoist religion emerging

increased state control of religion

Chou state rituals developing

Buddhism entering China

birth of main Chinese schools of Buddhism

syncretic lay sects growing despite persecution

theory of yin, yang, and five phases flourishing

MAJOR DYNASTIES:

HSIA (ca. 2200 - 1750)

SHANG (ca. 1750 - 1050)

CHOU (ca. 1050 - 256)

CH'IN (221 - 207)

HAN (206 B.C.E. - 220 C.E.)

PERIOD OF DISUNITY (220 - 589)

SUI (589 - 618)

T'ANG (618 - 904)

SUNG (960 - 1279)

YUAN (1279 - 1369)

MING (1368 - 1644)

CH'ING (1644 - 1911)

ROC (1911 -)
PROC (1949 -)

FIGURE 2.1. Time chart of Chinese religious history.

Three Sovereigns have been listed as Fu Hsi (Fu Xi: "Tamer of Oxen," who domesticated animals and instituted family life), Chu Jung (Zhu Rong: "Invoker of Heat," who invented fire), and Shen Nung (Shen Nong: "Divine Farmer," who invented agriculture). The list of Five Emperors is usually headed by the most important of all the ancient sages, Huang Ti (Huang Di: "Yellow Emperor"), who is the symbolic, and for some the actual, ancestor of all Chinese people. He and members of his court have been credited with inventing writing, music, medical practice, carriages, boats, wooden houses, cooking pots, bronze mirrors, silk cloth, and certain weapons as well as strategies of warfare. While the second and third of the Five Emperors are of minor significance, the final two, usually paired as Yao and Shun, have been adulated by Chinese from at least the time of Confucius. Yao and Shun have been adulated not so much for making inventions as for establishing a model of good government for all later Chinese rulers.

Oddly enough, among their virtues was the impartiality that each showed in passing over his own blood children in choosing a successor to his throne. Yao did so in selecting Shun from among the common people, as did Shun in naming his royal heir, who was Yü the Great. This was praiseworthy because, after Yao and Shun, Chinese rulers handed over the throne only to blood relatives. Yü the Great was thus the last Chinese ruler chosen solely on the grounds of his merit, which was great indeed. He saved China from the Great Flood by engineering a drainage system that prevented the floodwaters from inundating the land and, in the process, created China's major rivers. And since he passed the throne on to his own son, he is also remembered as the first emperor of China's first dynasty, the Hsia (ca. 2200–1750 B.C.E.). From available archeological evidence, however, there is little reason to believe this "dynasty" was anything more than China's first experiment with a family line from one clan exercising authority over neighboring clans and their combined territory (in a small area of North China).

Nevertheless, the archeology of ancient China has shown ever more clearly that the roots of China's classical tradition reach far back into prehistory. We know, for example, that the neolithic cultures that preceded the Hsia Dynasty had a hierarchical form of social organization based in part on agnatic lineages, that is, clans emphasizing lineal male kinship ties. We also know that, *religiously,* this was reflected in ancestor worship, complex burial customs, and rituals of communication with another world through animal bone divination and the aid of animal spirits.[3]

Development of these and other features of Chinese civilization continued during the Hsia era, but they are best known to us in the highly developed form attained under the next dynasty—the Shang. Not only is the Shang more fully described in China's classical histories, but writings from the period itself exist on certain oracle bones and bronze vessels that have been unearthed by archeologists.

---

[3] K. C. Chang, *Art, Myth, and Ritual,* p. 116; and by the same author, *The Archeology of Ancient China,* 3rd ed. (New Haven: Yale University Press, 1977), p. 110.

Shang Period (ca. 1750–1050 B.C.E.)

The Shang state was a theocracy led by rulers who held power due in part to their special relationship with divine beings. Like sacred kings in other ancient civilizations, they were held uniquely responsible for assuring that their people received the blessings and not the wrath of natural forces: wind, rain, rivers, etc. The Shang religion had gods representing these forces of nature as well as a supreme deity called Shang Ti (Shang Di: "highest divine ruler"). But in this religion, the leading role was played by deceased royal ancestors. It is believed that they were either directly in control of the Shang state's destiny or responsible for it indirectly as the Shang kings' link to their high god, Shang Ti.

When a Shang king wanted to communicate with his ancestors, oracle bone divination was used. Great care was taken in obtaining and preparing the bones, which were shoulder blades of cattle and water buffalo or plastral shells of turtles. After preparation, which involved cleaning and polishing as well as chiseling rows of hollows into each bone's surface, a rite was performed in which a hot implement was applied to the hollows to produce cracks.[4] The cracks were subsequently interpreted by court diviners. But no one today knows exactly how this was done, despite the fact that inquiries, and more rarely answers, were inscribed on many bones in the oracle bone script that constitutes China's earliest written language. What we do know, thanks to the many thousands of oracle bone inscriptions still in existence, are the kinds of questions asked by Shang kings: Should we attack state such-and-such? Should we go on a journey or a hunt in area so-and-so? Should a ritual sacrifice of such-and-such kind be performed on behalf of god or ancestor so-and-so? While these examples are not in the precise form of Shang divinatory questions, they do suggest the range of interest of these questions. And such questions did, in fact, extend into every area of the Shang state's affairs and its royalty's personal life.[5]

Perhaps even more important than the nature of divinatory questions put to Shang spiritual beings is the nature of the Shang spirit world itself. Its highest diety (Shang Ti) and the ancestral and natural spirits subordinate to him have already been mentioned. But it has not yet been sufficiently stressed how, even at this early time, all these spiritual beings were conceived to exist within a kind of divine political hierarchy. Sarah Allan has made this point in trying to suggest similarities between the Shang state cult and modern Chinese folk religion, as follows:

> Shang kings, like modern Chinese, believed that spirits were organized in a political and hierarchical fashion like living men. . . . The Shang spirit world was headed by

---

[4] The best source on methods of preparation and cracking oracle bones is David N. Keightley, *Sources of Shang History: The Oracle-Bone Inscriptions of Bronze Age China* (Berkeley: University of California Press, 1978).

[5] Thirty-nine different kinds of state activities that were inquired into through oracle bone divination are listed in David N. Keightley, "The Late Shang State: When, Where, and What?" in *The Origins of Chinese Civilization*, ed. Keightley (Berkeley: University of California Press, 1983), pp. 528–529.

Shang Ti, the "Highest Lord," who ruled the other world just as the Shang king ruled the earthly one, and is analogous to Yü Huang Ta Ti [Yu Huang Da Di, the Jade Emperor] in modern folk religion. He "ordered" (*ling*) the natural phenomenon [sic]—rain, thunder, clouds, and his "messenger" (*shih* [*shi*]) the wind—and he "sent down" (*chiang* [*jiang*]) drought to either bring favor or to curse the world below. The bones even refer to a court of "five ministers" (*wu ch'en* [chen]), perhaps . . . natural phenomenon [sic] or possibly the four directions and the center or earth spirit. Identical terminology is used when the earthly king orders his officers and ministers.[6]

As far as proper *relations* between the earthly king and the spirit world were concerned, such relations were maintained by frequent ritual offerings of cereals, horses, cattle, sheep, pigs, dogs, chickens and sometimes human sacrificial victims.

In addition to the record of ritual sacrifices provided by oracle bone inscriptions, bronze vessels surviving from the Shang period reveal not only a high level of artistic achievement but also yield further evidence of Shang willingness to devote large amounts of human and material resources to religious matters. For Shang ritual bronzes are religious in much of their identifiable decor, they seem to have been designed for ceremonial use, and they were perhaps even horded by the Shang and other states or clans as potent symbols of religio-political power.[7]

Early (Western) Chou Period (ca. 1050–770 B.C.E.)

In the middle of the eleventh century B.C.E. the Shang state was conquered by a western neighbor that had existed for some time in the shadow of Shang influence. The ruling family of this state then took its turn as the third and longest of ancient China's Three Dynasties: the Chou (Zhou, ca. 1050–256 B.C.E.). Because the Chou period is so long, it will be divided, according to precedent, into three periods. These periods reflect not only the declining fortunes of Chou but also the evolution of ancient Chinese thought and religious practice.

During its early period, called Western Chou because the capital was still in its original western location, near modern Sian (Xi-an), it established sovereignty over an unprecedentedly large area of northern and central China. It did so by establishing the most nearly feudal system ever adopted in China, one that was, moreover, founded on essentially religious principles. As a theocracy, the Chou Dynasty's greatest innovation was the idea of the Mandate of Heaven. While *Heaven* was replacing *Shang Ti* as the key term for an ultimate power in the universe, Chou rulers propogated the theory that this power had withdrawn its mandate from the previous

---

[6] Sarah Allan, "Shang Foundations of Modern Chinese Folk Religion," in *Legend, Lore, and Religion: Essays in Honor of Wolfram Eberhard on His Seventieth Birthday,* eds. Sarah Allan and Alvin Cohen (San Francisco: Chinese Materials Center, 1979), pp. 8–9.

[7] K. C. Chang, *Art, Myth, and Ritual* in fact presents the bold theory that political power in ancient China was integrally related with the possession of bronzes and other ceremonial objects.

dynasty and given it to the Chou rulers. This meant that, although the worship of royal ancestors remained a key part of state religion, the idea that the reigning king was a regent of Heaven (called the Son of Heaven) became the main justification for his sacred status. It also meant that the various nature deities subordinate to Shang Ti now had to share their prominence with the agricultural and territorial deities of the royal Chou domain and its feudatory states.

Honored as the progenitor of the Chou clan was an agricultural deity called Lord Millet (Hou Chi; Hou Ji), millet being chief among the staple crops in ancient North China. He was worshiped along with a deity of the earth or territory, thus establishing state worship of the Spirits of Land and Grain (She Chi; She Ji) that lasted into the twentieth century. According to later accounts, every territory that was established by the Chou king as a fiefdom maintained an earth-mound altar for the worship of these deities. This altar contained an actual lump of earth from the royal Chou altar, symbolizing both its own sovereignty and that of the Chou over it. From that time on, a key feature of Chinese capitals remained the presence of an ancestral temple south of the royal palace on the east, along with an outdoor altar for the worship of agricultural deities opposite it on the west.

Turning from official to popular religion, sources about early Chou culture yield our first glance at Chinese folk practices. The "Customs of the States" portion of the *Book of Odes* (one among five of China's ancient sacred scriptures) contains, or at least is based upon, folk songs about village life in early Chou China. Although it does not contain enough information to paint a detailed picture of ancient Chinese folk religion, what it does contain makes clear that the concerns of the early Chou peasant were often the same as those of his lord: the sacred earth, the family ancestors, and the ritual sharing of the earth's bounty with one's departed ancestors. Consider the following ode:

> *They sow the many sorts of grain,*
> *The seeds that hold moist life.*
> *How the blade shoots up,*
> *How sleek the grown plant;*
> *Very sleek, the young grain!*
> *Band on band, the weeders ply their task.*
> *Now they reap, all in due order;*
> *Close-packed are their stalks—*
> *Myriads, many myriads and millions,*
> *To make wine, to make sweet liquor,*
> *As offering to ancestor and ancestress,*
> *For fulfilment of all the rites.*
> *"When sweet the fragrance of offering,*
> *Glory shall come to the fatherland.*
> *When pungent the scent,*

> *The blessed elders are at rest."*
> *Not only here is it like this,*
> *Not only now is it so.*
> *From long ago it has been thus.* [8]

Also by the time of early Chou, rulers and populace alike had come to hold an interest in discovering their fate through divination. For the common people this probably involved using mediums to contact gods or departed ancestors, as in more recent Chinese religion. While there is no direct evidence of this for the early Chou period, there are several strongly suggestive facts: (1) Both Shang and Chou rulers employed human intermediaries in their efforts to communicate with spiritual beings; (2) ancient Chinese bronze and ceramic vessels display animal figures in a way that suggests these animals were spirit guides who assisted human mediums in otherworldly journeys, as in shamanism; (3) the ancient Chinese were obviously open to the idea of spirits entering humans, as it was a standard part of ancestral sacrifices to have a young descendant of the ancestor serve as a living receptacle for the ancestral spirit; and (4) early written sources refer to mediums called *wu* (usually translated "shamans") in contexts that indicate their major role in religious life. [9]

The most important source on ancient Chinese shamanism, the "Nine Songs" section of the *Elegies of Ch'u* (*Ch'u-tz'u; Chu-ci*), despite its late Chou date, deserves now to be quoted within the discussion of this topic. Each of the songs records a shamanistic seance in a love-poem-like portrait of the alluring performances of male and female shamans. Each shaman invokes a deity of the opposite sex and tells of the spiritual travels made in going out to welcome the deity or, later, wandering heartsick after it has departed for another realm. In the second of the "Nine Songs" the deity is a celestial male (The Lord Within the Clouds), and the shaman female; while in the third song the deity is an aquatic female (the Lady of the River Hsiang [Xiang]), and the shaman male. Here is the second song:

---

[8] Arthur Waley, trans., *The Book of Songs* (New York: Grove Press, 1960), p. 162; reprinted by permission of Grove Press, Inc. For the reader's information, some scholars have tried imaginatively to reconstruct the nature of ancient Chinese peasant life on the basis of these odes. The best known of these scholars is the French sociologist Marcel Granet. In English, see his work *The Religion of the Chinese People*, trans., Maurice Freedman (New York: Harper & Row, Publishers, Inc., 1977).

[9] The word *shaman* was borrowed from the Tunguz language of Central Asia, the home of *shamans*, narrowly defined as religious specialists of small-scale premodern societies who are considered to be uniquely capable of contacting the other world by means of spirit (out of body) travel. So defined, *shamans* are often distinguished from *mediums:* religious figures who receive messages from and/or are possessed by otherworldly spirits but never engage in spirit travel. In the case of Chinese religion, however, this distinction is not operable. Chinese *wu* and their various counterparts are hybrid shaman-mediums, mediumistic practices probably having developed in China under the influence of classical Central Asian shamanism. On shamanism in ancient China, see K. C. Chang, *Art, Myth, and Ritual*, Chap. 3 ("Shamanism and Politics"); and Arthur Waley, *The Nine Songs: A Study of Shamanism in Ancient China* (San Francisco: City Lights Books, 1973).

FIGURE 2.2. This spirit medium in trance represents a shamanistic aspect of Chinese religion that has existed since ancient times. Palace of the Consort of Heaven, Lukang, Taiwan.

We have bathed in orchid water and washed our hair with perfumes,
And dressed ourselves like flowers in embroidered clothing.
The god has halted, swaying above us,
Shining with a persistent radiance.
He is going to rest in the House of Life [shamanistic temple].
His brightness is like that of the sun and moon.
He yokes to his dragon car the steeds of god:
Now he flies off to wander round the sky.
The god had just descended in bright majesty,
When off in a whirl he soared again, far into the clouds,
He looks down on Chi-chou [Ji-zhou] and the lands beyond it;
There is no place in the world that he does not pass over.
I think of my lord with a heavy sigh,
And sad thoughts trouble my heart very sorely.

And some excerpts from the third song are as follows:

I look for my queen, but she comes not yet;
Of whom do I think as I play my reed-pipes?
North I go, drawn by flying dragons,
Bending my course to the Tung-t'ing [Dung-ting] lake. . . .

> *And over the great River waft my spirit:*
> *Waft, but my spirit does not reach her;*
> *And the maiden many a sigh heaves for me:*
> *While down my cheeks the teardrops in streams are falling,*
> *As with grieving heart I yearn for my lady.*[10]

While such shamanistic practices had become widespread by the end of Chou, they were not without their critics. The Confucian literati who wrote or edited so many of the records we have of Chou history refer to the *wu* shaman-mediums in distaste, and in the Han period they succeeded in prohibiting the *wu* as a hereditary class from holding government posts.

However, this did not mean that they, or their predecessors at the early Chou court, were opposed to divination as such. One of the Confucian scriptures, the *Book of Changes* (*Yi-ching; Yi-jing*), is a divinatory text whose roots go back to at least the early Chou. In fact, the form of divination connected with it was probably a part of Chou culture before the overthrow of the Shang Dynasty, for this event led to the replacement of Shang oracle bone divination by the *Book of Changes* method. This method is based on the manipulation of stalks from the milfoil plant (*millefolium,* the "thousand-leaved" plant), held sacred for its prolific fertility.

The momentous transformation in ancient Chinese culture that the *Book of Changes* represents was not, however, merely that from one kind of divination to another. It was a transformation, on the one hand, from viewing the universe as controlled by anthropomorphic deities like those of the Shang state religion to viewing it as having a regular pattern of impersonal processes. On the other hand, it was a transformation from naively assuming a relationship of interdependence between humanity and nature to feeling a need to define the character of this (now problematical) relationship. We see this transformation above all in the difference between the two sections into which the *Book of Changes* is itself divided, one containing actual "answers" to divinatory questions and another consisting of general philosophical writings. The first is very old and written in a cryptic ancient style of Chinese. The second, with its "ten wings" of commentary supposedly written by Confucius, contains a late Chou exposition of *yin-yang,* five phases cosmology that has had unparalleled influence in Chinese intellectual history.

Compared with Shang Dynasty divination ideology, this cosmological theory is much depersonalized. That is, it does not explain events by reference to personified natural powers (gods of wind, rain, etc.) or angry ancestors but, instead, by reference to a code of impersonal symbols representing the pattern of cosmic change. Yet still serving a divinatory function, it offers this code as a means for deciphering the pattern of change as it affects human affairs. The code is a binary one, its "plus" being represented by a solid (*yang*) line, and its "minus" by a broken (*yin*) one. Combining

---

[10] David Hawkes, trans., *Ch'u Tz'u: The Songs of the South* (Oxford: Clarendon Press, 1959), pp. 35–36; reprinted by permission of David Hawkes.

them to form all possible sets of three, the famous Eight Trigrams can be produced, as follows:

```
—    ..    ..    ..    —    —    —    ..
—    ..    ..    —    ..    —    ..    —
—    ..    —    ..    ..    ..    —    —
```

When the Eight Trigrams are themselves placed one atop another, so as to produce the Sixty-four Hexagrams, one is said to have a code expressing all the various cycles and subcycles of cosmic change. There is a passage in the divinatory section of the *Book of Changes* for each of the sixty-four hexagram-related cosmic possibilities, which actually run into the thousands when one considers the further mutations in hexagram formation that divination may yield. And various passages in the philosophical section of the book explain how all human affairs and cosmic events are related to one another and governed by the cycles of *yin* and *yang*.

However, from this single example, one should not conclude that the Chinese emphasized nature exclusively and failed to produce sacred histories like those that evolved elsewhere in the world—the oral mythologies of preliterate peoples, the written legends about heroes like the ancient Greek gods, or the scriptural revelations concerning God's role in history, such as one finds in the Bible. In fact, with the exception of the *Book of Changes*, each of the texts destined to have a place among China's classical Five Scriptures were in one way or another sacred histories. Two of them were specifically historical in nature: the *Book of History* (Shu-ching; Shu-jing) and the *Spring and Autumn Annals* (Ch'un-ch'iu; Chun-qiu). Together these cover events from before the Three Dynasties down to the time of Confucius. The remaining two texts are not strictly historical but they nevertheless record early Chou precedents that had for later Chinese an importance akin to that of the Bible in the West. One is the previously mentioned *Book of Odes*, with its uniquely poetic look at Chou life. The other is the *Book(s) of Ritual* (Li-ching; Li-jing), which describes and comments upon ritual as well as other aspects of religious and social behavior. The latter actually consists of three books: *Etiquette and Ritual* (Yi-li), *Chou Rituals* (Chou-li; Zhou-li), and *Ritual Records* (Li-chi; Li-ji), which often present a more ideal than real picture of early Chou behavior.

When carefully scrutinized, all these scriptures present not a static picture of ancient Chinese society but rather a society undergoing radical changes in belief and practice. Chronologically, the mid-Chou era to which we now move was the turning point in this drama of transition.

Mid-Chou (Spring and Autumn) Period (ca. 770–450 B.C.E.)

This era takes its name from the *Spring and Autumn Annals,* which is supplemented by a commentary of even greater historical value: the *Commentary of Tso* (Tso-chuan; Zuo-zhuan). The latter work helps us document the evolution of concepts that were just as important for Chinese social thought as *yin* and *yang* were for Chinese cosmological thinking. This will be demonstrated by looking closely at two of these concepts: *li* ("ritual") and *chün-tzu* (*jun-zi:* "gentleman").

Like similar practices elsewhere in the ancient world, Shang Dynasty religious sacrifices clearly reflected a *do ut des* ("I give so Thou may give") attitude in that they were made in hope of receiving specific benefits from the spiritual world. This same fact is also indicated by the etymology of the ancient Chinese character for *li*. Its left-hand element signifies contact with the spiritual world, and its right-hand element depicts food offerings. But by the Spring and Autumn period this was no longer its only or even primary meaning. Throughout the *Commentary of Tso*, it meant mostly other things: an aristocratic code of protocol, a criterion of social status, and sometimes even an ethical concept.[11] In the *Analects* of Confucius, who lived near the end of this period, *li* had become so ethicized that proper observance of the code of *li* was heralded as a key feature of the behavior of the morally perfect "gentleman," the *chün-tzu*.

Turning to the term *chün-tzu* itself, during the Spring and Autumn period it underwent a change in meaning similar to that undergone by the English word *gentleman*, which originally meant a person of noble birth but now usually means a person of proper moral character. In the most reliable source for the early Chou, the *Book of Odes*, *chün-tzu* always denoted superior social status: "lord," "sovereign," "nobleman," "officer," "husband," and so forth. With few exceptions, this is also true of the *Commentary of Tso*. But of sixty-eight passages in the *Analects* where it is used, only three perhaps have this meaning. In the rest it stands for Confucius' ethical ideal: the true Moral Gentleman.[12] Whether or not Confucius was uniquely responsible for this change is hard to say, and perhaps irrelevant, for it was but one sign of the intellectual revolution occurring in his day.

During the Spring and Autumn period, China entered the Iron Age, with the consequence that warfare and agriculture were revolutionized. This further broadened the scope of interstate rivalry and social mobility that were undermining the Chou feudal system. More important for China's religious history, the breakdown of this system was producing a social group that was ultimately responsible for the intellectual transformation that was taking place. Members of this group were identified by the word *shih* (*shi*), meaning at first something like "knight" and ultimately something more like "scholar." With no guarantee of livelihood through noble privilege, *shih* went forth to serve the rulers of surviving kingdoms with their personal skills: military, administrative, divinatory, philosophical, and so forth. From among them would come nearly all the major thinkers of ancient China, beginning with Confucius; and their criticism of old values often

---

[11] Statistics on the usage of the term *li* in various ancient sources are reported in Noah Edward Fehl, *Rites and Propriety in Literature and Life* (Hong Kong: The Chinese University Press, 1971), p. 141.

[12] On the exact nature of Confucius' ideal, see Chap. 5. On the specific topic of changes in meaning of the term *chün-tzu*, see Cho-yun Hsu, *Ancient China in Transition: An Analysis of Social Mobility, 722–222 B.C.* (Stanford: Stanford University Press, 1971), pp. 158–174.

went far deeper than the Master's redefinition of *ritual* and *gentleman*. This act of our drama was played out mostly during the period following Spring and Autumn, to which we now turn.

Late Chou (Warring States) Period (ca. 450–221 B.C.E.)

This era is called the Warring States period because China was then divided into numerous kingdoms competing to replace the royal house of Chou as it became progressively weaker. And the chaos of the period was ideological as well as military, for the ancient Chinese world view was disintegrating and countless thinkers were engaged in answering anew the question: What is the true Way? The Chinese have called this the time of the Hundred Schools of philosophy, as thinkers of every sort journeyed from kingdom to kingdom seeking a sympathetic audience or a ruler who would put their ideas into practice. In addition to the Confucians, there were the Taoists, the Mo-ists, the Legalists, and the Yin-Yang Cosmologists. The Mo-ists were religious utilitarians who argued that Heaven wants us to practice universal love and to distribute social goods more evenly. The Legalists were also utilitarians, but pragmatists rather than idealists, and authoritarians rather than populists, who therefore advocated the expedient use of rewards and punishments in an effort to mold a well-ordered society from what they considered to be self-seeking and potentially disobedient subjects. The Yin-Yang Cosmologists' theories about *yin, yang,* and the five phases explained how human society could best relate to the world of nature for mutual advantage. Since of all these, the Confucians and Taoists were most important for the course of later Chinese religious history, let us briefly discuss their state of development at this time. (The Legalists will also receive special attention, but only after we reach the time of the Ch'in Dynasty [221–207 B.C.E.], which founded itself on Legalist principles.)

During the Warring States period, the most illustrious follower of Master K'ung (Confucius) was Master Meng (Mencius, ca. 372–289 B.C.E.), the Second Sage of Confucianism. The spirit of this period is captured in the text bearing his name, which depicts him traveling from kingdom to kingdom preaching that the "golden age" has ended and that all kinds of false doctrines have arisen to confuse the people. This is a view Confucians would preach again and again throughout the course of later Chinese history. In one passage, when asked to explain why he is "so fond of disputation," he gives an eloquent justification of his mission. Beginning with a quotation about Wen and Wu, he takes us through the time of Confucius and to the sad state of affairs during his own era, as follows:

"I am not fond of disputation," answered Mencius, "I have no alternative. . . . The *Book of History* says,

> *Lofty indeed were the plans of King Wen!*
> *Great indeed were the achievements of King Wu!*
> *Bless us and enlighten us, your descendants,*
> *So that we may act correctly and not fall into error.*

"When the world declined and the Way fell into obscurity, heresies and violence again arose. There were instances of regicides and parricides. Confucius was apprehensive and composed the *Spring and Autumn Annals*. . . . No sage kings have appeared since then. Feudal lords do as they please; people with no official position are uninhibited in the expression of their views, and the words of Yang Chu [member of an egoist branch of Taoism] and Mo Ti [founder of Mo-ism] fill the empire. . . . Therefore I am apprehensive. I wish to safeguard the way of the former sages against the onslaughts of Yang and Mo and to banish excessive views. Then advocates of heresies will not be able to rise" (*Mencius* 3B:9).[13]

Even more than Confucius himself, Mencius thus felt that the true Way of the ancient sages was in danger of extinction.

At the same time, in his efforts opposing Yang, Mo, and other "heretics," Mencius succeeded out of necessity in doing far more than Confucius to define and defend the Literati Teaching. This was true not only of Mencius but in fact of the whole generation of Warring State period Confucians, including Hsun Tzu (Xun Zi, third century B.C.E.) and the authors of such early Confucian classics as the *Great Learning* (*Ta-hsueh; Da-xue*) and *Doctrine of the Mean* (*Chung-yung; Zhong-yong*).[14] In debating psychological and metaphysical issues that would have seemed foreign to Confucius, these thinkers grounded the Master's moral ideas in a new vision of the human individual's place in the universe. Whatever their differences on lesser issues, they all agreed that the individual had a unique relation to Heaven, source of the wisdom necessary to lead society. They also agreed that leadership consisted not so much in using force and legal measures as in setting a moral example and facilitating education in the "rituals" (*li*) of proper behavior.

Thus stressing the uniqueness of human moral qualities, and valuing distinctive features of human culture such as ritual, early Confucians were clearly at odds with their Taoist counterparts. As Chapter 1 has already made clear, early Taoist texts saw the obstruction rather than the fulfillment of human potential in just those human social conventions that Confucians held sacred. With great implications for Chinese religious history, early Taoists saw the human being as an individual who could, in fulfilling his or her potential, transcend the bounds of established social conventions: moral, political, ritual, or otherwise. The birth of this Taoist vision, so creative, challenging, and individualistic, was no doubt related to experiences with trance states. These states evolved from shamanistic practices like those described earlier, although the precise nature and extent of the relationship is a hotly debated issue.[15] The main evidence of a strong relationship lies in certain passages from *Chuang-tzu*. Perhaps the most

---

[13] D. C. Lau, trans., *Mencius* (Baltimore: Penguin Books, 1970), pp. 113–115; copyright © D. C. Lau, 1970; reprinted by permission of Penguin Books Ltd.

[14] These two works were preserved, initially, as chapters of the *Ritual Records* and, finally, as two of the Four Books (along with Confucius' *Analects* and *Mencius*). The Four Books were brought together and made famous much later in Chinese history, as we will see in discussing Neo-Confucianism later in this chapter.

[15] See the review article N. J. Giradot, "Part of the Way: Four Studies on Taoism," *History of Religions*, 11:3 (1972), pp. 319–337.

interesting of these is a description of the "fasting of the heart" that is
staged with Confucius teaching meditation to his favorite disciple, Yen
Hui (Yan Hui):

"I venture to inquire about the fasting of the heart" [said Yen Hui]. [Confucius replied]
"Unify your attention. Rather than listen with the ear, listen with the heart. Rather than
listen with the heart, listen with the energies [ch'i]. Listening stops at the ear, the
heart at what tallies with the thought. As for 'energy,' it is the tenuous which waits to
be roused by other things. Only the Way accumulates the tenuous. The attenuating is
the fasting of the heart.". . .

> *"Look up to the easer of our toils.*
> *In the empty room the brightness glows.*
> *The blessed, the auspicious, stills the stilled.*
> *The about to be does not stay still.*

This I call 'going at a gallup while you sit.' If the channels inward through eyes and
ears are cleared, and you expel knowledge from the heart, the ghostly and daemonic
will come to dwell in you, not to mention all that is human!"[16]

However uncertain we are about what may have inspired a passage like
this, we can be sure that this and similar passages themselves helped to
inspire the growth of a meditative tradition within later Taoist religion
and that this tradition was further inspired by exposure to Indian mystical
practices brought to China by Buddhism. But before this tale can be told,
we must tell the story of China's unification under the Ch'in and Han
dynasties, with all its implications for Chinese religious history.

Ch'in Period (221–207 B.C.E.)

The Ch'in Dynasty marked the beginning of China's imperial history, for
it eliminated the Chou system of feudal kingdoms and placed China under
direct central rule. Although this dynasty and its Legalist ideology were
often despised by later Confucian scholars, elements of its imperial system
were adopted by all subsequent dynasties. In fact, Legalism already had
strong historical as well as ideological links to both Taoist and Confucian
thinkers. Two of its early (fourth century B.C.E.) contributors, Shen Pu-
hai (Shen Bu-hai) and Shen Tao (Shen Dao) can with equally good reason
be listed among proto-Taoist thinkers. Moreover, its culminating theorist,
Han Fei Tzu (Han Fei Zi, third century B.C.E.), and its leading practitioner,
Li Ssu (Li Si), Ch'in prime minister until his death in 208 B.C.E., were
both students of Hsun Tzu, the outstanding Confucian of their time.

As for the ideological links between Legalism and the other two
schools, they are balanced, if not outweighed, by major differences. For
example, in accord with their ethics of following nature, the Taoists' ruler-

---

[16] A. C. Graham, trans., *Chuang-tzu: The Seven Inner Chapters and Other Writings from the Book
Chuang-tzu* (London: Allen and Unwin, 1981), pp. 68–69.

ship ideal was that of a sage who could rule magically "without action" (*wu-wei*), just as nature "rules" itself under the imperceptible influence of Tao. Such an ideal was easily accommodated to Legalist authoritarianism, especially since the early Taoist-*cum*-Legalist Shen Tao had already offered an almost satirical version of this ideal. According to Shen Tao, a ruler has the right and ability to rule on the basis of his "position" or "situation" (*shih; shi*) as the ruler. In the hands of Han Fei Tzu, this authoritarian "might makes right" conception of rulership came to full fruition, but without even abandoning the Taoist spiritual dimension. Thus, the ideal ruler was said to put in motion a system of administrative and penal statutes ("laws") that can run by itself, while he remains aloofly above it "as divine as Heaven and Earth." At the same time, the ruler is supposed to maintain firm personal control over the "two handles" of government: reward and punishment. He thereby keeps his subordinates in a state of simultaneous gratitude and fear while maintaining his own position as the magical center from which all power flows. This is necessary because, according to Han Fei Tzu's view of humans as basically self-seeking, one's subordinates will respond only to strict discipline.

Ironically, Han Fei Tzu did not live to fulfill his opportunity to serve as an advisor to the state of Ch'in. Having gone there to do so just over a decade before Ch'in completed its unification of China, he was imprisoned and forced to commit suicide by his fellow student Li Ssu. For Li Ssu contended that, as a former advisor to another state, Han Fei Tzu would never be loyal to Ch'in. Li Ssu thus remained the main advisor of the Ch'in ruler who finally subjugated and unified all the "warring states" and founded the Ch'in Empire. This ruler made Li Ssu his first prime minister and gave himself a title reflecting Han Fei Tzu's rulership ideal: Ch'in Shih Huang-ti (Chin Shi Huang-di), "the inaugural *huang-ti* of the Ch'in Dynasty." Although *huang-ti* has become the standard Chinese term for "emperor," prior to the Ch'in Dynasty, *huang* and *ti* were both terms used in referring to royal ancestors and divine beings, not living rulers. Now the first Ch'in ruler lived up to this title in both its dimensions— political (Legalist) and spiritual (Taoist). For better or worse, all of China had to yield to his authoritarian will *to standardize* measures, administrative districts, monetary usage, the size of carts, and the Chinese writing system as well as *to construct* grandiose landmarks of imperial power like the Great Wall. On the spiritual side, he associated himself with and worshiped a new array of imperial deities, such as the Supreme One (T'ai-yi; Tai-yi) and the Five Lords (Wu Ti; Wu Di), and he sought the help of numerous occult specialists (*fang-shih*) in a personal quest for immortality. In both regards, he set a pattern to follow for the emperors of the dynasty that would shortly replace the Ch'in.

Han Period (206 B.C.E.–220 C.E.)

Although the Han Dynasty attempted to define itself in opposition to the harsh and unpopular Ch'in, its ultimate accomplishment was the creation of a new religious cosmology around an imperial system of Ch'in origins.

It made a strong appeal to ideals associated with the "golden age" of early Chou, but its actual institutions more closely resembled those of the recent and hated Ch'in. Nevertheless, as the Confucian school came to have enough power to make Han institutions conform with Chou ideals, certain changes did occur. The gods worshiped by Ch'in and early Han emperors were ultimately replaced by Heaven as the main object of imperial worship. Occult specialists and the quest for immortality were replaced at court by Confucian officials and their more sober rituals.

The Confucian system that became dominant during this period was, however, much more obviously "religious" than the teachings of Confucius, who himself became an object of worship within a new Confucian temple cult. The new religious cosmology that developed simultaneously with this cult grounded imperial sovereignty in something quite different from the Legalist appeal to temporal power and humanly created laws. This cosmology featured the triad of Heaven, Earth, and Humanity, with the emperor as Humanity's unique agent. And it presented the entire cosmos as a moral realm, a *moral universe* within which all events had some humanly significant meaning, whether as portents of prosperity or omens of disaster. (The details of this religious cosmology will be given in a special section on Han Confucianism later in this chapter; now certain other trends in Han religion related to this cosmology command our attention.)

Not only Confucianism but all Han thought was influenced by the new religious cosmology. This new cosmology, which included the theory of *yin, yang,* and the five elemental phases, might appropriately be called the era's new "science." Divination during the Han period accommodated itself to this "scientific" theory. The *Book of Changes* completed its evolution as both a cosmological and divinatory text during this period. In addition, a kind of diviner's board, which also stressed the *yin-yang* cosmology, came into use at this time. The board itself was square, representing Earth (*yin*), and a disk that could be rotated on top of it was circular, representing Heaven (*yang*). Both the board and the disk had several bands of Chinese characters connected with cosmic cycles and spatial orientations. In several cases, the center of the circular disk featured the seven stars of the constellation Ursa Major (the Big Dipper), the closest thing in traditional Chinese religion to a "center of the cosmos." The circular disk was rotated over the square board for the purpose of "comprehending the appointed seasons of heaven and apportioning good and evil fortune" (to quote a Han period source).[17]

Chinese interest in the hereafter continued during the Han, which is in fact the earliest period for which we have considerable information about the purpose of burial rites, the destiny of souls, and related matters. And what we know points again to the dominating influence of *yin-yang,* five-phases cosmology. For example, bronze mirrors resembling Han diviner's boards in the symbolism that decorates their reverse sides are common finds at Han gravesites. Although their artistic value alone certainly could

---

[17] Cited in Michael Loewe, *Ways to Paradise: The Chinese Quest for Immortality* (London: Allen and Unwin, 1979), p. 77.

have made them worthwhile grave goods, their ultimate purpose was religious—a fact that becomes clear when they are viewed in relation to the diviner's board. In the words of Han historian Michael Loewe, "Their design emphasized the most favorable position that could be maintained by manipulating the two discs of the diviner's board," for "the mirrors were intended to set a man permanently in his correct relation with the cosmos and to escort him to a life in the hereafter."[18] The "hereafter" in this instance meant the heavenly abode in which one of two distinct souls ideally would reside after death, the other soul ideally remaining with the buried corpse. How long before this the Chinese believed in dual (or multiple) souls is hard to say, but from the Han period on, the natures of people's two souls, called the *hun* and the *p'o* (*po*), were explained by connecting them with *yang* and *yin* respectively.

A final example of the influence of *yin-yang* cosmology on Han religion can be seen in looking at the evolving festival calendar of that period. This calendar was based to some extent on the popular festivals of spring planting and fall harvest mentioned earlier as having roots in Chinese prehistory. For example, the influence of these festivals is seen in the rites of the emperor's Spring Planting Ceremony and the empress' Spring Silk Cultivation Ceremony. By the same token, popular festivals themselves would now have to conform to an official calendar prepared by a board of astronomy and promulgated by the emperor, at least in cases of national importance. The New Year festival, for example, always would be officially set for a date somewhere between our January 21 and February 20.[19]

Some, but not all, elements of folk religion were thus woven into the Han state religion. Certain popular religious forces that seem the antithesis of systematic state cult rituals lay dormant until they exploded into history at the end of the Han Dynasty as religious rebellions. Fed by egalitarian ideas of a future paradise on earth, and imbued with popular expectations of health and peace through divine dispensations, these forces helped give birth to religious Taoism in China. And they set the stage for the acceptance of Buddhism there. Yet since the key events in all this came late in the Han period, and belong in spirit to the next episode in Chinese religious history, they will be taken up in the next section.

WORLD TRANSCENDENCE AND INDIVIDUAL SALVATION

During the second stage in Chinese religious history, a native tradition (Taoism) more mystical than Confucianism grew in popularity, and a foreign faith (Buddhism) arrived in China offering a new mode of spiritual

---

[18] Loewe, pp. 80 and 83.

[19] On the popular and official composition of the Han religious calendar, see Derk Bodde, *Festivals in Classical China: New Year and Other Annual Observances During the Han Dynasty, 206 B.C.–A.D. 220* (Princeton: Princeton University Press, 1975), pp. 387–395.

salvation. But even more important, a classical world view in which the individual, society, and nature were considered to be a unity gave way to dualistic philosophies contrasting the ordinary world with a transcendent beyond and to practices that promised deliverance from ordinary existence. This growth of interest in world-transcending spirituality occurred in China during a period that saw the fall of the Han Confucian state and, following this, a long and chaotic Period of Disunity (221–589).

Moreover, the increased influence of Taoism and Buddhism was felt not only in the area of religious thought but also in the area of practice, not only among the elite but also among the common people. During this period, Taoism and Buddhism alike became responsible for a major innovation in Chinese religious life: the formation of "specifically religious groups" on a large scale. As indicated by sociologist of religion Joachim Wach, at some point in the history of every major civilization, "specifically religious groups" emerged.[20] Before this time, religious activities were an indistinguishable part of other social institutions: the family, the clan, the state. Afterwards, groups existed for the specific purpose of allowing individuals to engage in a personal quest for salvation. These were not groups into which one was born but which one could freely choose to join. Thus, on the one hand, they furthered the *individual spiritual quest* and, on the other hand, they were *voluntary organizations*. In some cases, such groups were short-lived and had only a handful of members. In others, they developed into universal religions, such as Buddhism and Christianity, bridging numerous peoples and cultures.

It is hard to say when the history of specifically religious groups began in China, but they were certainly not widespread before the Later Han era. Appearing at this time in a burst of energy that helped to crush the ailing Han, two Taoist movements first gained hold among the people. Combining ideas found in early Taoist texts with rituals and faith-healing arts long practiced by Chinese shamans and occultists, the leaders of these movements devised methods that they claimed could absolve people of their sins, cure them of their diseases, and ultimately remove them from all misfortune and deliver them into utopia. One such movement was responsible for the Yellow Turban Rebellion of 184, whose countless participants believed they had been made invincible through ritual for the purpose of bringing in a new age—that of the Yellow Heaven. Although this movement was finally suppressed, another that emerged elsewhere in China (Szechwan/Sichuan Province) at about the same time succeeded in establishing its own religious state. Not only did this state last for decades, but it also left as its legacy one of the main pillars of organized Taoism: the office of Celestial Master (*t'ien-shih; tian-shi*). First held by the movement's putative founder Chang Tao-ling (Zhang Dao-ling, second century), and thereafter remaining (ideally) in Chang family hands, it became the single most important religious office in Taoism, lasting down to the present day.

---

[20] Joachim Wach, *Sociology of Religion* (Chicago: University of Chicago Press, 1944), p. 57.

Period of Disunity (220–589)

The Way of Celestial Masters, as it came to be called, first appropriated elements of China's little tradition—shamanism, faith healing, ideas of the hereafter, utopian expectations—and created something that had all the features of a great-tradition religion. These included a priestly hierarchy, well-defined pantheon, formal rituals, and ultimately even canonical scriptures. As China's first Taoist "church," or "specifically religious group," the Way of Celestial Masters became the inspiration for several other movements which, along with it, are collectively known as religious Taoism. During the Period of Disunity, in fact, two of the other Taoist sects inspired by it had begun to thrive, namely, the Ling Pao (Ling Bao: "Spiritual Jewel") and Mao Shan ("Mao Mountain") sects.

Of the two dimensions of Taoist religion mentioned in Chapter 1—liturgical and mystical—the former was dominant in the early Way of Celestial Masters. But after Taoists of this and other sects had distinguished their rituals from "unorthodox" popular practices and made more of an appeal to members of the elite, the spiritual techniques and esoteric texts of Taoist mysticism evolved at a faster rate.[21] And they did so under the influence of Buddhism, whose activity in China dates from the Later Han period.

As for Buddhism itself, it brought to China a method of spiritual practice far more developed and institutionalized than anything produced by the Chinese themselves. As one of the world's universal religions, its message of salvation for all appealed to people of every social class, and its monastic form of organization provided a basis for evangelism and expansion. Taoism, despite being a native Chinese religion, therefore lagged behind Buddhism, whose growth during the Period of Disunity seems to have been incomprehensibly rapid, even when one considers that China was then divided north from south and suffering political chaos. Yet certain reasons for its growth can be suggested. In North China, power was held by non-Chinese rulers who already had a predisposition toward the foreign faith, while in South China, an émigré elite class turned more and more from worldly matters to private literary, philosophical, and spiritual pursuits.

This also meant that Buddhism developed differently in north and south. In North China, it nearly merged with secular powers to become a state religion, receiving so much support from state treasuries and wealthy royalty that it was able to produce such landmarks of religious art as the Buddhist cave sculptures at Yun-kang (Yun-gang) and Lung-men. In South China, it was not state patronage but fashionableness among intellectuals that aided its success. For this reason, the form of the religion then emerging in South China has been called Gentry Buddhism. In the world-away-from-the-world of Chinese literati who had been forced into exile by bar-

---

[21] See Rolf A. Stein, "Religious Taoism and Popular Religion from the Second to the Seventh Centuries," in *Facets of Taoism: Essays in Chinese Religion,* eds. Anna Seidel and Holmes Welch (New Haven: Yale University Press, 1979), pp. 53–82.

FIGURE 2.3. This temple mural of a fasting Buddha shows the element of Indian asceticism that Buddhism introduced into China. Lion's Head Mountain, Taiwan.

barian invasions in the north, Buddhist expositions upon Indian metaphysics and psychology were a welcome addition to debates about life's mysteries. And views that would be attacked as impractical and escapist at other points in Chinese history gained rapid acceptance. For this was an era when devaluation of the ordinary world as false and empty had for many become *de rigueur*.

However, it was not only royalty and intellectuals who had reason to turn to Buddhism during this age of change and instability; the common people had even more reason to embrace its message of otherworldly salvation. Far more than the foreign rulers of the north, or the gentry elite in the south, common people everywhere experienced the life and death realities of political chaos: food shortages, unpredictable market conditions, lack of relief from the results of natural disasters, unexpected shifts in rulership, and the continual threat of warfare. In the face of this, Buddhism offered them both spiritual solace and material aid. On the one hand, numerous Buddhist monks preached to the people about the power of Buddhas and Bodhisattvas to save the faithful. On the other hand, certain Buddhist leaders gathered people into religious organizations that gave them a sense of security and served them as mutual aid associations in times of need. Being among the earliest voluntary religious groups in China, some of these sects were organized with state support and approval. Others, however, followed the lead of Han period Taoist movements—waging religious warfare against the state and seeking to establish their own utopia on earth, now defined as the reign of the future Buddha, Maitreya.

Ultimately, it was not in the form of such sects that Buddhism would become most omnipresent in Chinese culture. Yet they helped bring the religion into the mainstream of Chinese folk religion, where its belief in *karma* and reincarnation would have a role along with beliefs in filiality and ancestor worship, and where Buddhas and Bodhisattvas would be worshiped right beside native deities. This, more than its coming into vogue among Chinese intellectuals, assured its place within Chinese society. By the time China was reunified under the Sui and T'ang (Tang) dynasties, Buddhism had become an indelible design on the fabric of Chinese religious life. In fact, within a new, more cosmopolitan era, it took its place alongside Taoism and Confucianism as one of China's Three Teachings.

The Sui (589–618) and T'ang (618–907) Periods

Little need be said of the Sui Dynasty here except that its relation to the T'ang was like that of Ch'in to Han. It provided the military power and autocratic firmness necessary to unify China but then stepped down from the stage of history and let other "actors" complete the drama of building a new imperial order. What was new with the T'ang imperial order was above all its cosmopolitanism, which extended into religious as well as other areas. This not only allowed for the coexistence of Confucians, Taoists, and Buddhists but also left room for Chinese Jews, (Nestorian) Christians, Manichaeans, Zoroastrians, and before the dynasty's end, China's first Muslims. Against this background, it is perhaps easier to understand how each of the Three Teachings could receive support from the people of T'ang Dynasty China and, with some exceptions, its emperors.

State patronage of Buddhism as established under the alien rulers of North China during the Period of Disunity was continued by the T'ang emperors. This meant that Buddhism was controlled as well as patronized by the T'ang state. A clerical bureaucracy was set up to screen applicants seeking to enter the Buddhist monastic order, for which purpose official ordination certificates were required. Buddhist temple construction and lay-group formation were similarly scrutinized, and the government was continually on the lookout for political activity among certain kinds of Buddhist believers, such as Maitreya worshipers, who had previously demonstrated subversive tendencies.

On the positive side, T'ang rulers incorporated Buddhist rituals into state ceremonies, such as imperial accessions and ancestral worship, and encouraged theological efforts to make the Chinese emperor an earthly equivalent of celestial Buddhas like Vairocana. The Buddhist clergy thus offered spiritual support for the T'ang imperial order, in return for which it received a good deal of material sustenance. Wealthy private aristocrats were just as glad as members of the imperial family to donate land and other resources to the clergy in return for spiritual merit. Gifts to Buddhist mendicants had become the accepted means of canceling the negative karmic debt of one's family members, especially one's deceased ancestors.

Buddhism's material wealth, in fact, became so great under the T'ang that this eventually did the religion more harm than good, making it the target of criticism. Ultimately, it was suppressed by the state on the grounds that it was a parasite draining the empire of both human and natural resources, without giving anything in return (due to its tax-exempt status). Near the end of the dynasty, in 845, when state suppression of Buddhism reached its height, Emperor Wu-tsung (Wu-zung) issued an edict expressing cultural as well as economic opposition to Buddhism and, at the same time, revealing the incredible extent of its wealth and influence:

> We have learned that up through the three dynasties (of Hsia, Shang, and Chou) there had never been any talk of Buddhism, and only since the Han and Wei has this idolatrous religion come to flourish. In recent times its strange ways have become so customary and all pervasive as to have slowly and unconsciously corrupted the morals of our land. . . . Now, when one man does not farm, others suffer hunger, and, when one woman does not weave, others suffer from the cold. At present the monks and nuns of the empire are numberless, but they all depend on agriculture for their food and sericulture for their clothing. The monasteries and temples are beyond count, but they are lofty and beautifully decorated, daring to rival palaces in grandeur. . . . More than 4,600 monasteries are being destroyed throughout the empire; more than 260,500 monks and nuns are being returned to lay life and being subjected to the double tax; more than 40,000 temples and shrines are being destroyed; several tens of millions of *ch'ing* [*ching*] of fertile lands and fine fields are being confiscated; 150,000 slaves are being taken over to become payers of the double tax. Monks and nuns are to be placed under the jurisdiction of the Bureau of Guests, to indicate clearly that Buddhism is a foreign religion.[22]

Since Emperor Wu-tsung died the year after issuing this edict, and his successor withdrew it, the measures it advocated had a brief though harsh effect on Chinese Buddhism. Institutionally, it relinquished its prior share of wealth and influence. But, fortunately, the spiritual and intellectual advances of Buddhism in T'ang China were not thereby negated.

It was during the T'ang period that each of the major schools of Chinese Buddhism formulated its doctrines by, on the one hand, gaining an accurate understanding of Indian Buddhism and, on the other hand, articulating a uniquely Chinese variation of the views imported from India. New accuracy in understanding was evident, for example, in the translations of certain Chinese monks who had studied in India, such as the famous Hsuan-tsang (Xuan-zang, seventh century), whose story in Chinese history and literature will be told in Chapter 4. Uniquely Chinese variations of Buddhist views are seen in the original works of the T'ang masters of nearly every school of Chinese Buddhism. In fact, although each school had its pre-T'ang patriarchs, these were usually overshadowed by their T'ang successors. For, in line with the Chinese love of antiquity and family geneology, each school called itself a "lineage" (*tsung; zung*) and claimed descent from the earliest eminent monk to whom its ideas could be traced, calling this figure its first "patriarch," or "ancestor" (*tsu; zu*).

---

[22] Kenneth Ch'en, *Buddhism in China: A Historical Survey* (Princeton: Princeton University Press, 1964), pp. 231–232.

While first patriarchs were thus not usually the important doctrinal founders for which we might mistake them, in turning to the first of four major schools of Chinese Buddhism that demand our attention, we must begin with an outstanding exception. The T'ien-t'ai (Tian-tai) School was established by Chih-yi (Zhi-yi, 538–597)—its first patriarch, most revered saint, greatest thinker, and the one who gave the school its name by establishing it on Mount T'ien-t'ai in modern Chekiang (Zhejiang) Province. His main doctrinal contribution typifies the syncretic spirit not only of his school of Buddhism but also of Chinese religion in general. This was the system of "dividing the teachings" (*p'an-chiao; pan-jiao*), by means of which he solved the problem of apparent disagreement among various scriptures imported from India by arranging them into five progressive stages of the Buddha's revelation of the Dharma. And by considering the *Lotus Scripture* representative of Buddha's highest teaching, he also gave it the central role it still has in this school of Buddhism.

Turning to a second school, called Hua-yen (Hua-yan), we find a similarly constructed system with the *Hua-yen Scripture* at its apex, though this system was not the work of the school's first patriarch, Tu-shun (Du-shun, 557–640), but rather of the great T'ang master Fa-tsang (Fa-zang, 643–712). Moreover, the latter's contribution went beyond this. His doctrine of the necessary interrelatedness of "noumenon" (or "principle," *li*) and "phenomenon" (*shih; shi*)—of essential and apparent reality—influenced later Chinese thought both in and outside of Chinese Buddhism (as we shall soon see in treating Neo-Confucianism).

Despite the fame of Chih-yi and Fa-tsang—each having preached at the imperial court during his lifetime—and the early prominence of the schools they represented, two other schools would ultimately dominate Chinese Buddhism: Ch'an and Pure Land. Although these two schools had pre-T'ang patriarchs of great renown, their fortunes were enhanced most of all by a series of T'ang masters too numerous to list. In the case of Ch'an, there is no doubt about the seminal importance of its first patriarch, Bodhidharma. It is said that around 520 he brought from India to China a special teaching passed down directly from Buddha himself. This was a transmission of Dharma outside of scriptures—from master to master or, as the Ch'an tradition says, "from mind to mind." But it is hard to say precisely what Bodhidharma taught, or even exactly who he was, since the story of his life has become embellished with so many legends. Moreover, it was rather late in Ch'an history that the unique form of Buddhist teachings called "Recorded Sayings" (*yü-lu; yu-lu*) emerged. Containing the words and deeds that so many modern Westerners identify with the Ch'an tradition, the "Recorded Sayings" preserve the heritage of such great mid-T'ang masters as Ma-tsu (Ma-zu, 709–788), Po-chang (Bo-zhang, 720–814), and Nan-ch'uan (Nan-chuan, 745–834).[23]

In the case of the Pure Land School, its first patriarch was among

---

[23] On this topic, see Yanagida Seizan, "The 'Recorded Sayings' Texts of Chinese Ch'an Buddhism," in *Early Ch'an in China and Tibet,* eds. Whalen Lai and Lewis R. Lancaster (Berkeley: Asian Humanities Press, 1983), pp. 185–206.

the most famous of all figures in early Chinese Buddhism, Master Hui-
yuan (who will be the subject of a special section in Chapter 3). However,
this figure was chosen more for his prestige than for his actual role in
formulating Pure Land doctrine. The formulation of doctrine was better
served by such leading T'ang masters as Shan-tao (Shan-dao, 613–681),
who was famous, among other things, for establishing the following list
of five key activities that can lead devotees to rebirth in the Buddhist
Heaven, the Pure Land or Western Paradise: namely, "(a) uttering the
name of the Buddha, (b) chanting the sutras [scriptures], (c) meditating
on the Buddha, (d) worshipping images of the Buddha, and (e) singing
praises to the Buddha."[24]

Dwelling on T'ang Buddhism at such length has been necessary because of the formative influence it has exerted on the subsequent development of Buddhism not only in China but also in Korea, Japan, Vietnam,
and now the West. Yet, as we shall soon see, T'ang Buddhists did not
completely eclipse their Taoist counterparts in spiritual prowess, for Taoists
also had reason to consider the T'ang Dynasty their golden age.

Sharing the surname Li with Lao Tzu, T'ang emperors claimed descent from this legendary Taoist patriarch. Li Yuan, the first T'ang ruler,
better known as T'ang Emperor Kao-tsu (Gao-zu), erected an ancestral
temple at the supposed birthplace of Lao Tzu. One of his successors, Emperor Hsuan-tsung (Xuan-zong), even succeeded for a time in replacing
the *Chou Rituals* and *Analects* of Confucius with Lao Tzu's *Tao-te-ching* as
the subject of state civil service examinations.[25] T'ang emperors frequently
had Taoist priests as their personal spiritual masters, certain ones having
had enough faith in their masters to eat immortality pills that reportedly
led to their death. Taoist ritual, moreover, was brought into the imperial
cult when, for example, official shrines were set up for the Taoist deities
associated with China's sacred mountains.

As far as the sects of Taoism were concerned, the one centered at
Mao Mountain surpassed all others in influence, especially at the imperial
court. The Mao Shan Taoists brought numerous T'ang notables into their
ken and also saw one of their scriptures, the *Scripture of the Yellow Court*
(*Huang-t'ing ching; Huang-ting jing*), incorporated into the state examination
system. The latter fact is even more remarkable than the similar use of
Lao Tzu's classic, because the Mao Shan scriptures had been produced
mainly in visionary revelations involving spirit writing—a practice hardly
fitting a so-called Confucian system. This serves to remind us that the
Literati Teaching was at this time only one dimension of state-supported
religion.

Although Confucianism was thus only one among three major religions of T'ang China, it was in a sense the best off among the three. As
Buddhism and Taoism were reaching a peak of institutional growth, from

---

[24] Translated in Ch'en, p. 346.

[25] John K. Shryock, *The Origin and Development of the State Cult of Confucius* (New York: Century,
1932; rpt. New York: Paragon, 1966), p. 132.

which they would inevitably fall, the Confucian tradition was rebuilding structures of influence like those it had once established under the Han Dynasty. And as Buddhists and Taoists sought to destroy one another in debates over which was historically older and spiritually superior, Confucian scholars were preparing for an intellectual revival that would reduce those debates almost to insignificance. Moreover, the most important emperor of the T'ang period—if not of all Chinese history—T'ang T'ai-tsung (Tai-zong, r. 626–649), enhanced the growth of a host of key Confucian institutions: national schools for training officials, civil service examinations, the system of seeking advice from publicly trained and appointed ministers, and last but not least, the cult of Confucian temples.

Perhaps the only T'ang emperor who could be called Confucian, T'ai-tsung had a unique influence on T'ang imperial history as the dynasty's second emperor. For his father, Kao-tsu, abdicated in his favor just after pacifying the empire. One of T'ai-tsung's first acts as emperor was to establish schools to train new officials. The schools he established at the capital were prestigious enough almost to guarantee their graduates a government job. And his subsequent expansion of the state examination system led to a situation in which, perhaps for the first time in Chinese history, a commoner could work his way through this system and into officialdom. Furthermore, despite the exceptions mentioned earlier in discussing T'ang Taoism, this system emphasized classical Confucian scriptures—especially as understood through the official interpretations of orthodox commentators like K'ung Ying-ta (Kong Ying-da, 574–647), a descendant of Confucius and contemporary of Emperor T'ai-tsung.

The direction in which the cult of Confucian temples developed under T'ai-tsung gives further evidence of his influence. Shortly after his accession (630), he decreed that all prefectures and districts have Confucian temples for sacrifices performed by literati in their capacity as government officials, not merely as private scholars honoring their patron saint. Later (647), he installed in the temples commemorative tablets for twenty-two orthodox Confucians of the Han Dynasty, for the first time using the cult to honor anyone who had lived after the time of Confucius. With these acts he expanded both the number and scope of Confucian temples but, perhaps unwittingly, also set in motion a process by which they became almost identical to other religious temples.

Within a century of T'ai-tsung's reign, Confucian temples had adopted the Buddhist practice of using carved images, instead of only tablets, to represent the figures whom they honored. These temples had, moreover, come to include a new group of ten Wise Ones (*che; zhe*). John Shryock's description of their basic form reveals how they could be mistaken for Buddhist temples if one were to imagine Buddhas, Bodhisattvas, and Buddhist worthies called Lo-han in place of Confucius, Yen Hui, the ten Wise Ones, the seventy-two disciples of Confucius, etc.:

There was a main hall, oblong, with the long side running east and west. Against the north wall was the image . . . of Confucius, with Yen Hui at one side. Against the east and west walls were the ten *Cheh* [*che*]. Before the main hall was a terrace, and below it a court, while on both sides of the court, east and west, ran cloisters. In these cloisters against the east and west walls, were the portraits, probably mural paintings in the T'ang temples, of two groups of men . . . the seventy-two disciples . . . [and] the group of later Confucians represented by T'ai-tsung's twenty-two names.

At present [1932] the absence of images makes the Confucian temples strikingly different from Buddhist and most Taoist temples; but when the images were there, the similarity to Buddhist temples, particularly those of the meditative school founded by Bodhidharma, must have been striking. In place of Confucius put the three Buddhas; instead of Yen Hui, and of three others who were placed with him as correlates in the Sung period, put the four great Bodhisattvas, and in place of the ten *Cheh*, put the Lo-han or the twenty-four deva kings. The arrangements are so similar that it is difficult to assume it as a coincidence.[26]

Even more interesting, the images and portraits used within this arrangement were not again replaced by tablets until the year 1530, after seven or eight centuries of efforts by Confucianism to distinguish itself from Buddhism and to set itself on a new nation-saving course. While these efforts can be traced back to the late T'ang era, they belong mostly to the third major period of Chinese religious history, to which we now turn.

RENAISSANCE OF THE CLASSICAL TRADITION

Beginning with the Sung period, representatives of the classical tradition once again took their turn at defining the parameters of socio-religious reality, as they had during the Han era. Yet they did so mostly at the upper echelons of society, while Buddhism and Taoism continued strongly to affect popular religious practice, at times spurring lay movements that opposed the ruling Confucians spiritually, politically, and even militarily. But did this attenuation of Buddhist and Taoist influence among Chinese intellectuals mean an abandonment of their concern with metaphysical speculation and individual spiritual cultivation? Of course not. This concern thoroughly pervaded the brand of literati thought that became current during and after the Sung period, thus yielding the strongest reason for our having decided to call it the "new" Confucianism.

Neo-Confucianism in the Sung (960–1279) and Later Periods

Just as Ch'an Buddhists insisted that Buddha's true Dharma was preserved in a transmission of mind, outside of scriptures, Sung Neo-Confucians distinguished the "transmission of political rule" (*cheng-t'ung; zheng-tong*) from the "transmission of the true Way" (*tao-t'ung; dao-tong*) of Confucius. They and their successors tried to be sages, not mere civil servants. This meant that they aspired inwardly to discover a higher self and outwardly, on a metaphysical plane, to realize their identity with the entire cosmos.

---

[26] Shryock, pp. 138–139.

Moreover, toward this end, they engaged in the practice of meditation or, in Neo-Confucian terminology, "quiet sitting" (*ching-tso; jing-zuo*). Yet, in contrast to Ch'an Buddhism, the goal of such meditation was (according to one opinion) "moral discrimination instead of mystical indiscrimination."[27] Another way of saying this is to describe the Neo-Confucian goal as that of *sagehood-in-action* and, furthermore, to point out that progress toward this goal involved continual *moral self-examination*.[28]

The Neo-Confucians' particular ideal of sagehood distinguished them not only from Buddhists but also from their own Confucian forebears. Early Confucianism, and Confucius in particular, wanted to place the nation's destiny in the hands of loyal but straightforward "gentlemen" (*chün-tzu*) who could properly advise their ruler. Han Confucians shifted responsibility onto the emperor who could manifest the "true king" (*wang*) ideal. And Sung Neo-Confucians envisioned the transformation of imperial bureaucrats into nation-saving "sages" (*sheng*) simultaneously capable of spiritual unity with the cosmos and enlightened service to their emperor. Moreover, the religious context in which the new ideal of sagehood resided was neither late Chou ethics nor Han cosmology but rather the Buddho-Taoistic quest for self-transformation. Thus, in the Neo-Confucian anthology *Reflections on Things at Hand*, we read: "Combine the internal and the external into one and regard things and the self as equal. This is the way to see the fundamental point of the Way."[29]

It was argued that this task was possible on the basis that self and all things universally possess Heavenly Principle (*t'ien-li; tian-li*), which the Neo-Confucians paired off against the material "life force" (*ch'i*) of physical substances, just as the Buddhists had set Principle opposite "phenomena" (*shih*). And the Neo-Confucians also set Heavenly Principle opposite "human desires" (*jen-yü; ren-yu*), defined as an obstruction to self-transformation, which further revealed their concern over psychological factors that were foreign to Confucius and his disciples. Whereas early Confucians saw the crucial problems "out there" in the socio-political realm, the aspiring Neo-Confucian sage looked for them first of all within himself. Chinese intellectual historian Thomas Metzger makes this point in comparing Mencius with the leading Neo-Confucians of the Sung and Ming periods respectively, Chu Hsi (Zhu Xi, 1130–1200) and Wang Yang-ming (1472–1529): "Whereas rulers obviously unwilling to institute good policies had been the enemy in Mencius' eyes, the enemy for Chu Hsi and Wang Yang-ming was overwhelmingly that 'inner' force within 'the mind' of the Confucian subject leading to corruption."[30] The new religious dimension in Sung and later Confucianism is thus found above all in a quest for sagehood

[27] Lai, p. 83.

[28] On Neo-Confucian sagehood, especially see Rodney L. Taylor, "Neo-Confucianism, Sagehood and the Religious Dimension," *Journal of Chinese Philosophy*, 2 (1975), pp. 389–415.

[29] Wing-tsit Chan, trans., *Reflections on Things at Hand: A Neo-Confucian Anthology Compiled by Chu Hsi and Lü Tsu-ch'ien* (New York: Columbia University Press, 1967), p. 85.

[30] Thomas A. Metzger, *Escape from Predicament: Neo-Confucianism and China's Evolving Political Culture* (New York: Columbia University Press, 1977), p. 76.

that not only incorporated metaphysical speculation about primal constituents of reality, such as Heavenly Principle and material life force, but also psychological concerns about being able to overcome evil within oneself through moral-spiritual cultivation.

As for the leading thinkers of the new Confucianism, the two most important ones have just been mentioned. These two figures (Chu Hsi and Wang Yang-ming), however, were the finalizers rather than the founders of Neo-Confucianism's two main branches. Chu Hsi is considered to be a direct intellectual heir of the early Sung period thinker Ch'eng Yi (Cheng Yi, 1033–1107); and their branch of Neo-Confucianism is generally known in China as the Ch'eng-Chu School. Similarly, its second major branch is known as the Lu-Wang School, since Wang Yang-ming followed the thought of the Sung scholar Lu Hsiang-shan (Lu Xiang-shan, 1139–1193), a contemporary and intellectual adversary of Chu Hsi.

Of all these thinkers, Chu Hsi had the most lasting influence on Chinese religious, philosophical, and political life. This is not only because his school of thought reigned supreme throughout most of the Yuan (1279–1368), Ming (1368–1644), and Ch'ing (1644–1911) dynasties, but also because his and Ch'eng Yi's commentaries on the scriptures of classical Confucianism constituted the basis for Chinese civil service examinations from 1313 to 1905. This was especially important in the case of the Four Books (Confucius' *Analects, Mencius, Great Learning,* and *Doctrine of the Mean*), which in fact owe their key role among Confucian scriptures to Ch'eng and Chu.

The basic teaching of the Ch'eng-Chu School, on which its debate with the Lu-Wang School hinged, concerned the realization of Principle through a process called the "investigation of things" (*ko-wu; ge-wu,* a term from *Great Learning* that gained utmost importance among Neo-Confucians). Some of their thoughts on the subject (Ch'eng's dictum and Chu's commentary) are as follows:

"There is principle in everything, and one must investigate principle to the utmost. There are many ways to do this. One way is to read books and elucidate moral principles. Another way is to discuss people and events of the past and present, and to distinguish which are right and which wrong. Still another way is to handle affairs and settle them in the proper way. All these are ways to investigate the principle of things exhaustively.". . .

[Chu Hsi commented] "We must investigate principle in the things and affairs we deal with. For example, when we read, we investigate principle in the printed word. When we listen to others, we investigate it in conversation. When handling affairs, we investigate it in the affairs themselves. Whether things are refined or coarse, big or small, we must investigate them all. After a long time we shall understand them, and the course will become refined and the small will become big."[31]

This process was meant to evoke a flash of enlightenment (for Ch'eng Yi also stated, "When one has accumulated much knowledge, he will naturally achieve a thorough understanding like a sudden release"). However, it

---

[31] Wing-tsit Chan, trans., pp. 91–92. The following comment from Ch'eng Yi appears on p. 92.

must be considered a *quantitative* approach involving broad learning, at least in comparison with the more *qualitative* approach of Wang Yang-ming. For Wang stressed the importance of "innate knowing" (*liang-chih; liang-zhi*), rather than broad learning, for attaining sagehood.

Despite the fact that Wang Yang-ming's challenge during the sixteenth century brought temporary victory for his school, the Ch'eng-Chu School became established as the ideological orthodoxy of late imperial China's ever stronger and more elaborate state religion. Its hold over the intellectual milieu of the time was accompanied by the increased exercise of imperial power and the glorification of this power through the state cult. When, for example, the Ming Dynasty founder, Emperor T'ai-tsu (Tai-zu), sought to revitalize ancient Chinese traditions in reaction to a century of foreign (Mongol) rulership, he established a trend. Idealized and costly versions of the rites described in classical scriptures such as the *Chou Rituals* became more important within Chinese government than they had been for centuries. The worship of imperial ancestors reached a level of particularly lavish splendor, as seen in the Ming and Ch'ing imperial tombs; and the Ming-Ch'ing capital of Peking became a sacred city of grandiose proportions, featuring a colossal Forbidden City of imperial palaces and throne halls.[32]

The Ministry of Rites, as the branch of officialdom most involved with these developments, not only expanded its duties connected with state rituals. It also increased the zeal with which it controlled nonofficial religious organizations from Taoist and Buddhist monasteries to "heretical" popular sects. Of course, in the case of Taoist and Buddhist monasteries, "control" only meant tighter restrictions on the construction of temples and ordination of clergy. Whereas in the case of "heretical" sects, it meant legal proscription and, if necessary, military suppression. Nevertheless, all these forms of religion thrived, including, if not especially, the popular sects that existed under continual fear of being banned and suppressed. Some of these, such as the Three Teachings Religion founded in the sixteenth century by the noted literatus Lin Chao-en (Lin Zhao-en, 1517–1598), were able to practice openly for long periods. Others, such as the White Lotus Religion to be covered in Chapter 3, had to persevere as underground movements from the Ming Dynasty down into the twentieth century.

Taoism and Buddhism in Late Imperial China
(ca. 1000–1900)

Taoism and Buddhism demonstrated their resilience by producing new sects and movements of their own just at the time when Confucianism was having its revival. Taoism, for example, gave birth to several new sects under the Chin (Jin) Dynasty, whose foreign rulers held North China

[32] On these two topics, see, respectively, Ann Paludan, *The Imperial Ming Tombs* (New Haven: Yale University Press, 1981) and Jeffrey F. Meyer, *Peking as a Sacred City* (Taipei: Orient Culture Service, 1976).

from the time they drove the Sung court south in 1127 until 1234, when the Mongols routed them in turn. Two of these, the Supreme Unity (T'ai-yi; Tai-yi) and Perfect Realization (Ch'üan-chen; Quan-zhen) sects, achieved considerable importance, the latter being largely responsible for preserving Taoist monasticism down into modern times. And in the area of liturgical Taoism, a resurgent Way of Celestial Masters showed its powers of perseverence. Throughout late imperial times, it was a highly coveted honor among Taoist priests to have received training and ordination from a Chang family Celestial Master on Dragon-Tiger Mountain in Kiangsi Province.

Of course, specialization in rituals did not mean abandonment of "mystical" self-cultivation, as the fifteenth-century Celestial Master Chang Yü-ch'u (Zhang Yu-chu) himself once argued in comparing other methods of cultivation with those of his own sect (under its alternative name of Cheng-yi [Zheng-yi: "Orthodox Unity"] Taoism):

> In recent years people take Zen Buddhism as seeking for cultivation of the nature (*hsing* [*xing*]); Taoism for cultivation of the life (*ming*); the Ch'uan-chen sect of Taoism, for dual cultivation of both the nature and the life, and the Cheng-[y]i sect of Taoism, for cultivation of rituals and ceremonies. But is not the learning of the *tao* simply the cultivation of nature and life and nothing else? Even the teaching of rituals and ceremonies is only for the learning of these two things.[33]

This passage also reveals the eclectic spirit of the era of late imperial times during which it was written—the Ming Dynasty. Perhaps only in such an eclectic era could the head of a Taoist sect refer to his religious adversaries with this kind of tolerance. Yet his being able to speak this way perhaps also reveals the generally favorable position of Taoism under Ming emperors as compared with their Mongol (Yuan) predecessors and Manchu (Ch'ing) successors, who favored Buddhism after the fashion of nearly all alien rulers of China since the Period of Disunity.

The Neo-Confucian tendency to borrow from Buddhism and the eclectic spirit of Ming Taoism are further paralleled by two themes that run throughout post-T'ang Buddhism: (1) syncretism within the religion and (2) its further accommodation to native Chinese religious values. After the T'ang period, the various Buddhist schools, which had worked so hard to define their unique positions, either disappeared or came to resemble one another closely. The two that did retain and even enhance their institutional strength, Ch'an and Pure Land, eventually entered into a *de facto* merger through sharing practices that had once been the defining feature of each tradition: Ch'an meditation and Pure Land chanting. The significant choice for a Buddhist in China was no longer between schools but simply between practices that either did or did not suit one's disposition. In the words of one author: "By the Ming period the well-known schools of Chinese Buddhism (T'ien-t'ai, Hua-yen, etc.) were becoming mere names, and the only meaningful divisions were those of contemplation (*ch'an*),

[33] Liu Ts'un-yan, "Taoist Self-Cultivation in Ming Thought," in *Self and Society in Ming Thought*, ed. Wm. Theodore deBary (New York: Columbia University Press, 1970), p. 306.

textual study (*chiang* [*jiang*]), and strict adherence to the monastic code (*lü*).[34]

The emphasis on shared practices rather than on doctrinal differences, which served as the basis for syncretism within Buddhism, was itself something Buddhism borrowed from the Chinese. This emphasis was perhaps even the key factor in Buddhism's accommodation to Chinese culture, despite the importance of so many other factors, such as (1) the ultimately Chinese character given to Buddhist deities in both the physical images and personal biographies created for them, (2) the transformation of Buddhist holy days into ecstatic folk festivals, (3) the bureaucratization of Buddhist heavens and hells by linking them with ledgers of karmic merit and demerit, and (4) the absorption of the time and energy of most Buddhist monks and nuns in handling familial rites for deceased ancestors. For an assumed emphasis on practice over doctrine, and world-affirming ethics over world-rejecting asceticism, lay beneath the efforts of all the key reformers in Chinese Buddhism from the Ming period's Chu-hung (Zhu-hong, 1535–1615) through the modern era's T'ai-hsu (Tai-xu, 1890–1947). The former figure, considered to be the inspiration for most later reformers, in fact placed an explicit stress on social ethics and lay practice, as seen in the following summary of his teachings:

> While the essentials of Chu-hung's lay teachings were drawn from Pure Land Buddhism, his movement was syncretic. It emphasized recitation of the Buddha's name (*nien-fo* [*nian-fo*]), non-killing, compassion both for one's fellow humans and for animals, and concretized this compassionate attitude in acts of social philanthropy and the release of animals from captivity and from slaughterhouses. Although there were precedents for all these, the late Ming movement was far more than just a revival of earlier movements. One principal reason for this was Chu-hung's success in making lay practice as well organized as the monastic order. Not only did he accord the lay believer the same attention as the *sangha*, but he also gave him detailed, programmatic advice on his religious practice. Chu-hung's choice of non-killing and the release of life as central themes in lay proselytization was another significant development. Since the Confucian tradition also gave great emphasis to the reverence for life, lay Buddhist practice could complement and even deepen the religious consciousness of lay devotees, facilitating the eventual syncretizing of Confucian and Buddhist values in their lives.[35]

Indeed Chu-hung's ecumenical consciousness seemed to have no bounds; he once even defended Confucian control over Buddhism as contributing to the latter's quality and endurance.

However, another event in his fascinating career better indicates the final importance for him of moral practice over spiritual doctrine. Matteo Ricci (1552–1610), a Jesuit who established the first Catholic mission in

---

[34] Leon Hurvitz, "Chu Hung's One Mind of Pure Land and Ch'an Buddhism," in *Self and Society in Ming Thought* (cited earlier), p. 452.

[35] Kristen Yü Greenblatt, "Chu Hung and Lay Buddhism in the Late Ming," in *The Unfolding of Neo-Confucianism*, ed. Wm. Theodore deBary (New York: Columbia University Press, 1975), pp. 130–131.

China, attacked the teachings of his contemporary Chu-hung and set off perhaps the first Buddhist-Christian controversy in history. Ricci contended that if one were to refrain from killing animals on the basis of Chu-hung's Buddhist argument—that in previous incarnations they might have been one's parents—the logical results would be ridiculous. One would not only have to stop killing animals but also stop using them to till land and, moreover, go on to outlaw marriage and the use of servants, since those to be married or employed might also have been one's parents in some previous incarnation! Chu-hung's response was essentially to show disbelief at what he felt was Ricci's sophistry in using words to compare such ordinary things as agriculture and marriage with the serious act of killing animals.[36] Nevertheless, as we shall soon see, balanced against later events in China's encounter with the West, Ricci's efforts to engage in dialogue with his Buddhist hosts in China deserves praise rather than condemnation.

RELIGION AND MODERNIZATION

In the nineteenth century, as the ailing Ch'ing Dynasty faced unprecedented domestic problems in the world's most populous nation, China suffered a series of humiliating encounters with Western nations and ideologies. Great Britain's victory in the Opium War of 1839–1842 resulted in unfavorable treaties with Britain, and subsequently with other Western powers. These treaties subjected China to unequal political and economic arrangements, including the opening of five Chinese ports to foreign residence as well as trade. While this might have had its good side, few Chinese took advantage of the opportunity to learn things from the West that could have helped China with its domestic problems. In fact, before China caught its breath after the Opium War, the domestic Taiping Rebellion (1850–1864) threw the country into a century of intermittent civil warfare. The Taiping Rebellion, the largest sectarian movement in Chinese religious history, was inspired by iconoclastically Christian rather than native millenarian ideas. For this reason, thousands of decimated Taoist, Buddhist, and other temples were left in its wake all over South China. Moreover, the Ch'ing state suffered further Western interference when it allowed France and Britain to "help" its strife-torn empire with the Taiping crisis. Later (1894–1895) China was even defeated by its own newly modernized Asian neighbor, Japan, which itself culminated the process of China's humiliation some two decades later by demanding capitulation to the infamous Twenty-one Demands. The date was May 7, 1915—afterward known as National Humiliation Day.

China's Response to Western Influence

Chinese intellectuals, particularly young ones, finally reacted when after World War I China's contribution to victory was overlooked, and German

---

[36] Greenblatt, pp. 114–115.

holdings in China were given to Japan, thereby further strengthening Japanese efforts virtually to colonize China. The response, known as the May Fourth Movement, was immediate and widespread. Student demonstrations in Peking on May 4, 1919 set off a month of boycotts, strikes, and further demonstrations against government leaders perceived to be weak, ineffectual, and above all, enslaved to the past. This event fired the furnaces of modernization that had been lit by the overthrow of the Ch'ing Dynasty in 1911. More specifically, it made a nationwide, multidimensional phenomenon out of the so-called New Culture Movement of a few young intellectuals, such as Ch'en Tu-hsiu (Chen Du-xiu, 1879–1942, who established the Chinese Communist Party in 1921), Hu Shih (Hu Shi, 1891–1962, who inspired a change in writing from classical to vernacular), and Lu Hsun (Lu Xun, 1881–1936, who wrote modern China's best-known vernacular fiction). Of all its dimensions, however, only one concerns us here: the antireligious movement.

This movement rarely favored opposition to all religion, for its proponents were generally just as much for religious freedom as they were for other modern ideas. What they were against, first of all, was the "Confucian" system of past dynasties. Secondly, they were against "superstitions," which meant primarily the beliefs and practices of Chinese folk religion, with its otherworldly system of rewards and punishments as well as its onerous concept of fate. Precisely how these might stand in the way of modernization one can judge for oneself from the opening paragraph of an extremely popular religious tract called *The Treatise of the Most Exalted One on Moral Retribution:*

> The Most Exalted One said: "Calamities and blessings do not come through any (fixed) gate; it is man himself that invites them." The reward of good and evil is like a shadow accompanying the body. Accordingly there are in Heaven and earth spiritual beings who record a man's evil deeds and, depending upon the lightness or gravity of his transgressions, reduce his term of life by units of three days. As units are taken away, his health becomes poor, and his spirit becomes wasted. He will often meet with sorrow and misery, and all other men will hate him. Punishments and calamities will pursue him; good luck and joy will shun him; evil stars will harm him. When the alloted units are exhausted, he will die.[37]

Believed to inhibit rather than aid modernization, folk beliefs and practices thus failed to meet the antireligionists' final criterion: "The value of a religion is in direct proportion to its benefit to society" (Ch'en Tu-hsiu, 1917).[38]

Organized religions fared better in the face of this criterion, and some reformers even felt that Buddhism or a revitalized Confucianism could serve as a spiritual basis for progress in the way that, in their view,

---

[37] Translated in Wm. Theodore deBary et al., *Sources of Chinese Tradition*, Vol. 2 (New York: Columbia University Press, 1964), pp. 287–288.

[38] Tse-tsung Chow, *The May Fourth Movement: Intellectual Revolution in Modern China* (Cambridge, Mass.: Harvard University Press, 1960), p. 329.

Christianity did for certain Western nations. The fortunes of Christianity itself, on the other hand, were quite mixed. As the dominant religion of successful Western nations, it was loved by some as the spiritual counterpart of modern science and hated by others as the religious bedpartner of imperialism. This created a special dilemma for a certain sector of Chinese youth, students of China's then numerous Christian schools, who in May 1919, for example, felt called upon to join in antigovernment, anti-Western demonstrations. We see this in a moving account by the American philosopher John Dewey and his wife about the closing of St. John's College near Shanghai on National Humiliation Day, written by them shortly after their arrival in China:

> Students walked to Shanghai, ten miles, on the hottest day to parade, then ten miles back. Some of them fell by the way with sunstroke. On their return in the evening they found some of the younger students going in to a concert. The day was a holiday, called the Day of Humiliation. The students stood outside of the door where the concert was to be held, and their principal came out and told them they must go to the concert. They replied that they were praying there, as it was not a time for celebrating by a concert on the Day of Humiliation. . . . Students said they were watching there for the sake of China as the apostles prayed at the death of Christ and this anniversary was like the anniversary of the death of Christ. The President told them if they did not go in he would shut them out of the college. This he did.[39]

Up to the present time, Christianity's international stature and Western support remain both its strength and weakness as a missionary movement in China, although Chinese Communist attitudes toward religion have naturally complicated the matter.

Religion and Chinese Communism

Like Christianity, Buddhism has reaped certain benefits as an international faith, especially because Chinese Communist Party leaders have since gaining control in 1949 sought to improve relations with Asian neighbors that have large Buddhist populations. However, it was before 1949, when Chinese Buddhism was in charge of itself, that it made the most substantial strides to enhance "its benefit to society." For, to some extent in competition with Christianity, it sought to further develop its own latent tendencies toward social philanthropy. And this trend continues today in places like Taiwan, Hong Kong, and elsewhere outside mainland China. But inside the mainland, where the religion exists as an official Chinese Buddhist Association pledged to social progress, its membership and resources have diminished so much that it has little impact as a social or religious force.

Organized Taoism is even worse off than Buddhism, both in and outside the mainland, as it has been throughout the twentieth century. It is not a universal religion with international support, and its fate may therefore be tied to the native Chinese folk tradition in which its priests serve.

---

[39] Chow, p. 323, note f.

It survives in Taiwan, where folk religion continues to thrive despite industrialization, and where the Sixty-Fourth Celestial Master Chang lives in
exile. It also hangs on in the mainland as the Chinese Taoist Association,
the Taoist counterpart of the state affiliated Chinese Buddhist Association
just mentioned.

Whatever the future holds for Taoism and Chinese Buddhism, it is
clear that they are not what is replacing Confucianism as China's new
orthodoxy. As the historian Arthur Wright has noted, for both China and
its Asian neighbors, today's trend is toward nationalism and various "secular faiths" that promise material rather than spiritual salvation. In his article
"Buddhism in Modern and Contemporary China," he concludes:

> Last, we might observe that throughout the whole of eastern Asia, the struggle today
> is for the new nations' survival as economically and politically viable units. The eyes
> of Asian people are turned to the ideologues who offer to relate present actions to
> future benefits, to the five-year planners, the technicians who seek to bring these people
> up to the level of life achieved over a period of two hundred crowded years by the
> West. We should be prepared therefore for a long period of secular faiths, of leadership
> that talks of economic and political salvation rather than the salvation of souls, of
> earthly utopias rather than heavenly cities.[40]

And among secular faiths, one that can be singled out for its zeal in demanding religiouslike popular support is Chinese communism. Many have argued
that communism is itself religious. And some would add that, because of
its own opposition to everything that it calls "religion," it is a faith that
cannot easily coexist with others. Unlike most traditional Chinese religion,
it is of the type that says "you shall have no other gods besides me."
Founded in the West just over a century ago by Karl Marx, it has spread
even faster than did the prophetic movements of Jesus and Muhammad
in their respective ages and, similarly, has divided the world into two opposing camps, each denouncing the other with religious fervor.

In the shape it took under Mao Tse-tung (Mao Ze-dong, 1893–1976),
in a nation just emerging from its involvement with traditional state and
folk religion, communism has been subject to religious colorations in China
even above and beyond its typical demand for repentence, conversion,
and unconditional allegiance. At the state level, Chinese Communist Party
leaders like Mao have at times had the status of official state deities; and
national holiday celebrations have perpetuated the atmosphere under which
the former state religion glorified emperors as semidivine Sons of Heaven.
At the folk level, the party first gained support not only because of its
mundane economic programs but also because of its utopian promises
of a future like the one envisaged by the religious millenarians of premodern
China. And it has kept the people's support not only by making economic
improvements but also by creating popular drama, music, and art in which
socialist themes have replaced traditional religious ones.

---

[40] Arthur F. Wright, "Buddhism in Modern and Contemporary China," in *Religion and Change in Contemporary Asia,* ed. Robert F. Spencer (Minneapolis: University of Minnesota Press, 1971), p. 26.

FIGURE 2.4. The new state religion is superimposed on the old, as patriotic slogans and Mao Tse-tung's portrait decorate the Gate of Heavenly Peace, outer entrance to Peking's Forbidden City.

Yet all this has not been done in a secret or sinister manner. It has been part of a conscious effort to make various popular activities serve the purpose of socialist progress at the same time that they provide recreation. Nevertheless, some have wondered whether this has involved a change only in objects of devotion rather than in social or religious consciousness. Consider Italian novelist Alberto Moravia's description of a procession of young Red Guards. He compares the procession to a religious parade of the kind traditionally held for a community god (such as on the god's birthday).

> As the flag moves closer to us, we can see the whole procession. The marchers are boys and girls, Red Guards, as we can guess from the scarlet bands they wear on their arms. All of them in blue trousers, white shirts, boys and girls alike, each with the little book of Mao clutched in his [or her] hand. At their head marches the standard-bearer, the flagstaff thrust into his belt. Then come two girls, carrying a portrait of Mao, framed in gold and decked with red festoons. And behind the portrait come the demonstrators, single file. . . . It need scarcely be said that the style of these processions, like that of the propaganda shows with their songs and music and dancing, is religious in the traditional peasant pattern of religion. In place of the red banner, set the standard of Confraternity, replace Mao's portrait with the patron saint of the village, and you'll scarcely be able to see any difference; basically, nothing has changed.[41]

---

[41] Alberto Moravia, "China Is an Immense School," in *Religious Policy and Practice in Communist China,* by Donald MacInnis (New York: Macmillan, Inc., 1972), pp. 346–347.

Now, in fairness, it must be pointed out that the events just described come from early in the Cultural Revolution (1966–1976), a radical sectarian movement matched in Chinese history only by the Taiping Rebellion of the nineteenth century. The often destructive excesses of its Red Guards have fortunately passed from the Chinese scene, along with Chairman Mao, and been replaced by more pragmatic and less repressive forces. One result of this has been an unprecedented growth of religious activities (Buddhist, Taoist, and even Christian) long held at bay. But whether this means a new beginning for organized religions in China, or only a temporary reprieve, remains to be seen. Let us turn now from this survey of Chinese religious history to selected periods and figures that deserve a more detailed treatment.

FORMATIVE PERIODS AND THEIR KEY FIGURES

According to theory about *yin* and *yang,* neither one of these cosmic forces can predominate for long; each invariably gives way to the other. Night is always followed by day; winter cold always leads into spring and then summer; a long and blistering drought inevitably ends in needed rainfall. And as the world of nature goes, so does the world of human history. Just as every individual is destined to lose youth's beauty, grow old, and die, so is there a limited term of life for every human institution from a merchant's shop to a royal dynasty.

Seeming to follow this universal law, Confucianism, sometimes called the *yang* dimension of Chinese culture, achieved a pinnacle of success during the Han era and then fell to its lowest level of influence in the era that followed. And that era, moreover, saw the growth of China's more *yin*like Taoist tradition and its foreign spiritual counterpart, Buddhism. Because of their special significance for Chinese religious history, each of these two eras will be described in detail. At the same time, two major figures from Chinese religious history, one from each period, will be discussed and compared. They are Tung Chung-shu (Dong Zhong-shu, ca. 179–104 B.C.E.), the grand architect of Han Confucianism, and Ko Hung (Ge Hong, ca. 283–340), an eclectic luminary who influenced Taoist developments during the Period of Disunity.

The Han Dynasty Confucian Triumph

When the unification of China was completed in 221 B.C.E., the new Ch'in ruler wasted no time in taking steps to eliminate all vestiges of the Chou Dynasty feudal system. For example, his Legalist prime minister, Li Ssu, made a proposal to the throne advocating the burning of books and the execution of scholars at odds with Ch'in policies. In his proposal, he indicated that the characteristically Confucian love for past traditions could not coexist with the pragmatic goals of the new government:

> In their discussion, the scholars speak of ancient times in order to decry the present. They use false examples to stir up confusion in the actual state of affairs, and they

proclaim the excellence of the doctrines they have studied to abuse what your majesty has established. . . . This being the case, unless we take action, the authority of the sovereign will be abased, the association of the malcontents will grow powerful. It is necessary to prevent this. Your subject proposes that the histories (of the feudal states), with the exception of that of Ch'in, shall all be burnt. With the exception of those holding the rank of "Scholars of Great Learning," [seventy men appointed by the emperor] all men in the entire empire who possess copies of the *Shu Ching*, the *Shih Ching*, and the works of the Hundred Schools, must all take these books to the magistrate to be burnt. Those who dare to discuss and comment upon the *Shu Ching* and *Shih Ching* shall be put to death and their bodies exposed in the market place. Those who praise ancient institutions to decry the present regime shall be exterminated with all the members of their families. Officials who condone breaches of this law shall themselves be implicated in the crime. Thirty days after the publication of this decree, all who have not burnt their books will be branded and sent to forced labor on the Great Wall.[42]

This decree was approved, many scholars perished, and the various books covered by the ban were sought out and burned with the same steadfast efficiency that the Ch'in ruler used in his military campaigns and work on the Great Wall. How was it then possible for the Confucian School— a main target of the decree's prohibitions—to survive and even make strides toward becoming China's state orthodoxy within the next two centuries? Part of the answer to this question lay in the past, for Confucianism's roots reached deep into the soil of ancient China and could not be torn out by one brief attack, however severe. But the rest of the answer lay in events yet to take place, for Confucianism had to undergo a major redevelopment before gaining its dominant position.

ORIGINS OF CONFUCIAN INFLUENCE. In 201 B.C.E., shortly after overthrowing the Ch'in and restoring order in the country, Emperor Kao (Gao) of the Han Dynasty held his first New Year Court Audience, an ancient ceremony meant to strengthen the ties between the emperor and the various nobles and ministers below him. According to the famous *Records of the Historian*, written a century and a half later by Ssu-ma Ch'ien (Si-ma Qian), the ceremony occurred as follows:

In this ceremony, before dawn, the Internuncios directing the ritual led them [nobles and ministers] according to rank through the gate to the hall. . . . At the foot of the hall, the Gentlemen of the Palace, several hundred of them, flanked the stairs. The ministers of merit and full marquises, the generals and military officers, took their places according to rank on the western side, where they faced the east, while the civil officials, from the Chancelor downward, took their places on the eastern side, where they faced the west. . . . Then the Emperor, in this imperial conveyance, emerged from his apartment, and the standard-bearers of the hundred officials alerted (the assembled multitude). The vassal kings and marquises, down to the officials of six hundred bushels, were led forward according to rank to offer their felicitations, and there was no one, from vassal kings and marquises downward, who did not quake with fear and awe.

[42] C. P. Fitzgerald, *China: A Short Cultural History* (New York: Frederick A. Praeger, 1954), pp. 144–145.

> Upon the conclusion of this ceremony, wine was served in an orderly manner. All those seated in attendance in the hall bowed their heads to the floor and then, in order of rank, arose and wished long life (to the Emperor). . . . Thereupon Emperor Kao said: "Today I know the nobility of being Emperor."[43]

This account lets us see what was perhaps Confucianism's greatest advantage over other schools. Probably without exception, Chinese emperors loved ceremony and saw the need for it in government; and the Confucians were ahead of all others as ritual experts. While they also held much else in their hand, this was their trump card. In fact, where early Han emperors were concerned, the Confucians' advice on ritual matters was at least as important as their advice on political ones.

Under the famous Emperor Wu, when Confucianism made its greatest advances, this emperor's love for ritual was again a factor. But it was not the whole story. On the throne for forty-six years (141–187 B.C.E.), Emperor Wu (the "martial emperor") was known for his efforts to expand the borders of the empire and pacify all the territory that lay within them. In these efforts, the help of his Confucian ministers played no small role. In the *History of the Former Han Dynasty,* Emperor Wu is shown at court graciously seeking their advice on matters of state. In the following episode, for example, he appears as a paragon of sincerity and concern for his people:

> The Emperor Wu said, "I have received the throne from the former rulers and I should put their principles into practice, but the responsibility is so great that I cannot sleep. I wish to perfect the state, and so I collect the scholars and loyal men of the country to discuss thoroughly the Great Principle [of good government]. I am happy that you have come to advise me. . . . You know the Tao ["Way"] of the ancient rulers better than I. Reveal it to me and conceal nothing. Help me to adopt the good and correct the evil, so that a good government may be created for future generations. Do your best, hide nothing from me, and I myself will diligently examine these things."[44]

In this case, the response to his request was provided by Tung Chung-shu, whose solutions will be discussed later. First let us consider some general principles of Han Confucianism.

HAN CONFUCIAN IDEOLOGY. The most fundamental principle of Han Confucianism concerned the close relationship between humanity and nature, and especially between the emperor, as Son of Heaven, and Heaven itself, as the ruler of nature. Not explicit in the teachings of Confucius, this principle developed as the Confucians incorporated ideas from other schools, particularly the Yin-Yang School. According to their new theory, the emperor's political decisions, and also his performance of state rituals, were supposed to follow nature in the specific terms defined by *yin-yang,* five-phases thinking. The basis for the whole theory was found in the se-

---

[43] Translated in Bodde. Copyright © 1975 by Princeton University Press. Excerpt, pp. 146–147, reprinted by permission of Princeton University Press.

[44] Shryock, p. 49.

quence of these phases and in the numerous correspondences between them and other aspects of life, as shown in the following table of selected examples:

Elemental Phases

	wood	*fire*	*earth*	*metal*	*water*
Direction	east	south	center	west	north
Season	spring	summer	whole year	autumn	winter
Color	green	red	yellow	white	black
Grain	wheat	beans	panicled millet	hemp	millet
Virtue	benevolence	wisdom	faith	rightness	decorum
Animal	sheep	fowl	ox	dog	pig

This set of correspondences became basic to Chinese state religion. It determined the details of all imperial sacrifices by specifying the time, location, colors, and so forth, that were appropriate to a particular object of worship.

The new theory further specified that, in addition to thus conforming to natural patterns in his rituals, the ruler had to keep an eye out for unusual phenomena that might be a message or warning from Heaven. Of course, he did not personally do this but instead had court astronomers to assist him, just as he had ritual, financial, military, and diplomatic specialists to help him perform other key functions of government. And as the number of posts for such functions grew, and more and more followers of Confucius came to fill them, something began to evolve that would thereafter remain an identifying feature of Chinese civilization: the so-called Confucian bureaucracy. At first, of course, officials in the different posts were from different schools of thought, but as time went on, only the Confucian School succeeded in offering a world view and political system suitable in scope for the empire-building enterprise of the Han Dynasty.

EXPLAINING CONFUCIAN SUCCESS. What, we must ask, were the Confucian qualities that allowed for this success? *First,* of course, the Confucians were great traditionalists and thus the custodians of a voluminous literature of ancient classics. Confucius had himself said: "I would rather transmit than create; I believe in and prefer the teachings of antiquity" (*Analects* 7:1). In fact, in contrast to the predominantly military or priestly character of the ruling class in many other ancient cultures, China's Confucian elite remained so distinctly oriented to scholarship that they have been, quite appropriately, called literati. *Second,* the Confucians honored government service and insisted that once one accepted a post under a (virtuous) ruler, he should serve his lord with utmost devotion, a quality that would be desired by emperors of the Han or any other dynasty. During his own time, Confucius was asked by a ruler to describe how he should employ the services of his officials and how they in turn should serve him.

The Master replied: "A ruler should employ his officials according to the traditional code of ritual and etiquette; and the officials should serve the ruler with unswerving devotion to duty" (*Analects* 3:19). *Third,* as the quotation indicates, the Confucians placed great emphasis on *li:* the traditional code of ritual and etiquette. As the Han system of state sacrifices and court ceremony became more and more complex, the Confucians' knowledge in such matters greatly enhanced their image in the eyes of Han emperors. *Fourth,* and also indicating the importance of ethico-religious factors for the Confucian success, was the ancient Mandate of Heaven theory, which held that Heaven appointed but one legitimate sovereign— the Son of Heaven—for all the civilized world (i.e., the Chinese empire). This theory guaranteed that a reigning emperor had the moral and religious right to rule. At the same time it stipulated that he must rule virtuously or risk the loss of his divine appointment. *Fifth,* and finally, with the Mandate of Heaven theory as a basis, Han Confucians weaved a great system linking all natural and human events together into one all-encompassing whole. The comprehensiveness of this system was extremely well suited to the Han rulers' desire to bring stability and unity to an empire that had, for the first time, incorporated that great area of eastern Asia now known to us as China.

Ultimately, Han Confucianism deified Master K'ung, insisted that it possessed orthodox truth, and laid a monopolistic claim to all the official functions needing to be performed for the Son of Heaven. Thus a grand scheme was completed—a scheme that matched the scale of the Han imperial enterprise. In order to understand more fully the nature of this scheme, it will be worthwhile to have a close-up look at the man most responsible for creating it, the Han scholar and court advisor Tung Chung-shu.

Tung Chung-shu: Grand Architect of Han Confucianism

According to *History of the Former Han Dynasty,* Tung Chung-shu was in his time "the leader of all the literati."[45] This work also informs us that although he never held high office, he was widely respected as a teacher and writer; and it reports on the dialogue between him and Emperor Wu to which reference was made earlier. From that dialogue was previously quoted the emperor's humble request for guidance. Now here is part of Tung's answer:

> I have studied in the *Spring and Autumn Annals* what a great ruler should be. The essential is uprightness. The ruler follows uprightness, and is close to Heaven. The principle of government is to follow the action of Heaven by governing with uprightness, for the ruler must act as Heaven acts.
>
> The Tao of Heaven summons the Yin and the Yang. Yang signifies virtue, while Yin

---

[45] Fung Yu-lan, *A History of Chinese Philosophy,* Vol. 2, trans. Derk Bodde (Princeton: Princeton University Press, 1953), p. 18.

signifies punishment or killing. To emphasize virtue is to aid growth. Yang is the source of life in the spring, while Yin destroys in the fall. From this we can see that Heaven also emphasizes Yang. Yang is used to give life and is assisted by Yin, for without Yin, Yang is not complete. The ruler merely carries out the intention of Heaven, and so he should endeavor to develop virtue and education, not depending upon punishment. . . .

Confucius said, "If you punish without educating the people, that is cruelty."

A year is a unit and exhibits the greatness of all things. It must have a foundation of unity, in order that all may prosper, and therefore a ruler of men, like the year, must unify his heart, making it upright, for if his heart is rectified, the state will have unity and uprightness. Then the officials will follow his example, the people also, until the whole world will be upright and things far and near will possess unity. In such a land, evil will hardly appear, Yin and Yang will be harmonized, wind and rain will come at the right seasons, while life will be peaceful and the people settled in good order. Harvests will be plentiful, even the grass and trees will flourish, and the whole world will be richly nourished.[46]

From this single passage, we can grasp many key features of Han Confucianism as set forth by Tung Chung-shu. First, it explains that the source of his inspiration was the *Spring and Autumn Annals,* which he believed to contain important judgments on history made by Confucius, whom Tung considered to be a godlike sage on whom Heaven had secretly conferred its mandate. Second, the passage points to the Confucian principle of government that "the ruler must act as Heaven acts." Third, it explains that the ruler can do so by comprehending how Heaven employs *yin* and *yang* in its operation. Fourth, it tells us that in a government modeled on Heaven the stress is on education and exemplary behavior, not on strict punishments. Finally, it argues that when the ruler's good example is followed by his officials and the people, not only the social but even the natural world will flourish.

All these and other essential principles of Han Confucianism were weaved by Tung into one great religio-political system. Here these various principles will be discussed under three headings: (1) Tung's view of the human as a microcosm of the universe; (2) his presentation of the Confucian ruler as a man among men—the Son of Heaven; (3) his understanding of the world as a single organismic whole.

THE HUMAN AS MICROCOSM. In his *Luxuriant Dew of the Spring and Autumn Annals* (an exposition of the truths expressed by Confucius in the *Annals* themselves), Tung made this key statement:

Heaven, Earth, the *yin* and *yang,* and wood, fire, earth, metal and water [the five elemental phases] make nine; together with man they make ten. Heaven's number is with this made complete.[47]

---

[46] Shryock, p. 51.

[47] Fung, p. 19.

It is thus due to the existence of humanity that the essential components of the universe come to number *ten*—Heaven's number and a Chinese symbol of perfection. More than this, each human being has a body, an inner nature, and feelings that uniquely represent—in microcosmic form—the components of the universe as macrocosm. The five phases correspond to the body's Five Viscera (heart, liver, spleen, lungs, and kidneys). The inner nature is *yang*, while the feelings are *yin*. Humanity is uniquely bestowed Heaven's Mandate and forms part of the great cosmic trinity of Heaven, Earth, and Man. And who is it that can make this trinity a working unity? It is the Son of Heaven, the man among men, the one and only legitimate king in the civilized world.

THE SON OF HEAVEN. Tung's most important pronouncement on the subject of kingship is as follows:

> The ancients, when they invented writing, drew three (horizontal) lines which they connected through the center (by a vertical stroke), and then called this "king" [pronounced *wang* and written 王]. These three lines represent Heaven, Earth, and man, while the connecting of them through the center represents the (king's) penetration of their (interrelated) principles. Who, indeed, if not a (true) king, could take the central position between Heaven, Earth, and man, so as to act as the connecting link between them? Therefore the king models himself on Heaven. He takes its seasons as his model and gives them completeness. He models himself on its commands and circulates them among all men. He models himself on its numerical (categories) and uses them when initiating affairs. He models himself on its course and thereby brings his administration into operation. He models himself on its will and with it attaches himself to love (*jen*).[48]

It is in exercising Heaven's will and loving the world as does Heaven that the king both enjoys his privileges and bears his responsibilities as the Son of Heaven. His main responsibility is to lead as well as to *educate* the people, which is not so much a matter of teaching them how to read and write as it is of *completing their natures*. Because the nature each person receives from Heaven is potentially good but incomplete, the king, in his personal behavior, must exemplify the principles of proper conduct for all others to follow. Only by acting in this way can he expect that the people will obey him and that Heaven will let him remain on the throne. But what is proper conduct for the Son of Heaven? This question is answered in Tung's organicistic theory of the universe.

THE UNIVERSAL ORGANISM. Just as the human body is for Tung a microcosm of the universe, so is the universe for him an organism that operates like the human mind and body. When one's appendix (or even one's finger) becomes inflamed, other parts of the body are affected, for all events in the body are correlative, that is, mutually related to one another. Thus, inflamation in one part of the body may lead to excessive heat throughout the body (a fever). In a similar way, Tung would argue,

---

[48] Fung, pp. 46–47.

each event in the universe is connected with all other *like* events. Thus his world view is governed by a principle of "like responds to like," as stated, for example, in the following passage:

> If now water be poured on level ground, it will avoid the parts that are dry and move toward those that are wet. Whereas if (two) identical pieces of firewood are exposed to fire, the latter will avoid the one that is wet and catch to that which is dry. All things avoid that from which they differ and cleave to that to which they are similar. Thus forces that are similar meet each other, and tones that match respond to each other. Experience makes this evident. . . . There is nothing supernatural in this. . . . In the same way, when an emperor or king is about to arise, auspicious omens first appear, whereas when he is about to be destroyed, evil auguries likewise first appear. Thus it is that things of the same kind call to one another.[49]

Therefore, in governing, the king must watch out for the warnings and reprimands of Heaven as expressed in unusual astronomical phenomena, unseasonal weather, or natural disasters. He must also pattern himself upon Heaven in the most exact way possible, keeping his political as well as ritual behavior in accord with the course of the seasons. Tung specified a proper way of governing for each season, telling us of the ideal king: "With his beneficence he duplicates warmth and accords with spring, with his conferring of rewards he duplicates heat and accords with summer, with his punishments he duplicates coolness and accords with autumn, and with his executions he duplicates coldness and accords with winter."[50]

In addition to being concerned with the four seasonal ways of governing, the Son of Heaven must also pay careful attention to the color of his clothes at seasonal rituals, the directions in which he travels at different times, the number of officials who serve him at various levels, and so forth. For all these things have their correlational significance according to the system of *yin, yang,* and the five phases. Why are the actions of this one man such a delicate matter? It is so because the natural and social world wherein he stands is a very subtly balanced one. Just as a stone tossed into the center of a pond causes waves to reach its banks, the influence of acts performed by the Son of Heaven reaches to the four corners of the world. If his acts are evil or disharmonious, thus will the whole world become.

For this reason, perhaps, Tung was obsessed with creating a complete and perfect system of correspondences for all natural, social, and individual acts. He wanted to create a system that could serve all the purposes of the one man who must govern "all under Heaven" (the phrase traditionally used to designate the Chinese empire). To meet this aim, Tung took the idea of the human being as a microcosm of the universe and gave it significance on a truly imperial scale, thus fashioning the great vision of Han Confucianism.

This vision, with its skillful synthesis of religion and politics, would

---

[49] Fung, p. 56.
[50] Fung, p. 48.

leave its impression on all later Chinese dynasties. Yet when the Han Dynasty disintegrated and Confucian theorists lost their official support, a period of national disunity followed that left them without a centralized national bureaucracy in which to serve. The new social and political climate did not encourage further development of the Confucian path toward sagehood through service to state and society. Instead, it encouraged the emergence of spiritual paths leading away from such service and toward world-transcending liberation.

Taoism, Immortality, and Anticonventionalism in the Period of Disunity

The fall of the Han Dynasty in China has been compared to the fall of Rome in early European history, for both followed upon barbarian invasions and led to the disintegration of a great centralized culture. However, although later Chinese historians would call the era that ensued an "age of confusion," it would be wrong to call it a "Dark Age." For despite its being characterized by political disunity, it was a very lively era from the intellectual and spiritual point of view.

In the Han period, the Confucian tradition became wed to the imperial government and was transformed into a state religion. During the Period of Disunity, Taoism became a religion linked with Chinese folk traditions as well as court intellectual life, and Buddhism brought China a whole new set of fascinating spiritual concepts from India. While the Han Dynasty was thus famous for the development of China's orthodox system of government and state rituals, its demise opened the door for an era of experimentation with new and, from the Confucian perspective, "unorthodox" practices. Mirroring events that have occurred elsewhere in the history of religions, China's increased interest in metaphysical speculation, voluntary religious groups, and individual spiritual liberation were all part of a pattern. And the heart of this pattern can be expressed in a single word: *transcendence*.

Sometimes the quest to transcend the ordinary temporal world is only vaguely visible in religions beneath layers of social convention, monotonous liturgies, priestly vestments, and practical considerations tied up with their physical survival. But, at other times, the quest for transcendence breaks through to the surface of religious life. The desire for direct, unmediated contact with the spiritual dimension takes precedence over the practical concerns facing a religious group, society, or nation. One such time was the period of Chinese religious history we are now describing. Like their Han predecessors, Chinese thinkers of this period still dealt with the same issue—the human being's place in the universe—and even continued to do so by conceiving of the human individual as microcosm and the universe as macrocosm. But the similarities ended there. This new breed of thinkers turned from Confucian to Taoist models in conceiving the microcosmic-macrocosmic relationship. They turned from worldly goals, such as empire building and government service, to transcendent ones, such as Taoist immortality and Buddhist *nirvāna*. And they turned from social conformity to individualistic nonconformity in defining the ideal of human behavior. In what follows, something will be said about each of these shifts in perspective.

TAOIST MODELS OF MICROCOSM AND MACROCOSM. The introduction to Taoism in Chapter 1 credited this religion with making the most of the Chinese idea that the essential structure and energies of the whole universe are present in each of its constituent parts. Now we have a chance to see precisely how this is so. According to Taoist views formulated during the Period of Disunity, each human body is a dynamic configuration of cosmic Life Force, or Breath (*ch'i*), made unique by its own peculiar Essence (*ching; jing,* which also means "semen" in the case of male bodies), and guided by a conscious Spirit (*shen*). These three fundamentals of life have parallels in several other aspects of the Taoist microcosmology of the body, such as the Three Fields, Three Palaces, and Three Vermin.

Of the Three Fields, the one associated with Spirit is located in the head, the one connected with Life Force in the chest, and that linked with Essence in the abdomen, below the navel. These three energy centers are known, more specifically, as *Alchemical* Fields (*tan-t'ien; dan-tian*), and they have a central role in the Taoist mystical practice called Internal Alchemy (soon to be discussed under the Taoist quest for immortality). The Three Palaces are located precisely where the Three Fields are found. Being further divided into nine palaces each, they represent a detailed conception of the forces that run the body—a conception probably inspired by the actual palace compounds of Chinese emperors. In the head, for example, where the controlling Spirit dwells, we find the most complex arrangement of palatial structures, halls and offices for nearly every conceivable kind of royal dignitary and divine official, including the Jade Emperor.

Furthermore, as in the macrocosmic universe, there are gods outside these palace compounds for every part and function of the human microcosm. Some of the more important ones inhabit the internal organs, divided into Five Viscera (heart, liver, spleen, lungs, and kidneys) and Six Receptacles (stomach, gall bladder, large intestine, small intestine, bladder, and, taken together, esophagus/interior stomach canal/urethra). According to one account: "These gods command 18,000 [other] gods." And, the account continues:

> When a man concentrates his thought upon them, the 18,000 gods do not scatter; when they do not scatter, Heaven causes 18,000 other gods to come down so as to complete the inside of the body, making 36,000 gods in all, who together lift the whole body and bring it up to the Three Heavens. Then the man becomes a Divine Immortal; his transformation is without fault.[51]

Thus can proper treatment of the body's indwelling gods lead to immortality. But, conversely, the body also has indwelling evil spirits that are bent

---

[51] Translated in Henri Maspero, *Taoism and Chinese Religion,* trans. Frank A. Kierman, Jr. (Amherst, Mass.: University of Massachusetts Press, 1981), p. 347. On the topic of the Three Palaces, see pp. 326–329, and on the Three Vermin, pp. 332–337.

on its early destruction and death. Primary among these are the Three Vermin associated with the body's Three Fields and Three Palaces.

Called Old Blue, White Maiden, and Bloody Corpse, the Three Vermin are considered to be responsible for maladies of the three respective areas where they dwell: head, chest, and abdomen. These nemeses of life seek to take advantage of every human error—spiritual, moral, or physical—precisely in order to subtract time from a person's life span. They seek to drive off a person's indwelling good spirits. They report misdeeds to the heavenly Director of Destiny, petitioning that a certain number of days be taken off one's life. And they encourage and delight in dietary imprudence, such as gluttony, as an opportunity to cause disease. In every way, then, they are the counterparts of those evil-doing ghosts and demons that inhabit the macrocosmic universe according to Taoist cosmology.

The Taoist Master must, therefore, be just as much on guard against these internal enemies as he is against external ones, and not only for his own sake but also for that of the community he serves—his "diocese" (to borrow a term from Catholicism). In addition, reflecting the extreme importance of the microcosmic-macrocosmic relationship in Taoism, his internal success can have great benefits for the external world. Reporting on the way this still works in modern Taiwan, Kristofer Schipper explains it as follows:

> At each ceremony during the liturgical year, the *ch'i* of the master's body are upgraded and, thanks to the system of the integration of the faithful with the *lu* of the master ["register" of deities he can call upon for aid], the whole community and country is also elevated in spiritual status. The *hsing-tao* [*xing-dao:* "practice of the Tao"] of the Taoist Master is the way of salvation for all that live within his diocese. It is traditionally said that Legendary Immortals rise up to Heaven accompanied by their entire families as well as with the dogs and chickens of their wards. *The external world depends on the internal world of the Taoist.*[52]

Now we shall see what occurs within the Taoist Master's "practice of the Tao."

THE QUEST FOR IMMORTALITY. The various Taoist methods for attaining immortality can be grouped under either External Alchemy or Internal Alchemy, as long as these terms are defined broadly enough. External Alchemy was quite in vogue during the Period of Disunity but was later abandoned almost completely. It must be taken to include the ingestion of powerful drugs as well as the more narrowly alchemical procedure of transmuting benign, commonplace materials into gold or elixirs of immortality. Little will be said of it here except to point out that it frequently led to death and was probably abandoned for this reason. It nevertheless had its value, as did alchemy in the West, within the development of science in China. Internal Alchemy is the real focus of this discussion of the Taoist quest for immortality. It must be taken to include the dietary and calisthenic

---

[52] Kristofer Schipper, "The Taoist Body," *History of Religions,* 17:3–4 (1978), p. 381 (italics added).

practices that prepared one for the inner circulation of *ch'i*, which itself constituted the specifically "alchemical" dimension of Taoist mystical practice.

The dietary and calisthenic practices that prepared one for doing Internal Alchemy were conceived of by reference to the Taoist internal "cosmology" just described. One was instructed to consume what would destroy the inner Three Vermin and to avoid foods that would sustain them; and one was required to perform a rite of propitiation for the god inhabiting any part of the body about to be exercised. Likewise, it was in the Three Alchemical Fields of the human microcosm that the mystical practices of Internal Alchemy were to occur. In the Three Fields were believed to exist three furnaces where alchemical "firings" could be done in conjunction with the circulation of *ch'i* through channels supposed to connect the fields with one another. Now Taoist calisthenics probably had an actual effect upon physical health and was closely linked with the evolution of Chinese gymnastics and martial arts. And the respiratory exercises underlying the practice of circulating *ch'i* presumably benefited both mind and body. But whatever the psycho-physiological effects may have been, they were not the ultimate goal of these "alchemical" practices, which was to generate a spiritual "embryo" instead of a physical drug. The spirit-infant thus created was considered to be the true elixir of immortality: a spirit-body that could become one's immortal vehicle after the physical body died.

The belief that this goal was a real possibility shaped the evolution of the Taoist religion during the Period of Disunity and was passionately defended by leading writers of the period, such as Ko Hung, whose views will soon be described. Yet at the same time there were those who, having already rejected the Confucian quest for official position and social reform, did not take the Taoist quest for immortality, or anything else, very seriously. These were the nonconformists and anticonventionalists of their age; and without describing them, our picture of the era would be incomplete.

SEVEN WORTHIES OF THE BAMBOO GROVE. Near China's northern capital of Loyang late during the Wei Dynasty (221–265), at a place known as Bamboo Grove, scholars gathered to engage in what were called pure conversations (*ch'ing-t'an; ching-tan*). These were discussions untainted by worldly concerns, delving into abstruse problems, and perhaps ending in silent smiles or roaring laughter that expressed common understanding of truths beyond words. This place was not far from the estate of a certain Hsi K'ang (Xi Kang, 223–262), perhaps the leader of a group known to posterity as the Seven Worthies of the Bamboo Grove. He was among those in this group who left important Taoist philosophical writings behind. In one of his writings, he expressed the group's overall attitude toward worldly wealth and glory, as follows:

Is it necessary to have glory and splendor before one has honor? Cultivate the field to raise rice and weave clothing. When these are sufficient leave the wealth of the world alone. Do as a thirsty person drinking from a river. He drinks happily enough but does not covet the voluminous flow. . . . This is how the gentleman exercises his mind, for he regards rank and position as a tumor and material wealth as dirt and dust.[53]

Others in the group, such as Wang Jung (Wang Rong, 234–305) and Hsiang Hsiu (Xiang Xiu, ca. 221–300), are also remembered for their philosophical contributions. These were contributions to a movement in Chinese thought known appropriately as Abstruse Learning (*hsuan-hsueh; xuan-xue*). Yet, as a whole, the Seven Worthies gained their reputation more for representing a way of life than for writing philosophy. They termed their way of life "wind flowing" (*feng-liu*), a phrase that has since come to denote bohemianism, amorousness, and eccentricity. For them, it meant naturalness or spontaneity as opposed to behavior conforming to conventional morality. Examples of the spontaneous acts and witticisms attributed to them and their likeminded contemporaries are amply recorded in a fascinating book called *Tales of the World*, written late in the era under discussion (fifth century). Several examples from this book are given below.

Many tales about the Seven Worthies touch upon the role of wine drinking in helping them overcome the fears and inhibitions of ordinary men. Of one Liu Ling (third century), perhaps the greatest imbiber among them, it states:

On many occasions Liu Ling, under the influence of wine, would be completely free and uninhibited, sometimes taking off his clothes and sitting naked in his room. Once when some persons saw him and chided him for it, Ling retorted, "I take heaven and earth for my pillars and roof, and the rooms of my house for my pants and coat. What are you gentlemen doing in my pants?[54]

Two other notorious drinkers among the seven were Juan Chi (Ruan Ji, 210–263) and Juan Hsien (Ruan Xian, 234–305), of whom *Tales of the World* relates:

The Juans were all great drinkers. When Juan Hsien arrived at the home of any of the clan for a gathering, they no longer used ordinary wine cups (*pei* [*bei*]) for drinking toasts. Instead they would use a large earthenware vat (*weng*) filled with wine, and sitting facing each other all around it, would take large drafts. One time a herd of pigs came to drink and went directly up to the vat, whereupon pigs and men all proceeded to drink together.[55]

In addition to uninhibited spontaneity, such as wine may induce, tales about the Seven Worthies also laud calm self-composure in the face of danger or suffering. The *Tales of the World* account of the execution of

[53] Wm. Theodore deBary et al., *Sources of Chinese Tradition*, Vol. 1 (New York: Columbia University Press, 1960), p. 246.

[54] Richard B. Mather, trans., *A New Account of Tales of the World*, by Liu I-Ch'ing with commentary by Liu Chün (Minneapolis: University of Minnesota Press, 1976), p. 374.

[55] Mather, pp. 375–376.

the leader of the Seven Worthies, Hsi K'ang, well exemplifies this. Sentenced to death at the instigation of enemies at court who resented Hsi K'ang's arrogance and sharp tongue, he maintained an attitude of tranquil indifference. Even on the eve of his execution, "his manner and spirit showed no change"; and he spent his time calmly plucking a zither. Thus it was that another of the Seven Worthies, Shan T'ao (Shan Tao, 205–283), said of him: "As a person Hsi K'ang is majestically towering, like a solitary pine tree standing alone."[56] Such an image, indeed, expresses a whole array of values for which the Seven Worthies stood: aloofness, imperturbation, freedom, solitude, and transcendence.

Although these are typical values of the Period of Disunity, we have not chosen one of the Seven Worthies to exemplify the religious-philosophical trends of this period. Nor have we chosen one of the many Taoist priests or Buddhist monks of the period who played such a definitive role in shaping these two traditions, then still so young. Instead, our selection has been Ko Hung, an independent thinker who, because of his impassioned defense of the quest for immortality and his cataloging of its many methods (alchemical, respiratory, sexual, etc.), has nonetheless been appropriated by the Taoist tradition as somewhat of a patriarch. His links to Taoism, moreover, go beyond this. He was a member of the southern aristocracy during an era when foreign "barbarians" took over in the north and made South China the main theater of developments in "Chinese" culture—developments that included the Ling Pao and Mao Shan sects of Taoism as well as the Gentry Buddhism referred to in our historical survey earlier. Interestingly, it was his family and one related to it by generations of intermarriage that produced the basic texts of the Ling Pao and Mao Shan sects.[57] Let us now turn to a portrait of the man himself.

Ko Hung: The Master Who Embraced Simplicity

Ko Hung had no taste for the "pure conversations" continued by northern scholars in exile at the southern capital, where he was a native, and he detested those who drifted into drunken licentiousness in the name of Lao Tzu and Chuang Tzu. In addition, he was an individualist who was not afraid to criticize the ancient classics when reason or experience called for it. Yet, ultimately, this apparently rational individualist arrived at a strong belief in immortality and spent much of his life seeking it, which may seem difficult to understand. Fortunately, under the name of his self-chosen sobriquet, "the Master Who Embraces Simplicity," he left behind some writings that let us see the unity underlying his many different dimensions: rationalist and spiritualist, concerned social critic and mountain-dwelling recluse, Confucian scholar and Taoist alchemist.

The text of *The Master Who Embraces Simplicity* is itself divided into

---

[56] Mather, pp. 180 and 309.

[57] See Michel Strickmann, "The Longest Taoist Scripture," *History of Religions*, 17:3–4 (1978), p. 332, on the Ko family's links to the Ling Pao Sect; and "On the Alchemy of T'ao Hung-ching," in *Facets of Taoism* (cited earlier), p. 126, on its links to the Mao Shan Sect.

"outer" and "inner" sections dealing in one case with social philosophy
and in the other with the individual religious quest; and Ko himself described them, respectively, as "Confucian" and "Taoist."[58] In the Confucian
section, he depicts the corruption and ineffectiveness among social leaders
of his time in a way that helps us to understand why he ultimately chose
the life of a recluse. In fact, the first chapter of the Confucian section
constitutes a defense of this way of life in the form of a dialogue between
a recluse and "a man who ran to power." Consider the following excerpts
from the dialogue:

> [The "man who ran to power"] said "If we are to come to the aid of a society with
> many difficulties, we must employ extraordinary abilities. To stand in a high place and
> salute with clasped hands someone who is drowning is not the genuine practice of
> benevolence. To embrace the Way in one's heart but let the country fall into disorder
> is not the action of a sage. . . . I sincerely hope that now, since you have not gone
> far in your lost path, you will return."
>
> At this, the recluse looked off in the distance in an aloof manner. His spirit wandered
> in the thoroughfare of the heavens. It was far away. It was as if nothing was by his
> side. He lowered his head and replied, "Ah, how can you speak like that? The highest
> sage is without purposeful actions. He rests his spirit in the vastness (of nature). He
> does not permit his will to serve for salary, position, or material gain. Thus harm and
> insult cannot reach him. He does not pace back and forth in a dangerous place. Thus
> collapses and falls cannot cause him difficulty. . . . He looks just like the masses of
> people but in his heart he is happier than a king. . . .
>
> Thus I rest in my good points and correct my shortcomings. Although I have not the
> merit to stand in the court or the ability to be a warrior, I can study with young people,
> enlarge the Tao, and cultivate the straight—different paths to the same result (contribut-
> ing to society)."[59]

Despite the personal choice to stay out of office that is defended
here, Ko Hung was not unconcerned about the plight of his times. In
other of his "outer chapters," he detailed the many signs of moral decay
evident in his times: gambling, drinking, licentiousness, vile language, slov-
enly dress, arrogance on the part of those in power, and disobedience
among those below them. He compared the society of his day to a seriously
ill individual, needing strong medicine for severe problems. Thus, to argue
in favor of strict treatment for criminals, he used the body-state analogy,
a form of microcosmic-macrocosmic theory. Like Tung Chung-shu and
so many other Chinese thinkers, Ko considered society and the universe
to be organisms similar to the human body and subject to the same laws
of operation. Of course, while Tung's views on the individual, society,
and the universe were based on Han Confucianism's theory of correspondences, Ko built his ideas upon medicinal knowledge that was familiar to

---

[58] Stated in his autobiography as translated in Jay Sailey, *The Master Who Embraces Simplicity:
A Study of the Philospher Ko Hung*, A.D. 283–343 (San Francisco: Chinese Materials Center, 1978),
p. 265.
[59] Sailey, pp. 10–11 and 23–24; reprinted by permission of Chinese Materials Center.

him from the Taoist quest for immortality. However, this quest itself was not mentioned in the discourse on social problems in his "outer chapters." Instead, he placed all discussion of this quest in a separate part, the "inner chapters," because he felt it would be viewed askance by those who lacked the proper background and open-mindedness.

IMMORTALITY. Ko considered it correct not only to believe in Immortals but also to think of becoming one. As he saw it, in this universe of continually marvelous occurrences and miraculous transformations, beings far more advanced than humans must surely exist. For having the same essence as the universe itself, and already having discovered many of its life-nurturing secrets, humanity must be close to discovering the way toward an infinitely long and perfect life. What keeps most people confined to their limited mode of existence is their small-mindedness, he argued, their inability to conceive of things on a scale appropriate to the wonders of the universe. But what about the open-minded individual who withdraws from the world and seeks to become an Immortal? What methods are at his disposal? The "inner chapters" of *The Master Who Embraces Simplicity* give us one of China's earliest and fullest answers to this question.

Assuming that the human body is a microcosm of the universe, Ko Hung adopted the previously described belief that it was populated by numerous kinds of spirits. And he further believed that, for purposes of self-cultivation, it is necessary for one to give the inner gods a pleasant abode within a healthy body and to preserve the "breaths" (*ch'i*) which animate that body. The importance of the inner gods and breaths was explained by Ko as follows:

> It is through perfect freedom that the empiric comes into existence; form requires the inner gods in order to be. Then the empiric becomes the palace of perfect freedom, and bodies become the abodes of the inner gods. Therefore, to adopt a comparison with a dike, remember that when the dike crumbles, water is no longer retained. Similarly, when the breaths are exhausted, life itself ends. When the roots are worn out and the number of branches are excessive, vigor departs from the tree; when the breaths are worn out and desire gets the upper hand, the inner spirits leave the body. There is no time set for the return of the departing, and the decayed lacks the principle of life. These facts are sincerely regretted by the man who knows God.[60]

What the translator of the above passage renders as "perfect freedom" is the key Taoist metaphysical concept *wu* ("nonbeing"); by "the empiric" he means the phenomena of the material world; and by "God" he means the Tao. Thus, as all material things are grounded in *wu*, so does the life of the body depend upon the inner gods and breaths.

MYSTICAL TECHNIQUES. To nurture these inner forces and thereby attain "Fullness of Life" (*ch'ang-sheng; chang-sheng*) requires using the whole

---

[60] James R. Ware, trans., *Alchemy, Medicine, Religion in the China of* A.D. *320: The Nei P'ien of Ko Hung* (Cambridge, Mass.: M.I.T. Press, 1966), pp. 98–99.

repertoire of techniques connected with Taoist mystical physiology. Ko mentions three of the most essential of these techniques in the following passage:

> The *taking of medicines* may be the first requirement for enjoying Fullness of Life, but the concomitant practice of *breath circulation* greatly enhances speedy attainment of the goal. Even if medicines are not attainable and only breath circulation is practiced, a few hundred years will be attained provided the scheme is carried out fully, but one must also know the *art of sexual intercourse* to achieve such extra years. If ignorance of the sexual art causes frequent losses of sperm to occur, it will be difficult to have sufficient energy to circulate the breaths.[61]

However, for Ko, these techniques are only preliminary ones; the truly essential one is taking the elixir of immortality. All other methods are useful only to keep oneself whole until the elixir has been successfully compounded. The elixir itself, he instructed, can be compounded from gold and cinnabar, substances that had become synonymous with immortality because, according to Taoist lore and alchemical experience, they could withstand repeated chemical processing. The physical endurance of gold and cinnabar was translated into spiritual terms—their transmutation could make one an Immortal.

It might therefore be said that the belief in an elixir compounded from gold or cinnabar was based upon the "like affects like" principle that was also important in Tung Chung-shu's thought. It was surely a similar principle that guided later developments in Taoist mysticism, wherein all the various inner gods were given specific physiological responsibilities, just as the various deities of the Taoist universe had specific cosmological tasks. And most important, the inner gods were meditated upon in order to realize the identity believed to exist between each part of the human body and its corresponding star or planet in the firmament. In fact, all this may even have been a result of the same drive to oversystematize the theory of human-cosmic harmony that led to Han Confucianism. But the main thing is not whether this theory was, in specific cases, under- or over-systematized, expressed with sophistication or crudeness, or used by a Confucian empire-builder or a Taoist recluse. The main thing is that the theory kept reemerging as a key feature in the pattern of China's religious past.

---

[61] Ware, p. 105 (italics added).

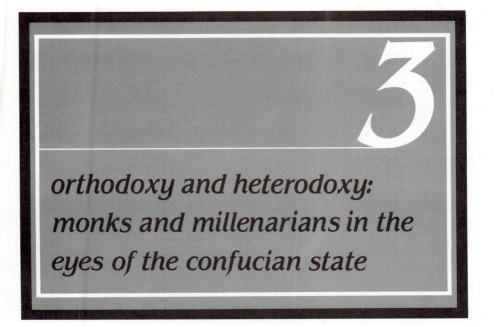

3

orthodoxy and heterodoxy: monks and millenarians in the eyes of the confucian state

Wars, persecutions, book burnings, inquisitions, witch hunts, and mass executions have all been known to occur in the defense of religious orthodoxy. Although such phenomena played a smaller role in China's history than in our Western past, they inevitably occurred there also. And their occurrence was almost always instigated by the state rather than by any church or other specifically religious institution. There are a number of reasons for this: (1) Only the state in China had the kind of organization and power that could effect religious controls; independent religions, such as Taoism and Buddhism, never developed anything approaching the sophisticated structure and pervasive influence that the Roman Catholic Church had in medieval Europe, for example. (2) Confucianism, the Chinese tradition most concerned with worldly matters, did not become an independent faith challenging state authority but instead took a course by which it became the religious dimension of the state itself. (3) Under the influence of Confucian ideology, the state conceived of itself as having a duty not only to rule but also to educate the people, safeguarding them from heterodox teachings as parents protect their children from outside evils. (4) Finally, often under the pretext of protecting the people from heterodox views, the state sought to prevent autonomous religious groups from attaining a level of size and unity at which they could challenge state authority.

For these reasons, the discussion of orthodoxy and heterodoxy in China must focus on the problem of religion and state, acknowledging that the state itself had a strongly religious dimension—one defined largely by its association with Confucianism. Doing so, we shall first treat Confucianism's relationship with traditional China's imperial government as constituting the first of three possible forms of religion-state relations: *mutual support*. Later, we will turn to the kinds of religious groups that represented the other two possible forms of religion-state relations: *indifference* and *mutual opposition*.

CONFUCIAN ORTHODOXY: RELIGIOUS DIMENSION OF THE CHINESE STATE

Regardless of their origins, all the major religions ended up stressing those among their teachings that best met the functional needs of the societies and governments they served in the course of history. The Confucian tradition was no exception—even to the extent of frequently forgetting the creative ideas and reformist spirit of its founder. These will be described in a later chapter. Now we shall describe only its conservative role as an institution concerned with preserving itself and the state with which it became identified. The historical summary of the previous chapter explained how it came to serve as the orthodox ideology of the Chinese state. Here we must go a step further by describing (1) the content of this ideology and (2) the way in which it was imposed on society at large, especially where this affected the existence and practice of other religions.

In describing the content of Confucian orthodoxy, the emphasis will be on four key values: rationalism, conservatism, familism, and organicism. Confucian *rationalism* was simply the attitude that the world could be understood and its problems solved through the use of human reason alone, which left little room for things like ghosts and spirits, miracles, or supernatural aid. This attitude could be traced to Master K'ung himself, who, when questioned on the subject, responded: "Not yet being able to serve people, how can one be able to serve the souls of the dead? . . . Not yet understanding life, how can one presume to understand death?" (*Analects* 11:11); and: "Strive to perform what is right for the people, and, while showing respect for souls of the dead and spirits, keep your distance from them; this can be called wisdom" (*Analects* 6:20). On the basis of such sayings, later Confucians attacked the common person's efforts to obtain divine aid by hiring Taoist priests and Buddhist monks or otherwise wasting their resources on "superstitious" and "useless" methods.

However, what many later Confucians failed to realize about human reason was that it should be tailored to meet each new situation, not codified into a set of unchanging principles. Making Confucius and other ancient sages into the sole legitimate source of reason, they produced a kind of intellectual *conservatism* that was perhaps even more stultifying than Western beliefs in Supernatural Reason revealed to humanity through the Bible alone. Nonetheless, it must be stressed that Confucian "conservatism" did not mean invariable resistance against reform and progress. In fact, the most important thing about Confucianism was its *dual role* as the religious dimension of the Chinese state. On the one hand, it supported imperial

FIGURE 3.1. This Temple of Confucius reveals the solemn grandeur of the tradition it represents. Taichung (Tai-zhong), Taiwan.

institutions and legitimized imperial power, like a typical state religion. On the other hand, it also sought reform of those institutions and dared to challenge imperial power, more like the politically active sects that exist in modern society under the separation of church and state (and unlike most traditional Chinese Buddhism and Taoism). However, whether supporting or reforming imperial institutions, legitimizing or challenging imperial power, Confucians always sought inspiration from their ancient sages and classical scriptures. This is what we mean in calling "conservatism" a Confucian value. Others have made the same point in referring to Confucian "fundamentalism," defined, for example, as "the belief that all truths were essentially realized in the Three Dynasties and expressed in the classics."[1] Whatever we call it, this value's result in practice was that new institutions were too rarely created to solve emerging social problems, and old institutions were preserved more because of their time-honored status than their practical value.

The oldest of such institutions was the family clan; and, as pointed out earlier, *familism* (along with ancestor worship) was the oldest and most

---

[1] Thomas A. Metzger, *Escape from Predicament: Neo-Confucianism and China's Evolving Political Culture* (New York: Columbia University Press, 1977), p. 193. Also see Wm. Theodore deBary, "Some Common Tendencies in Neo-Confucianism," in *Confucianism in Action,* eds. David S. Nivison and Arthur F. Wright (Stanford: Stanford University Press, 1959), pp. 25–49, in which fundamentalism is similarly defined and listed along with the values of restorationism, humanism, rationalism, and historical-mindedness.

basic of Chinese religious conceptions. Filiality, the root of familism, was praised in all the ancient scriptures; in fact, one—the *Book of Filiality*—was exclusively dedicated to this topic. Allegedly written by Tseng Tzu (Zeng Zi), it is a dialogue between Master K'ung and this famous disciple of his; and it attributes to filiality a most extraordinary importance. For example, at one point Tseng Tzu says: "I beg to ask whether there is truly nothing in a sage's virtuous behavior which surpasses filiality?" And the Master responds:

> Among all things bestowed by Heaven and Earth, human nature is most noble; and among all forms of human behavior, nothing is greater than filiality. . . . It is on the basis of reverence for his own parents that the sage teaches others about respect; and it is on the basis of affection for his parents that he teaches others about love. Thus, although not strict in his teaching, the sage succeeds; and although not severe in his governing, he maintains order. What he thus takes as his basis is a fundamental principle (of the universe). The principle of the parent-child relationship is bestowed by Heaven; and it defines what is proper in the ruler-subject relationship. Parents give birth to people—no bond is greater than this. The ruler affectionately cares for them—no form of generosity is more important than this (Chapter 9).

Why was filiality thus given such extreme importance? Precisely because it was considered to be a *natural* basis for all moral and political behavior. And the most biologically rooted of all human institutions—the family—was likewise considered to be a model for all human social organization, including government.

Further employing biological metaphor, the Chinese conceived the family, the state, and other human institutions upon the model of a living organism. In the Confucian case, this *organicism* was given a distinctly hierarchical flavor. There was, thus, a superior and an inferior status assigned to each participant in almost every social relationship. For example, with the exception of the relationship between friends, this was true of all the famous Five Relationships: father-son, ruler-subject, husband-wife, elder-younger (brothers), and friend-friend. Even the division of society into ruled and ruling classes was believed to have a natural basis, as implied in this quotation from *Mencius:* "Those who work using their minds rule others; and those who work using their strength are ruled over by others" (3A:4). Moreover, the entire Chinese empire was conceived as a hierarchically ordered organism with the emperor and his officials as its "head." Because this organism was at the same time conceived as a family, the role of China's leaders was also like that of the head of a family. That is to say, ideally at least, their role involved the responsibility to care for and to educate morally all the empire's subjects, just as if these subjects were their own children. Of course, in this instance, education usually meant guiding them toward the path of orthodoxy and away from heterodox teachings.

Despite their self-appointed role as society's moral authorities, Confucian officials were actually quite liberal "parents" when it came to enforcing belief in orthodox doctrines. On the whole, they took a rather subtle approach, based on several broad principles: (1) The actual ranks of officialdom must be kept closed to those holding heterodox views. This was accomplished primarily through the state examination system, which promised success only to those who had for years dedicated themselves to studying Confucian scriptures. (2) Those who become officials should spread the orthodox teachings through exemplary acts and other subtle ways of persuasion, without normally using force or legal sanctions. Thus, in addition to performing their official duties with incorruptible dedication, they should help build ancestral halls and support clan organizations wherein their influence could reach less educated kinsmen. They should also write and lecture on classical scriptures for the benefit of others and donate funds for the construction of monuments commemorating virtuous deeds. (3) Popular belief in an otherworldly system of rewards and punishments need not be interfered with as long as this system keeps people from performing immoral deeds and encourages them to be good subjects. (4) The only time unorthodox beliefs must actually become the focus of attention for state authorities is when such beliefs are professed by *organized* religious groups.

In the case of such groups, state officials exercised their "educational" role as parents of the people to oversee and, if necessary, control religious activity. This could legitimately be done through the Ministry of Rites, an organ of government established in ancient times for the purpose of handling state religious rituals. Later, when, for example, Buddhism grew in popularity and the number of its monasteries increased, it naturally fell on the Ministry of Rites to oversee the registration of monasteries and grant certificates to ordained Buddhist monks. If Buddhist monasteries seemed to be gaining control over too much land, or if too many young men were entering the monkhood (perhaps seeking to avoid being drafted for military campaigns or state work projects), the Ministry of Rites could set quotas restricting the number of monasteries and monks that could legally exist. While monastic groups could thus be controlled with relative ease, lay religious groups presented a rather different problem. First, their members were not as easily identified as licensed monks; second, their leaders were often suspected of being charlatans or even rebels; third, their teachings were considered to be even more dangerous than the foreign doctrines of Buddhism (from which, moreover, they often borrowed); and fourth, such teachings might infect the entire lay populace, not only a monastic minority. For these reasons, lay groups often had to live a precarious existence as unlicensed associations. They grew when the state ignored their presence and shrank into secrecy, or responded in rebellion, when the state sought to suppress them.

The Confucian fears about lay sects that denied these sects an open role in Chinese society may have been justified from at least one point of view: while a group of monks could, at worst, be characterized as social parasites *indifferent* to social affairs, a group of lay sectarians was in a position to serve as the basis for *opposition* to the state. As we shall see, the key factor bearing upon the Confucian perception of a group's malignance as a form of heterodoxy was whether it tended toward indifference or opposition with regard to the state.

INDIFFERENCE AND OPPOSITION TOWARD THE CONFUCIAN STATE

Although a religion such as Buddhism stands in tension with the world, it is not so much interested in changing the world as in changing the individual's attitude toward it. Yet, in China, simply by maintaining a world-transcending attitude, Buddhism ran counter to established orthodoxy. In other words, merely in following their exemplary founder, Buddhists were required to shave their heads, leave their families, and perform other non-Confucian acts. As a result, they often had to exist under state supervision as a tolerable but heterodox religion. Yet they were able to exist openly, which, as we will see, was mainly because they were successful in showing that they did not constitute a threat to the state. The same was also true of Taoism's mystics and ritual priests, who, being even more loosely organized than the Buddhist clergy, were deemed politically safe as well.

By contrast, groups that formed themselves around "heterodox" prophets constituted something quite capable of challenging state authority. First of all, holding forth a divine message of imminent world change, those who founded these groups could lead masses of disenchanted peasants into rebellion. Secondly, even when this was not the intention of such groups, as was normally the case, they still seemed to oppose everything Confucianism stood for. In the face of Confucian rationalism, they tempted the people with dreams of a new world in which life would be miraculously simple and comfortable; and they challenged the hierarchical, familist, and organismic character of traditional institutions by attempting to realize egalitarian utopias within their own communal organizations. Finally, groups inspired by a prophetic message of world transformation were by nature evangelistic. And by seeking openly to spread their teachings, they automatically tread upon the territory of Confucian literati as exclusive moral educators of the people.

Just as monastic groups were less feared by Confucian authorities than prophetic sects, then, the difference in spiritual perspective between Buddhist monks and sectarian laypersons determined their respective positions of indifference and opposition vis-à-vis the Confucian state. The two examples that follow bear colorful testimony to this. One concerns an early Chinese defender of monastic Buddhism, the other a syncretic lay sect inspired by Buddhism many centuries after its acceptance in China.

Hui-yuan and the Defense of Buddhism

We have already referred several times to Buddhism's differences with native Chinese culture, but now we wish to treat them more systematically in order to provide some background for discussing a famous defense of Buddhism written in the year 404 by the monk Hui-yuan (344–416). The various differences worth discussing can be grouped under three headings: intellectual, cultural, and political. Intellectually, due to the world-affirming rather than world-rejecting nature of their classical tradition, certain Chinese have argued down to the present day that the Buddhist world view is nihilistic and pessimistic. That is to say, they have considered Buddhism's search for transcendence to be based on the false assumption that the world is illusory and life naught but sorrow. Both Indian and Chinese thought agreed that the world was characterized by ceaseless change. But only in India was the conclusion drawn that, because things are ever-changing, they are therefore metaphysically nonreal and an inevitable source of sorrow for those who become attached to them. Thus, the Chinese found it hard to accept not only the Buddhist goal of transcending the world of change but also its method of detachment from the ways of ordinary life.

In fact, it was ultimately cultural issues connected with Buddhist monastic life, rather than philosophical differences, that became crucial in fueling anti-Buddhist sentiments and initiating state persecutions of the religion. While wandering religious mendicants were from ancient times part of Indian culture, there was no ready place for them in Chinese society, where each person had a clearly defined set of obligations corresponding to his or her place within the family and related social institutions. To give up the obligations and associated joys of ordinary social life was considered to be *unnatural,* especially considering the debt and filial respect owed to one's parents and ancestors. A child was expected to contribute to society for the sake of the family name and, in addition, to produce offspring to carry on the family line. Since Buddhism required one to reject all this, to disfigure one's body—the most precious of all parental gifts—by shaving the head, and to adopt foreign religious garb, it naturally drew harsh attacks from China's cultural elite.

Despite these attacks, however, Buddhism grew rapidly during its early history in China, yearly attracting thousands of new monks and nuns, absorbing large tracts of land free from taxation, and using valuable resources and precious metals to construct religious images and temples. This led, in turn, to criticism of Buddhism from the political and economic point of view. The problem was further aggravated by the fact that Buddhist clergy members, on the basis of their monastic rules, declined from paying obeisance to secular authorities, including the Chinese emperor. At first, this seemed quite natural, for during Buddhism's first century or so in China all its monks were foreign and therefore lived under conditions similar to what we now call extraterritorial immunity. Later, however, the Buddhist clergy was swelling with Chinese subjects and, for the reasons just given, suspected of having too much influence.

It was under these circumstances, early in the fifth century, that Huiyuan was called upon to defend Buddhism in general, and its refusal to pay obeisance to the Chinese emperor in particular. His arguments are important to us, however, not only as a defense of Buddhist theory and practice, but also as a clear statement of a religion's stance of indifference vis-à-vis a state.

At the beginning of the fifth century, a crisis arose in relations between Buddhism and the Eastern Chin Dynasty (317–420, in South China during the Period of Disunity). An ambitious official named Huan Hsuan (Huan

Xuan) had usurped the dynastic throne (402) and sought to purge the Buddhist clergy of undesirable elements. At the same time, he required all its members to begin paying obeisance to him. (In China, obeisance to the ruler was performed by repeatedly kneeling and touching one's head to the ground.) In his view—strongly supported by China's classical scriptures—the emperor was Heaven's exclusively appointed authority and source of benefit for all the empire's subjects. Therefore, he could not countenance that among these subjects there were those (the Buddhist clergy) who received the benefits of life in his empire while contributing little to its maintenance and, moreover, refused to pay him due respect. Huan Hsuan was not, however, against all Buddhists. He admired those who were sincere in their practice and sought only to return to lay life those who were "unworthy." In fact, he so admired one Buddhist master that he decided to exempt the master's entire community from scrutiny and even to seek the master's advice on the issue of the Buddhist clergy's status in general. This was Master Hui-yuan.

By the time Huan Hsuan approached Hui-yuan for advice, the latter had already become the leader of South China's most prestigious Buddhist center, the Monastery of the Eastern Grove at Lu-shan in Kiangsi (Jiangxi) province. When the issue of the Buddhist clergy's proper attitude toward secular authority was referred to him, his sincere and persuasive response so impressed Huan Hsuan that he soon decreed (403) that no Buddhist cleric need perform the customary acts of obeisance to secular authorities (a policy reversed, nonetheless, under most later Chinese rulers). In the following year, Hui-yuan elaborated and clarified his argument in the famous "Treatise on Why Buddhist Clerics Need Not Pay Obeisance to Kings," whose salient points are summarized below.

Hui-yuan's argument was rooted in a distinction between clerical and lay Buddhists. On the basis of this distinction, he justified the clerical Buddhists' attitude toward secular authority by saying, in essence, that they were *in but not of this world*. Lay Buddhists, on the other hand, were said to form a separate category of subjects who continue to remain in and of the world, enjoying its illusory pleasures and remaining subservient to its authorities in every way. This is made clear early in Hui-yuan's treatise, as follows:

> If one examines the broad essentials of what the teachings of Buddha preach, one will see that they distinguish between those who leave the household life and those who remain in it. . . . Those who in the home revere the Law [the teachings of Buddha] are subjects, who are obedient to [the ordinary world of] Change. Their feelings are not inclined to changing the way of the world, hence their course is within the common boundaries. Therefore, this way of life includes the affections of natural kinship and the proprieties of obedience to authority. . . . Thus acquiescence is made the common rule, and the natural way is not changed. Why? Because when one makes much of one's person and fosters life, one encumbers oneself with the restrictions of existence. When the roots are deep and firmly embedded, and the erroneous notion of self not yet destroyed, then one makes the passions one's garden, sounds and colors one's promenade. Immersed in worldly pleasures one cannot escape and leave them. Therefore the restrictions imposed by the Doctrine set their limit here, and do not explain

what lies beyond [i.e., the way of those who enter the clergy]. As long as what lies beyond is not explained, it is largely the same as acquiescence in Change. Hence one may not benefit by (the ruler's) virtue and neglect propriety, bask in his kindness and cast aside his due respect. Therefore they who rejoice in the way of Śakya [Buddha] invariably first uphold their parents and respect their lords.

As far as laypersons are concerned, then, Buddhism does not interfere with but rather fosters a respectful attitude toward superiors. In this regard, they are, at the very least, the same as the emperor's other subjects.

Buddhist clerics, however, are another breed of being altogether. They have dedicated their lives to severing attachments to the world of change, and they have no interest in sharing either its joys or obligations with ordinary subjects of the empire. In Hui-yuan's words:

He who has left the household life is a lodger beyond the limits, his traces are cut off from those of the beings. The Doctrine by which he lives enables him to understand that woes and impediments come from having a body, that by not maintaining the body one terminates woe. He knows that continuing life comes from undergoing Change, and by not acquiescing in Change he seeks the First Principle. . . . If the termination of woe does not depend on the maintenance of the body, then he does not treasure the benefits that foster life. This is something in which the Principle runs counter to the body and the way is opposed to common practice. Such men as these commence the fulfilment of their vows with the putting away of ornaments, and realize the achievements of their ideal with the changing of their garb. Therefore, in general, they who remain outside the household life all flee the world in order to attain their ideal, and change their way of life in order to reach their way. If they have changed their way of life, then their garb and distinctive marks cannot share the rules of the secular codes. . . . Therefore, though inwardly they may run counter to the respect of natural relationships, yet they do not violate filial piety; though outwardly they lack the courtesy of upholding the sovereign, yet they do not lose hold of reverence. Looking at it in this way, one knows that if one crosses to beyond Change in order to seek the First Principle, then the reason is profound and one's resolve sincere.[2]

Thus, in Hui-yuan's mind at least, one who has set his foot on the Buddhist path with sincere resolve has, in a way, already left the world. By virtue of his resolve, and the profound reason underlying it (belief in the Buddha's message), such a one was no longer of this world, although it remained the arena in which he must work toward liberation. Like the lotus blossom, which Buddhism takes to symbolize its spiritual aspirations, this person remained rooted in the mire but hoped to rise radiantly above it—in but not of the world.

It was remarkable that Chinese society opened up a place for persons claiming such a status, for, according to its classical roots, everyone in the world was *of* it—that is, each had his or her role within the great hierarchically ordered "family" headed by the Chinese emperor. Equally remarkable, then, was Buddhism's establishment of itself as an institution

---

[2] Leon Hurvitz, " 'Render Unto Caesar' in Early Chinese Buddhism," *Sino-Indian Studies* 5:3–4 (1957), pp. 97–99 and 99–100. Reprinted by permission of the author.

FIGURE 3.2. The "in-but-not-of-the-world" aspect of Buddhism is found in the mountainside settings of many of its monasteries. This one is located atop Lion's Head Mountain, Taiwan.

at least partially free from state control and able to exist according to its own monastic rules. As we saw in the previous chapter, one reason for its success was the relative weakness of orthodox Confucian institutions during the period of its initial growth in China. Another reason was that even when these institutions reasserted themselves during the Sui, T'ang, and later dynasties, Buddhism had already become a needed refuge for many who had no secure place in Chinese society, such as orphans and those last born in families with too many mouths to feed. But not only orphans and paupers were drawn to the religion. Many who could have easily achieved worldly success were attracted to the Buddhist world away from the world, where in the tranquility of mountainside monasteries they could lead a life of spiritual cultivation.

Buddhism may not have been the first and only religion to hold forth an "in-but-not-of-the-world" ideal. One finds it, of course, in Christianity, whose early history also saw a crisis emerge over doing acts of obeisance to secular rulers (Roman emperors) and their images. However, although the problem was the same, the outcome was different. Whereas Chinese Buddhists adopted an attitude of indifference to society and the state, early Christians moved toward a stance of tension with the world and its powers.

Awaiting the destruction of this world and its evil ruler (the Anti-Christ), they believed they belonged to a future millenium over which Christ would reign. Like millenarian groups elsewhere, they initially adopted a stance of opposition toward the state; only later did they compromise and join forces with the state. In China, it is also toward groups of this kind that we must look if we wish to examine the existence of oppositional relations between religion and state.

White Lotus Millenarians

Interestingly, Hui-yuan is connected, at least by legend, with the establishment of a Buddhist lay sect called the White Lotus Religion. That is to say, when this religion came to exist centuries after his death, its leaders claimed him as their original founder and sometimes even went so far, in founding their own groups, as to dig a pool and plant a lotus in imitation of his legendary establishment of a "lotus association." However, while they stressed this connection, their more orthodox Buddhist critics did their best to deny it, as in the following quotation from a Ming Dynasty Buddhist source criticizing White Lotus groups:

> In the world there are vagrant evil elements who falsely use the Buddha's name to assemble the people and plot illegal and rebellious activities. Their false statements include, "Sakyamuni Buddha has declined; Maitreya Buddha shall govern the world." This is certainly not the Mount Lu Lotus Association (*lien-she* [*lian-she*]) of Hui-yuan.[3]

In fact, Hui-yuan's association may not even have had the word "lotus" in its name; but due to the strength of Hui-yuan's legend, numerous Buddhist lay groups were founded during the Sung, Yuan, and Ming dynasties. These groups called themselves lotus associations. Such groups often had close connections with monastic Buddhism and did not generally incur governmental opposition. However, the course of White Lotus development made it different from lay groups connected with monasteries and led it toward inevitable conflict with the state.

Almost since the time of Hui-yuan, Chinese Mahāyāna Buddhism had been producing groups with methods quite different from the ascetic path inspired by the life of Śākyamuni Buddha. These groups emphasized the broad salvational powers of other Buddhas, such as Amitābha and Maitreya. In addition to stressing universal salvation, they accommodated themselves to the world view of ordinary folk with simplified rituals, vernacular scriptures, evangelism, and congregational worship. They nearly all stressed chanting such Buddha's names as a means for gaining religious merit and salvation; and their practices often incorporated vegetarianism and other features borrowed from monastic Buddhism.

---

[3] Translated in Daniel L. Overmyer, *Folk Buddhist Religion: Dissenting Sects in Late Traditional China* (Cambridge, Mass.: Harvard University Press, 1976), p. 37. The information about the legend of Hui-yuan's lotus association (p. 87) and many other details in what follows were learned from this work.

Most of these groups were in the Pure Land tradition, and their members were model citizens just in the way they should have been according to Hui-yuan's treatise quoted earlier. They lived ordinary lives and hoped that, through good behavior and chanting praise to Amitābha, they could have an improved life, and, ideally, a rebirth in Amitābha's Pure Land. But a good number of such groups were not Pure Land but rather Maitreyan, at least in spirit if not in name. By Maitreyan we mean oriented toward a belief in the Buddhist "millenium," the future reign of Maitreya Buddha or something similar.

While not a central feature of Indian Buddhism, the idea was expressed in Indian Mahāyāna texts that Maitreya waits in the Tushita Heaven for his turn (following Śākyamuni Buddha) to come to earth and preach the Dharma. While, according to these texts, this event would occur thousands of years in the future, after a certain virtuous ruler had established the Dharma in the world, many Chinese versions of the event placed it in the immediate future. These versions were created by and for millenarian groups who believed that the Maitreyan age of peace and prosperity would soon replace the reigning dynasty, and whose leaders sometimes claimed to be the virtuous ruler connected with Maitreya's coming, or even Maitreya himself. Understandably, such groups were not popular with the dynasties under whom they existed; and pressure from state authorities had the predictable result of further intensifying the groups' millenarian expectations. For such is the nature of the relation of mutual opposition between religion and state.

Turning specifically to the White Lotus Religion, from what little is known about its early history during the Southern Sung Dynasty (1127–1279), it was at first not much different from Pure Land groups discussed earlier. However, being slightly more heterodox and autonomous than most of these groups, it became subject to official criticism and censure. This, along with the fact that it answered certain social needs and was actively evangelistic, accounted for its further growth as an independent sectarian movement. At some point, perhaps due to increasingly bad relations with the state and worsening socioeconomic conditions, Maitreyan (millenarian) features became paramount in the group's ideology; and later, these beliefs were turned into practice—a religious rebellion against the reigning dynasty. Beginning in 1351, this rebellion contributed significantly to the overthrow of the foreign (Mongol) Yuan Dynasty and the establishment of the native Ming (1368–1644).

Ironically, a few decades earlier, one of the Mongol emperors (who were generally friends and patrons of Buddhism) had issued a decree to end persecution of White Lotus groups. In this decree of Emperor Jen-tsung (Ren-zong), we also see something of the massive, yet benign character of the religion at that time (1313):

There are those who don't understand Buddhism who have destroyed some of these [White Lotus] temples. . . . In these Buddhist temples (*fo-t'ang* [fo-tang]), built with their own contributions, they regularly chant sutras, pray for prosperity and long life for those in higher positions, and carry out other beneficial activities. . . . (All responsible officials) are hereby ordered to stop prosecuting and suppressing this religion. . . . Further, all the Lotus temples, water and land, people, rolls of cloth, gardens and forests, mills, shops, (supplies for) feasts, sutra storehouses, bathhouses and boats which belong to this sect are neither to be molested nor confiscated.[4]

Here we have a picture of an independent religious movement, without any apparent political motivations, that seems to have well served many social needs. But this was hardly the way authorities *normally* viewed it; they attacked it precisely because it was a movement that was independent of both monastic Buddhism and the state, and which, moreover, dared to serve needs that the family and state officials should serve according to orthodox Confucian theory. Its independence from monastic Buddhism was clearly determined by its having married clergy, and its differences with the Confucian state were exacerbated by its disseminating heterodox religious literature. For this activity was easily regarded as constituting a challenge to the "educational" role of state authorities.

With their social services, independent leadership, and unorthodox scriptures that had a popular appeal because they were written in the vernacular style and employed common folk motifs, White Lotus groups effected a concentration of spiritual forces that otherwise remained diffusely spread throughout Chinese folk religion. This was made possible, above all, by prophetic, charismatic leadership. In contrast to Confucian officials and Buddhist monks, for example, prophetic leaders do not have religious authority by virtue of holding a position in a state cult or church hierarchy. They have *charismatic authority,* to which people respond out of a belief in their individual sanctity, and with a depth of piety not easily inspired by state or church authorities.

When a charismatic leader delivers a message of impending world transformation and calls upon his followers to raise up in arms and put their weight to the already moving wheel of cosmic change, then we have millenarian rebellion. This is what happened in mid-fourteenth-century China, when the White Lotus leader Han Shan-t'ung (Shan-tong), announcing the descent to earth of Maitreya Buddha, called for rebellion against China's Mongol rulers. It is hard to determine the extent to which the White Lotus Religion should be held responsible for what ensued; for Han Shan-t'ung not only appealed to the religion's Maitreyan ideology. He also appealed to nationalism by claiming descent from the native Chinese line of Sung emperors, and even to popular beliefs adopted from the Manichaean religion of a coming King of Light. Moreover, it was neither Han nor even his son (Han Lin-er) who finally brought the rebellion to its successful conclusion. It was Chu Yuan-chang (Zhu Yuan-zhang), who had been an officer under Han Lin-er for ten years, but who had the latter drowned and denounced the White Lotus movement just two years before founding the Ming Dynasty in 1368.

The episode ended in one of the great ironies of Chinese history.

---

[4] Overmyer, p. 97.

After capitalizing on the success of the White Lotus millenarian armies, and naming his new dynasty with a term (*ming:* "bright," "light") from the religion's title for its King of Light (*ming-wang*), Chu Yuan-chang soon issued (1370) imperial statutes against heterodox religion which, in the opinion of one author, "became the backbone of official suppression until 1911" (when China's imperial history ended with the Republican revolution).[5] There is good reason to believe that, for Chu personally, this was a strictly political precaution. But such an explanation hardly suffices to cover the generally deep-seated hostility toward heterodox lay sects on the part of Confucian officials. Since such sects adhered to a syncretic mixture of unorthodox Buddhist, Taoist, and other (e.g., Manichaean) elements, they naturally invited ideological criticism. But hostility toward them was probably based on something even more fundamental than differences in beliefs and ideas, something that we can understand if we return to what was said about monastic Buddhism.

The "in-but-not-of-the-world" life style of the Buddhist clergy was something never accepted by certain Confucian conservatives, whose ideal world was a *single* great "family" with a productive role for every member. How much more they must have resisted the formation of nonfamilial, voluntary associations with otherworldly religious ideals. Indeed, nothing could be more threatening to their world view than to see their "children" (the common people) forming groups outside the pale of orthodox living, especially when such groups had a millenarian flavor. For this meant nothing less than entire groups of ordinary people claiming to be in this world but not of it. Their world was the coming millenium, and their aim was to make their lives conform with that future vision rather than with present reality.

For example, the religious literature of White Lotus groups reveals a belief (which coincided with their efforts to live in egalitarian, mutual-aid associations) in a future world where there would be new categories of time, new standards of longevity, and greater equality in social status. One of their sacred texts states:

> Eighteen kalpas [Buddhist cosmic eras] have already been completed, and the form of all things is about to change. (In this new time) a year will have eighteen months, a day eighteen (Chinese) hours . . . a month forty-five days, and a year eight hundred ten days. In heaven and earth there will be neither completeness nor deficiency, among men there will be neither youth nor old age, birth nor death and there will be no distinction between men and women. This then is the Great Way of Long Life, in which all will live for 81,000 years. The time destined by heaven has been fulfilled, and a new world is being established.[6]

The belief in such a new world, ushered in by a Buddhist "messiah," violated all orthodox sensitivities with its bold assertions that there were standards of time, life, and culture other than those established by Heaven

---

[5] Overmyer, p. 100.

[6] Overmyer, p. 159.

to be upheld by the Son of Heaven and his Confucian officials. Therefore, groups that dared to hold beliefs of this sort, and to behave in accord with them, were from the Confucian point of view the ultimate in heterodoxy. Officials of China's last two imperial regimes, Ming and Ch'ing, never rescinded the laws proscribing such groups nor ceased in their efforts to root them out. For these officials, the name "White Lotus Religion," in particular, was synonymous not merely with "heterodoxy" but even with "sedition."

Why, one then must wonder, did White Lotus groups continue to survive and, moreover, succeed in organizing rebellions? For this they certainly did. As late as the nineteenth century, they were still active in spectacular fashion. A White Lotus rebellion that lasted for eight years and affected several provinces of North China was finally suppressed by the Ch'ing government in 1803; and a decade later, in 1813, another shocked the government, despite its smaller scale, when some of the rebels maneuvered their way into the imperial palace compound of Peking's Forbidden City.[7] Obviously, there were continually people willing to risk their lives in millenarian causes. For them, it seems, the Confucian ideal of all living together in harmony as one big family was not an actuality. Perhaps economic hardships or natural disasters had left them drifting apart from the secure ties of kin and community. Or perhaps the Confucian ladder of success, promising stable employment through impartial examinations, had for them turned out to be an oppressive network of corruption and favoritism. Whatever the reason, they responded to something in the White Lotus Religion that was totally absent from Confucianism—a vision of immediate universal salvation dependent for its realization more on divine deliverance than on human effort. Of course, Confucianism, rationalistic and conservative though it was, had its own utopian vision of restoring the order achieved long ago by China's ancient sages. But not everyone shared this orthodox vision, despite Confucian educational efforts. Inevitably, some found greater promise and appeal in alternative religious visions.[8]

---

[7] See a fascinating account of the 1813 rebellion in Susan Naquin, *Millenarian Rebellion in China: The Eight Trigrams Uprising of 1813* (New Haven and London: Yale University Press, 1976), which also gives details concerning the previous White Lotus rebellion on pp. 65–66.

[8] Those further interested in this key issue should see the volumes *Orthodoxy in Late Imperial China* and *Heterodoxy in Late Imperial China*, ed. K. C. Liu (Berkeley: University of California Press, forthcoming).

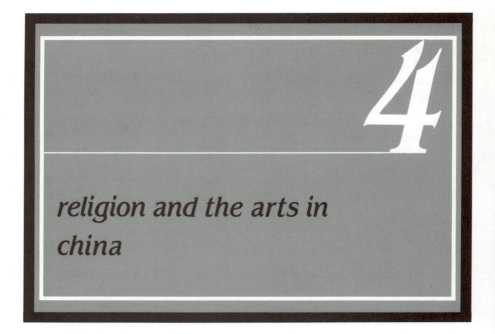

4

religion and the arts in china

Whether we turn to Europe, the Middle East, Africa, or India, we find that in traditional times the arts were all dominated by religious themes and created to serve religious purposes. To a large extent, the same was true in China, especially where the common people were concerned. The best of architecture, sculpture, and painting in their rural environment was found at local temples. Their main contact with drama, dance, and music was in the religious folk operas held at temple celebrations. And, for those among them who could read, much of their "literature" was made up of the moral tracts, simplified scriptures, and hagiographies available through temples or local religious groups.

The close connection between religion and the arts in traditional societies was more than coincidental. In the first place, to the extent that there is a specifically religious experience, this experience of ultimacy, wholeness, otherness, etc., is also given rise to by music, drama, painting, sculpture, and other art forms. For they can also transport one's consciousness to that realm of *intuitive* perception that is beyond words and ordinary ways of thinking. In the second place, as forms of nonverbal communication, the arts are preeminently *symbolic*. This is to say they are vehicles for pointing to "truths" that can be expressed in words only with great difficulty, and certainly not in a way that the average person can understand. The arts thus serve as perfect handmaidens of religion, expressing—especially for the theologically unsophisticated masses—concepts that even great minds find hard to put into words.[1]

Both as an aid to intuition and the vehicle of specific symbolic contents, the arts have long served as windows through which to look into the realm of the holy. And they are thus a prime indicator of the nature of the holy as conceived in a particular culture. Looking at the arts of traditional China, we can see that there the holy was most often conceived by making reference to the world of nature, whose processes were considered to be sacred and, therefore, worthy of human imitation. Some may even feel that certain Chinese art forms express nature itself, but it is best to say that they express a certain conception of the natural world—namely, the holistic, organicistic, and sometimes hierarchical world view described in previous chapters as underlying all of Chinese religious life.

RELIGION IN VARIOUS REALMS OF ARTISTIC EXPRESSION

In this chapter we wish to see how the basic Chinese world view was given artistic expression with regard to both the intuitive and symbolic functions of art. This means keeping in mind that we find in China, on the one hand, artistic efforts to intuitively perceive and creatively imitate nature's essential processes and, on the other hand, attempts to consciously produce symbolic systems representing the universe conceived of as an organismic and hierarchically ordered whole. As we will see, one or the other of these will be prominent in the case of each of the chosen examples of art discussed in this chapter: music and ritual, painting, architecture, and literature.

Music and Ritual

Among the performing arts, music and ritual almost everywhere have a key role in religious practice. And because of their dynamic nature as performing arts, their impact on the mind is likely to be deeper than that of two or even three-dimensional arts. The strength of this impact was well understood by the Chinese, as indicated in the classical sources that will be quoted. Before discussing these sources in detail, a few general remarks must be made. First, such sources took for granted that music and ritual were interrelated, both being essential dimensions of any large-scale ceremonial event. Second, both were considered to have an important role from the ethical as well as esthetic point of view. This was especially true of ritual, as we will now see.

In China's classical sources on the subject, we meet the central concept *li*, which actually had a much broader scope than did the English word

---

[1] These two dimensions of art (intuitive and symbolic) have been treated, with special reference to Chinese religion, in Laurence G. Thompson, "Efficacy and Afficacy in Chinese Religion," *Bulletin: Society for the Study of Chinese Religions*, No. 6. (Fall, 1978), pp. 31–49.

ritual. For *li* indicated appropriate behavior among people (or between people and spiritual beings) on all ceremonial occasions, such as were found in every area of life. A quotation from the *Ritual Records* (one of China's Five Scriptures, described in Chapter 2) gives us some idea of the various contexts in which ceremonial rules (*li*) applied:

> These rules (set forth) the way of reverence and courtesy; and therefore when the services in the ancestral temple are performed according to them, there is reverence; when they are observed in court, the noble and the mean have their proper positions; when the family is regulated by them, there is affection between father and son, and harmony among brothers; and when they are honored in the country districts and villages, there is proper order between old and young. . . . The ceremonies at the court audiences of the different seasons were intended to indicate the righteous relations between ruler and subject; those of friendly messages and inquiries, to secure mutual honor and respect between the feudal princes; those of mourning and sacrifice, to indicate the kindly feelings of ministers and sons; those of social meetings in the country districts, to show the order that should prevail between young and old; and those of marriage, to exhibit the separation that should be maintained between males and females. These ceremonies prevent the rise of disorder and confusion, and are like the embankments which prevent the overflow of water.[2]

Precisely why the performance of ceremonial behavior in so many contexts had *esthetic* and *ethical* functions is another matter, one that was eloquently approached by the early Confucian thinker Hsun Tzu, from whom the *Ritual Records* borrowed much of its theory about the functions of *li*.

Being keenly aware of the potential harm of hidden emotions and untamed desires, Hsun Tzu saw *li* as channels for their appropriate and controlled expression. "Appropriate," for him, meant having a suitable esthetic form; and "controlled" meant conforming to the moral standards of society, which were in turn grounded in nature. As we all know, a celebration without unifying rules and symbols can become raucous and ugly, and an uncontrolled expression of sorrow can be equally unappealing to the eye. In Hsun Tzu's theory of ritual, its purpose is to "ornament" feelings of joy and sorrow, reverence and majesty, and so forth, thereby giving them a beauty like that of a painting, play, or piece of music dealing with such feelings. In the following passage, he indicates how many features of a ritual performance serve this purpose:

> Smiles and a beaming face, sorrow and a downcast look—these are expressions of the emotions of joy or sorrow which come with auspicious or inauspicious occasions, and they appear naturally in the countenance. Songs and laughter, weeping and lamentation—these too are expressions of the emotions of joy and sorrow which come with auspicious or inauspicious occasions, and they appear naturally in the sound of the voice. . . . The wearing of ceremonial caps, embroidered robes, and patterned silks, or [by contrast] of fasting clothes and mourning clothes and sashes, straw sandals, and hempen robes—these are expressions of the emotions of joy and sorrow which

---

[2] James Legge, trans., *The Li Ki,* Vol. 3 of *Sacred Books of China: The Texts of Confucianism* (Oxford, 1885), pp. 258–259.

come with auspicious and inauspicious occasions, and are expressed naturally in one's manner of dress. . . . The beginnings of these two emotions are present in man from the first. If he can trim or stretch them, broaden or narrow them, add to or take from them, express them completely and properly, fully and beautifully, seeing to it that root and branch, beginning and end are in their proper place, so that he may serve as a model to ten thousand generations, then he has achieved true ritual. But only a gentleman of thorough moral training and practice is capable of understanding how to do this.[3]

Hsun Tzu's final sentence may make one wonder why and how the performance of ritual is connected with morality, especially since in the modern world many find ritual to be empty formal behavior without moral content. But, according to early Confucian thinkers, nothing could be further from the truth. They considered their ritual rules (*li*) to be sacred creations of ancient sage kings, perfectly consonant with both the social and natural worlds. In practice, it was believed, these rules could express the utmost reverence toward other beings, whether human or divine. Ritual behavior was therefore conceived of as a vehicle for exchanging deeply moral feelings of mutual respect. And the rules guiding such behavior were believed to determine the supremely *civilized* way of treating another human *as human*, not as a beast.

Moreover, in addition to having a role in interpersonal relations, rites (*li*) were considered to be the finest way of harmonizing all of society and the cosmos. In Hsun Tzu's words:

Through rites Heaven and earth join in harmony, the sun and moon shine, the four seasons proceed in order, the stars and constellations march, the rivers flow, and all things flourish; men's likes and dislikes are regulated and their joys and hates made appropriate. Those below are obedient, those above are enlightened; all things change but do not become disordered; only he who turns his back upon rites will be destroyed. Are they not wonderful indeed?[4]

While the harmonizing effects of ritual were thus described in superlative terms, it was actually music that the traditional Chinese took to represent the ultimate in harmony.

The word for "music" used in classical sources (*yueh; yue*) incorporates the dancelike, ritual movements performed to the musical rhythm and sounds of a ceremonial event. Also, because the written character for *yueh* can be read with a different sound (*le*) and, then, mean "joy," the ancient Chinese, ever fond of word play, said the entire dance-music performance had the expression of joy as its ultimate purpose. Of course, music was believed to be capable of expressing not only joy but, in fact, a full range of human qualities, as indicated in this passage on the "symbolism of music" by Hsun Tzu:

[3] Burton Watson, trans., *Basic Writings of Hsun Tzu* (New York and London: Columbia University Press, 1967), pp. 101–102.

[4] Watson, p. 94.

This is the symbolism of music: the drum represents a vast pervasiveness; the bells represent fullness; the sounding stones represent restrained order; the mouth organs represent austere harmony; the flutes represent a spirited outburst; the ocarina and bamboo whistle represent breadth of tone; the zither represents gentleness; the lute represents grace; the songs represent purity and fulfillment; and the spirit of the dance joins with the Way of Heaven. The drum is surely the lord of music, is it not? Hence, it resembles Heaven, while the bells resemble the earth, the sounding stones resemble water, the mouth organs and lutes resemble the sun, and the scrapers resemble the myriad beings of creation. How can one understand the spirit of the dance? The eyes cannot see it; the ears cannot hear it. And yet, when all the posturing and movements, all the steps and changes of pace are ordered and none are lacking in the proper restraint, when all the power of muscle and bone are brought into play, when all is matched exactly to the rhythm of the drums and bells, and there is not the slightest awkwardness or discord—there is the spirit of the dance in all its manifold fullness and intensity![5]

Beginning by associating various human qualities with different musical instruments, and then moving on to associate various features of the universe with them, the passage concludes by describing the goal of an ideal dance-music performance: a spirit of perfectly spontaneous authenticity, without "the slightest awkwardness or discord."

This spirit of spontaneous authenticity was a quality desired in all of Chinese esthetics. For just as the Chinese sought to capture nature's rhythms and shapes in concrete symbolism, they also tried to grasp the spirit of natural creativity in the production of art. Thus, though ultimately human creations, works of art were expected to be created with the same direct and unfeigned spontaneity with which nature seems to bring forth its creations. This is a view perhaps best exemplified by looking at the art of monochrome ink painting that is often associated with Ch'an (Zen) Buddhism.

Monochrome Ink Painting

Long before China produced monochrome ink painting (in which plain black ink is used against an equally plain but white background, and which is hereafter referred to simply as "ink painting"), natural forms and processes were the main inspiration for artists and artisans. And long before Ch'an Buddhism existed, the idea of imitating nature's spontaneous authenticity had stirred the minds of Chinese thinkers, especially the early Taoists. As far back as history takes us, in fact, zoomorphic and botanical images dominate Chinese artistic expression. Thus, Chinese landscape painting, which the rest of the world sometimes takes to represent all Chinese art, is actually a late variation on an old theme. Yet regardless of its particular form, explains art historian Michael Sullivan, Chinese art holds its universal appeal precisely because of its sympathetic grasp of nature. Speaking of the response to it of average Westerners, he states:

[5] Watson, pp. 117–118.

Do they sense, perhaps, that the forms which the Chinese artist and craftsman have created are natural forms—forms which seem to have evolved inevitably by the movement of the maker's hand in response to an intuitive awareness of a natural rhythm? Chinese art does not demand of us, as does Indian art, the effort to bridge what often seems an unbridgeable gulf between extremes of physical form and metaphysical content; nor will we find in it that pre-occupation with formal and intellectual considerations which so often makes Western art difficult for the Asian mind to accept. The forms of Chinese art are beautiful because they are in the widest and deepest sense harmonious, and we can appreciate them because we too feel their rhythms all around us in nature, and instinctively respond to them. These rhythms, moreover, this sense of inner life expressed in line and contour, are present in Chinese art from its earliest beginnings.[6]

This means more than that the subject matter of Chinese artworks is often taken from nature; it also means that nature is itself imitated in the techniques of creation. And it is the latter fact that must be emphasized here.

While some may consider religious or philosophical training to have little to do with one's ability to paint, many masters of Chinese ink painting have, up to the present day, required their students to practice meditation or to read spiritual texts. This is said to be necessary because the spirit of spontaneous authenticity that this style of painting aims to capture is not simply an artistic technique. It is an attitude toward life.

When the Ch'an school of Buddhism developed and, later (Sung period), showed a special interest in ink painting, the cultivation of this attitude through Buddhist meditation gained a role within the world of Chinese art. From the point of view of Ch'an Buddhism, ink painting was, like meditation, a means of developing the desired attitude toward life. In the following passage from D. T. Suzuki, a well-known modern Japanese spokesperson for the Ch'an (Zen) tradition, ink painting is in fact compared to life itself:

Life delineates itself on the canvas called time; and time never repeats, once gone forever gone; and so is an act; once done, it is never undone. Life is a *sumiye* (ink) painting, which must be executed once and for all time and without hesitation, without intellection, and no corrections are permissible or possible. Life is not like an oil painting, which can be rubbed out and done over time and again until the artist is satisfied. With the *sumiye* painting any brushstrokes painted over a second time results in a smudge; the life has left it. All corrections show when the ink dries. So is life. We can never retract what we have once committed to deeds, nay, what once has passed through consciousness can never be rubbed out. Zen therefore ought to be caught while the thing is going on, neither before nor after. . . . This fleeting, unrepeatable and ungraspable character of life is delineated graphically [in ink paintings] by Zen masters who have compared it to the lightning or spark produced by the percussion of stones.[7]

[6] Michael Sullivan, *The Arts of China*, rev. ed. (Berkeley and Los Angeles: University of California Press, 1977), p. 14.

[7] Reprinted by permission of Schocken Books Inc. from *The Chinese on the Art of Painting* by Osvald Sirén; copyright © 1963, pp. 106–107.

FIGURE 4.1. *The Sixth Patriarch Cutting Bamboo* by Liang K'ai (Liang Kai, 13th cent.). Simple brush strokes create a living image of a monk engaged in one of the everyday tasks that typify Ch'an Buddhist practice. Courtesy of Tokyo National Museum (photographed from *Zen Painting* by Yasuichi Awakawa, trans. John Bester; reprinted by permission. Copyright © 1970 Kodansha International, Ltd., Tokyo and New York).

To the extent that the Ch'an painter succeeds in graphically expressing a moment of life, he has become nature's mirror. In Ch'an's own terms, he has succeeded in expressing, not his own mind, but the Universal Mind, which can only be characterized as "void" or "empty" (*k'ung*; *kong*).

One may further speculate that it was the Ch'an view that voidness was more basic than substantiality, as a characteristic of phenomena, which led Ch'an painters to make as much of empty space as of brushstrokes in their works. Consider the following comment on Ch'an Buddhism and painting by Osvald Sirén, the late dean of Chinese art historians:

We need hardly to dwell on the well-known fact that the Chinese painters, and particularly those who worked in Indian ink, utilized space as a most important means of artistic expression, but it may be pointed out that their ideas of space and their methods of rendering it were far from the same as in European art. Space was not to them a cubic volume that could be geometrically constructed, it was something illimitable and incalculable which might be, to some extent, suggested by the relation of forms and tonal values but which always extended beyond every material indication and carried a suggestion of the infinite. . . . When fully developed as in the composition of the Ch'an painters, where the forms often are reduced to a minimum in proportion to the surrounding emptiness, the enveloping space becomes like an echo or a reflection of the Great Void, which is the very essence of the painter's intuitive mind. The correspondence may not be demonstrable . . . yet it seems quite obvious when we know something about the psychological attitude which was developed by the Ch'an training. The painters who had arrived at an experience of the inner meaning of things or the essence of reality could hardly avoid using symbols of the same kind as the [Ch'an] philosophers. As the things which they conceived were parts of their own consciousness, alive with their own vitality, they were given an added significance by their relation to the illimitable space, which is a symbol of ultimate reality.[8]

As this passage suggests, it was intuition rather than conscious calculation that guided the creation of ink paintings. Yet such works of art nevertheless explicitly manifested many features of the Chinese organicistic world view, frequently employing subjects from the natural world and always balancing dark and light, brushstrokes and empty space, *yin* and *yang*.

However, while Chinese ink paintings provide a striking example of the effort to intuitively grasp the natural process at work, they are hardly the best place in Chinese art to look for a detailed and explicit expression of the *structure* of the Chinese universe. As we shall see, this is far easier to find in the world of Chinese architecture.

Architectural Sacred Space

In Chapter 1 we discussed the traditional use of geomancy (*feng-shui*) in China to select for every new structure a building site where nature's *ch'i* (physical/spiritual "life force") was well constituted. Here we will discuss yet another dimension of the way in which structures were built in compliance with religious conceptions about the nature of the universe, the emphasis now being on the principles of *shape* and *directional orientation* that lent sacredness to certain structures on the traditional Chinese landscape. Of such structures, it was of course temples, as the palaces of gods, that most obviously constituted zones of "sacred space." But since many other structures shared the same basic architectural plan as temples, one suspects there was something sacred about the plan itself. In the following paragraphs, we aim to explore just what this may have been.

Coming up to a temple, other public structure, or large private estate, one finds it surrounded by an outer wall with a high, decorated main gate in the center of its south face. Thus, like the buildings within, the compound opens up to the south (associated with warm and beneficent *yang* influences) and has its back to the north (the direction of baleful *yin* influences). If the compound is large, there will be another gate within, which will probably have three separate doorways, the central one being reserved for the god, emperor, or other appropriately exalted guest or host. Farther within the compound, one will find the main hall occupying a central position, with halls of lesser importance to the sides and back. In a family estate, the main hall would be reserved for the ancestors; in a government office compound, for business and ceremony of the highest level; and in a temple, for the main god's throne and altar.

---

[8] Sirén, p. 97; reprinted by permission of Schocken Books Inc.

FIGURE 4.2. A Chinese temple presents an image of balanced symmetry, while also yielding hints of otherworldliness. New Ma-tsu Temple, Lukang, Taiwan.

Thus, in a typically religious way, the spatial center is also the most important and holy place; and moving away from it, one finds concentric zones of lesser and lesser sacredness. Moreover, because of the connection of north with *yin* and south with *yang,* all the major halls and gates are located along a single north-south axis. And when there are important structures on the two sides, they balance one another in their placement, size, and grandeur. Thus, the concepts of sacred space underlying Chinese architecture are dominated by these three principles of concentricity, north-south axiality, and east-west symmetry, all reflecting the Chinese sense of cosmic order. (In Chapter 6, this will be made especially clear in treating the ceremonial sites of China's last imperial capital, Peking. Figure 6.2, Plan of Peking's Forbidden City, in particular, illustrates all three of the principles just mentioned.) By means of these principles, the Chinese defined as sacred a *general* architectural plan, not only *particular* hallowed places, trees, rivers, or mountains. And just as with the forms of ritual (*li*) discussed earlier, it was considered to be sacred because it was believed to reflect the essential structures of a sacred cosmos.

If we can in our mind's eye imagine a state ceremonial hall or local folk temple with a ritual event in progress, it should now be possible to see how traditional Chinese religious conceptions were expressed and reinforced in several different but equally artistic ways: (1) a certain architectural plan marked the place off from its surroundings as *sacred space;* (2) the dramatic performance of tradition-honored rites, showing reverence for imperial ancestors or invoking a popular god to descend for a feast, also marked off a *sacred time;* and (3) the beauty and frequently religious nature of the decor in the hall or temple helped to stimulate *emotive responses* of a kind we often associate with religious experience. Now let us turn to the final realm of artistic expression to be discussed.

Literature

Here we will explore in detail how one of the most widely enjoyed Chinese novels, *Journey to the West,* presents the traditional Chinese religious world view. By way of introduction, it should be pointed out that all of China's popular novels contain religious themes. First of all, the world of popular novels was the same vast and fantastic universe that formed the backdrop for Chinese folk religion, with its countless deities and demons, ghosts and ancestors. Secondly, in their plots, these novels never departed from the idea of moral retribution, originally Buddhist but so basic to Chinese religion, according to which one will always be punished for evil deeds, if not by fellow humans, then by divine beings or (as was most likely in fiction) the ghosts of those whom one had wronged. Finally, they often made direct or allegorical reference to the path of individual spiritual cultivation by means of which humans became gods, Buddhas, Taoist Immortals, or Confucian sages.

At least one reason for the Chinese novel's many religious features was that its early evolution was so much a part of Chinese religious history. In fact, several accounts agree that Buddhist monks were China's first professional storytellers.[9] At least as early as the T'ang period, they publicly delivered simple didactic tales that expressed their religious doctrines and moral principles in a form the common people could understand. Later, when they and secular storytellers imitating them produced theatrical prompt books as an aid for delivering somewhat longer tales to the public, the basis for the Chinese novel was born. And, ironic as it may seem, it was a prohibition against public storytelling by Buddhist monks during the Sung Dynasty that helped secular storytellers to flourish and, thus, hastened the appearance of China's first full-length novels.

It should therefore be no surprise that it was the transmission of tales about a famous Chinese Buddhist monk's journey to India that emerged, late in the sixteenth century, as China's first and most enduring fantasy novel (*Journey to the West*). For present purposes, the main thing is that the embellishments added to this novel during the course of transmission make it a fascinating introduction to the world of Chinese religion.

---

[9] On this and what follows, see C. T. Hsia, *The Classic Chinese Novel: A Critical Introduction* (New York and London: Columbia University Press, 1968), pp. 6–8; Daniel L. Overmyer, *Folk Buddhist Religion: Dissenting Sects in Late Traditional China* (Cambridge, Mass.: Harvard University Press, 1976), pp. 176–179; and Anthony C. Yu, trans. and ed., *The Journey to the West,* Vol. 1 (Chicago and London: University of Chicago Press, 1977), pp. 22–23.

THE CHINESE RELIGIOUS WORLD VIEW IN
JOURNEY TO THE WEST

At about age thirty, a T'ang Dynasty monk named Hsuan-tsang (Xuan-zang, ca. 596–664) secretly joined a merchant caravan and headed toward India in search of Buddhist wisdom. He spent four years reaching his goal and, then, another twelve in India studying Buddhism and gathering texts. After a return trip that lasted only about a year, he was not only pardoned by the T'ang emperor (T'ai-tsung) for illegally leaving the country seventeen years earlier but was also granted a personal audience during which he greatly impressed the emperor with his knowledge of foreign cultures. Thereafter offered an official post by Emperor T'ai-tsung, he turned it down so that he might spend the rest of his life translating the texts he had acquired on his trip. He had returned from India with a total of six hundred and fifty-seven items of textual material, and it was thus appropriate that he was later given the honorific Buddhist title of T'ang San-tsang (Tang San-zang: "Tripitaka of the T'ang Dynasty"). Tripitaka (Sanskrit for "three baskets") refers to the Buddhist canon in its three divisions, and it is the name by which Hsuan-tsang is generally known in China, since this is what he is called in the novel that made him famous: *Journey to the West.*

The Tripitaka of the novel makes his journey to the West and back in only fourteen years, which is perhaps the only thing about the trip that the novel "underexaggerates." Everything else about the novel shows that its author, probably Wu Ch'eng-en (Wu Cheng-en, ca. 1506–1582), conceived the journey as religious allegory, myth, and fantasy on the grandest scale. As most Chinese will be able to tell you, each of the novel's main characters is supposed to represent a dimension of human life or personality. Tripitaka is simply the ordinary man: frail, anxious, bumbling, and selfish, though striving to be compassionate. All his companions on the trip are superhuman but hardly beyond having human faults. First, there is a divine monkey, who represents the mind—creative, unbridled, and sometimes dangerous. Second, we have a gargantuan pig, surnamed Chu (Zhu: "pig"), and clearly symbolic of sensual lust and desire. Finally, we have a once ferocious water monster who, after his subjugation and conversion to Buddhism, is called Sha Monk (*sha* meaning "sand" and referring to his former river-bottom home). Less outstanding and assertive than the other characters, he has been appreciated by the Chinese as a symbol of quiet sincerity.

Going beyond this more obvious symbolism, some have interpreted the whole journey as an inner, spiritual one rather than one of actual combat with demons and other physical ordeals. For example, the editor of the first (1592) edition of the novel had this to say:

> For demons are the miasmas caused by the mouth, the nose, the ears, the tongue, the body, the will, the fears, and the illusions of the imagination. Therefore, as demons are born of the mind, they will be also subdued by the mind. This is why we must subdue the mind in order to subdue the demons; we must subdue the demons in order

to return to truth; we must return to truth in order to reach the primal beginning where there will be nothing more to be subdued by the mind. This is what is meant by the accomplishment of the *Tao*, and this is also the real allegory of the book.[10]

To the extent that such an interpretation is true, it still only presents half the picture. While all the ordeals that are undergone by Tripitaka and his disciples may be unreal and imaginary at the level of Buddhism's ultimate truth, they are quite real at the common-sense level on which the pilgrims, like most of us, face life's difficulties. And, moreover, it is on the second level that the pilgrims are ultimately judged and rewarded for their good deeds, which also have a certain reality.

Therefore, we have two complementary religious views represented in the novel, one in which all events are illusory and must be met with an attitude of detachment, and another in which they are real and can be understood from within an ordinary moral perspective. Thus it is that the novel is able to represent to us elements of the spiritual quest as interpreted by China's Buddhist and Taoist elite at the same time that it preserves popular religious conceptions concerning moral retribution. Furthermore, what is most important for us is that it presents all this against the background of a universe that could have been born only within the Chinese popular imagination. This is a universe run by a great divine-human bureaucracy, headed by the Jade Emperor and the nobles and officials of his Heavenly court, who are aided on earth by their human counterparts. Opposed to these preservers of order in the cosmos, there exist every conceivable kind of villain, rebel, demon, and monster. And most important, this universe is conceived on a scale that constitutes a religious vision in itself—one that cuts the problems of ordinary life greatly down to size. In introducing *Journey to the West* as a source book of Chinese religious life, our chief aim will be to offer the reader some feel for this vision.

The Monkey King's Rise to Power

Beyond the seas exists the great Flower-Fruit Mountain, where there was once an immortal stone.

Since the creation of the world, it had been nourished for a long period by the seeds of Heaven and Earth and by the essences of the sun and the moon, until, quickened by divine inspiration, it became pregnant with a divine embryo. One day it split open, giving birth to a stone egg about the size of a playing ball. Exposed to the wind, it was transformed into a stone monkey endowed with fully developed features and limbs. Having learned at once to climb and run, this monkey also bowed to the four quarters, while two beams of golden light flashed from his eyes to reach even the Palace of the Polestar.[11]

---

[10] Cited in Yu, Vol. 1, p. 34; reprinted by permission of University of Chicago Press.

[11] Yu, Vol. 1, p. 67; reprinted by permission of University of Chicago Press. Even where not specifically acknowledged, the following is based upon Yu's complete four-volume translation of *Journey to the West* (Chicago and London: University of Chicago Press, 1977–1981).

It was thus that the Jade Emperor (who reigns the universe from his position at the polestar) learned about the monkey's birth. Unaware of the trouble this mischievous ape would cause in the future, the Jade Emperor was unimpressed and calmly declared: "These creatures from the world below are born of the essences of Heaven and Earth, and they need not surprise us."[12].

As for the monkey, because of his rare talents, he quickly became head of a monkey kingdom on Flower-Fruit Mountain. After three or four hundred years as Monkey King, he became alarmed about his future, realizing that as a mortal being he would be subject to the will of Yama, King of the Underworld. Vowing to become an immortal and escape Yama's death appointment, he left his happy kingdom to search for a Taoist master who could teach him the practices that lead to immortality. He found one who was willing to accept him as a student, and who gave him the surname Sun and the religious name Wu-k'ung ("Awake-to-Vacuity"), which is a reference to the Buddhist doctrine that all phenomena are metaphysically "void" or "empty" (*k'ung*). An outstanding student, before long Monkey learned the secret practices that lead to immortality, and soon afterward he departed from his master.

Returning to his monkey kingdom a great hero, Awake-to-Vacuity (Sun Wu-k'ung), swelling with pride, went on a rampage of mischief that upset a variety of powerful beings in the universe. Even the Jade Emperor heard about it—for he received memorials from those whom Awake-to-Vacuity had offended. The first such memorial stated:

> From the lowly water region of the Eastern Ocean at the East Pūrvavideha Continent, the small dragon subject, Ao-kuang [Ao-guang] humbly informs the Wise Lord of Heaven, the Most Eminent High God and Ruler, that a bogus immortal, Sun Wu-k'ung, born of the Flower-Fruit Mountain and resident of the Water-Curtain Cave, has recently abused your small dragon, gaining a seat in his water home by force. He demanded a weapon, employing power and intimidation. . . . We presented him with the divine treasure of an iron rod and the gold cap with phoenix plumes; giving him also a chain-mail cuirass and cloud-treading shoes, we sent him off courteously. But even then he was bent on displaying his martial prowess and magical powers, and all he could say to us was "Sorry to have bothered you"! We are indeed no match for him, nor are we able to subdue him. Your subject therefore presents this petition and humbly begs for imperial justice.

And a second memorial, from the Minister of Darkness and the Bodhisattva Ti-tsang (Di-zang; Sanskrit: Kśitigarbha), who are in charge of the underworld realm where everyone's destiny is officially recorded, said the following about Sun:

> He caused great confusion in the Palace of Darkness; he abrogated by force the Record of Names, so that the category of monkeys is now beyond control, and inordinately long life is given to the simian family. The wheel of transmigration is stopped, for birth

---

[12] Yu, Vol. 1, p. 68; reprinted by permission of University of Chicago Press.

and death are eliminated in each kind of monkey. Your poor monk therefore risks offending your heavenly authority in presenting this memorial. We humbly beg you to send forth your divine army and subdue this monster, to the end that life and death may once more be regulated and the Underworld rendered perpetually secure.[13]

Despite his bold offenses, Sun was not tracked down and punished. Instead, upon the wise advice of a counselor to the Jade Emperor, he was invited to take an official post among the ranks of the celestial officials, where his actions could be closely watched.

However, when Sun found out that his post was a lowly one, he left in rebellion, to return only after being granted the title of "Great Sage, Equal to Heaven." And still later, after being appointed to look after the Garden of Immortal Peaches, he launched into another spree of disobedience, which he began by consuming dozens of sacred peaches from the garden. Unable to find any way to subdue him, the Jade Emperor finally appealed to Buddha, whose powers transcend those of the Heavenly court and even, we shall see, the Great Sage, Equal to Heaven—Sun Wu-k'ung. Believing he was a match for anyone, Sun was tricked into making a wager with Buddha. He bet that he could jump free of the Buddha's hand, using his "cloud-somersault," and he agreed to subjugation on the earth below should he fail to do so.

With a great leap, Sun reached a place where there were five great pillars supporting the sky, and he took this place to be the edge of Heaven. In order to prove that he had been there, he wrote the words "The Great Sage, Equal to Heaven has made a tour of this place" on the central pillar and urinated at the base of the first pillar. Then, returning to his starting place, he announced to Buddha that he went to the edge of Heaven. But, as he was immediately informed, he had never left the Buddha's hand. The words he had written on the pillar at the edge of Heaven were on the Buddha's middle finger, and a puddle of his own urine lay at his feet. Thus did our monkey king learn of Buddha's infinite wisdom and power, which could put to shame an immortal like himself or even overshadow the Jade Emperor and all his Heavenly soldiers and officials. Subjugated on earth within the Five-Phases Mountain (made by the transformation of the Buddha's fingers into the five elemental phases: wood, fire, earth, metal, and water), Sun would not be heard from for another several hundred years.

Tripitaka and His Mission

Coming down to the time of the early T'ang in China (seventh century), the Buddha announced from his Spirit Mountain in the West his intention to give his holy scriptures to the people of T'ang China. He stated:

---

[13] The two memorials (which have been abridged here) are in Yu, Vol. 1, pp. 112–114; reprinted by permission of University of Chicago Press.

> They are scriptures for the cultivation of truth; they are the gate to ultimate goodness. I myself would like to send these to the Land of the East; but the creatures in that region are so stupid and scornful of the truth that they ignore the weighty elements of our Law and mock the true sect of Yoga. Somehow we need a person with power to go to the Land of the East and find a virtuous believer. He will be asked to experience the bitter travail of passing through a thousand mountains and ten thousand waters to come here in quest of the authentic scriptures, so that they may be forever implanted in the east to enlighten the people.[14]

His request is answered by the Bodhisattva Kuan-yin (in India a male deity, this Bodhisattva has become popular in China as a *goddess* of mercy), and the "virtuous believer" she finds after going to the Land of the East is, of course, Tripitaka. As the tale further unfolds, Tripitaka turns out to be Buddha's former disciple, Golden Cicada, who had been expelled to earth for being inattentive during a sermon by Buddha and was (as Tripitaka) serving out the tenth, and last, of his incarnations on earth. This gave him something in common with the other pilgrims who would join him. For all had been banished to horrid existences on earth—Pilgrim Sun (the monkey) having played havoc with his hosts in Heaven, the pig pilgrim having drunkenly dallied with the moon goddess, and Sha Monk having broken a crystal cup at a Heavenly feast.

In fact, while still on her way east to find Tripitaka, Kuan-yin met and converted each of the other pilgrims. First she met the monster of Flowing Sands River, who had been condemned to a life of eating helpless travelers seeking to cross the river. Giving him the surname Sha ("sand") and the religious name Wu-ching (Wu-jing: "Awake-to-Purity"), she revealed to him the place he would have in Tripitaka's westward pilgrimage. Next, she met the pig, who also led a life of killing and eating passing strangers—so that he could maintain his life and home on the Mountain of the Blessed Mound. Surnaming him Chu ("pig") and giving him the religious name Wu-neng ("Awake-to-Power"), she likewise told him to be on the lookout for a Buddhist pilgrim heading west. Finally, she met Pilgrim Sun, who was more than willing to convert to Buddhism and help with the pilgrimage, so long as he be freed from his imprisonment.

Thus, we see that each of the assistant pilgrims is a delinquent convert to the faith; and that all of them, including Tripitaka himself, are working off the bad *karma* of their previous acts. For this reason, their pilgrimage represents a good opportunity to cancel the karmic effects of past evil deeds and, moreover, to store up great merit on the positive side of the divine moral ledger. Indeed, above and beyond the quest for sacred scriptures, there are many ordeals (eighty-one in all) during which numerous evil demons are slain, and numerous helpless victims saved, by Tripitaka's superhuman assistants.

However, there is no way they can eliminate for Tripitaka the trials he must undergo *as a human*, before he may acquire the scriptures. For example, when he, Monkey, and Pig get to the Flowing Sands River and

[14] Yu, Vol. 1, p. 184; reprinted by permission of University of Chicago Press.

meet the water-monster who (without their knowing it) will soon become their companion, the following conversation ensues between Monkey and Pig:

> "Elder Brother," said . . . [Pig], "if it's so easy all you need to do is carry Master [Tripitaka] on your back: nod your head, stretch your waist and jump across. Why continue to fight this monster?" . . . "If you can't carry him [said Monkey], what makes you think I can? There's an old proverb which says: 'Move the T'ai Mountain, and it's as light as the mustard seed, but carry a mortal and you won't leave the red dust [i.e., the mortal world] behind!' Take this monster here: he can use spells and call upon the wind, pushing and pulling a little, but he can't carry a human into the air. And if it's this kind of magic, old Monkey knows every trick well, including becoming invisible and making distances shorter. But it is required of Master to go through all these strange territories before he finds deliverance from the sea of sorrows; hence even one step turns out to be difficult. You and I are only his protective companions, guarding his body and life, but we cannot exempt him from these woes, nor can we obtain the scriptures all by ourselves. Even if we had the ability to go and see Buddha first, he would not bestow the scriptures on you and me.[15]

Master Tripitaka is not only a burden from the point of view of his divine assistants. As one of Buddha's most virtuous disciples, he is also a greatly desired prize from the point of view of every demon and demoness in the universe. Thus, the former wish to capture and eat him, and the latter want to seduce and have intercourse with him, since they may thereby add to their power and life span.

For example, when the pilgrims come to the Heaven-Reaching River, which measures eight hundred miles across, the Great King who rules the river from its depths devises a plan to capture Tripitaka. He causes the river to freeze and, after the pilgrims are on their way across, opens a great hole in the ice into which they all fall. Monkey flies into midair; while Pig, Sha Monk, and even the Master's horse (a former water dragon) are all at home in the cold water and easily escape. But Tripitaka himself gets caught—to be saved only after a prolonged river-bottom struggle with the Great King of the Heaven-Reaching River.

Time after time this kind of scene repeats itself, until the pilgrims finally reach a western land where only the most beautiful pines and jewel-like flowers grow, and where all the people live pious and peaceful lives. Thus do they know that they are coming close to Buddha's abode. Soon they meet an immortal who shows them how to make the final leg of their journey to Spirit Mountain, having been long ago appointed this task by Kuan-yin. Yet, even following his instructions, the pilgrims find they still have one more river to cross, one that apparently can only be traversed by using a narrow bridge made of slim tree trunks connected end to end. It turns out, however, that this is not just another dangerous river. It is the Cloud Transcending Stream, and crossing it will not be just another ordeal for the pilgrims. Rather, it will be their liberation.

---

[15] Yu, Vol. 1, p. 436; reprinted by permission of University of Chicago Press.

FIGURE 4.3. This three-dimensional mural shows the main characters from *Journey to the West*. Tripitaka is at the lower right, and the words above read: "Tripitaka going to fetch the Scriptures." Cave of the Purple Clouds, Ch'ing-shui (Qing-shui), Taiwan.

As they are bickering about how to cross the river, unexpectedly a boat with a man in it yelling "ferry, ferry" arrives. Relieved at first, Master Tripitaka then becomes hesitant about getting on board when he sees that the boat has no bottom. It is necessary, in fact, for Monkey to push his master on board; for only he can see that the ferryman of this bottomless boat is the Buddha in charge of conducting souls to salvation. As the boat crosses the river, Tripitaka's anxiety does not subside, but rather grows, since he now sees his and his disciples' bodies floating swiftly away downstream. Only afterwards, freed from ignorance, does he realize that he has only lost his fleshly shell and the corruption of its senses. For he and his disciples have reached the Other Shore (i.e., salvation).

Ironically, however, they find there the same kind of ceremonial and bureaucratic procedures that existed in the world they left behind. Buddha himself carefully checks their passports before turning the pilgrims over to his assistants, the famous disciples Ānanda and Kāśyapa, who are instructed to give them the desired holy scriptures. But since Tripitaka is not able to produce "a few little gifts" for the two Buddhist bureaucrats, they are at first reluctant to give him any scriptures at all and later decide to cheat him by handing over mere blank scrolls. Moreover, when their deception is discovered, Buddha, with cunning wit, tells them that the blank scrolls are, after all, the *true* scriptures. He then tells Ānanda and Kāśyapa to fetch some scrolls with writing on them for the still foolish and ignorant people of the East. Finally, after giving them his last possession, a gold begging bowl once presented to him by the emperor of China, Tripitaka leaves for home with his disciples and a load of holy scriptures.

Returning to the Court of T'ang China, the pilgrims of course receive a warm welcome and—after again having their passports examined—are invited to a great imperial banquet. But the worldly honor thus conferred upon them is of little consequence; for the real end of their journey comes after they return, mission completed, to Buddha's Spirit Mountain to receive Heavenly ranks in reward for the merit achieved during their arduous journey. Tripitaka and Monkey become Buddhas; Sha Monk becomes an Arhat (an enlightened being somewhat lower in status than a Buddha or Bodhisattva); and Pig, with due regard for his still untamed appetite, becomes Cleanser of all altars in the universe where Buddhist offerings are made. Our heroes thus rejoin the ranks of the divine bureaucracy which, according to both Chinese popular religion and literature, exists in the Heavens as a perfect mirror image of the human bureaucracy here on earth.

In *Journey to the West*, the traditional Chinese religious world view thus comes alive in its aspect of supernatural fantasy, where spiritual beings of every rank and kind are believed to exercise their powers to save the worthy and punish the wicked. It has another aspect, of course, both less supernatural and more serious, which is better represented by China's classical philosophical texts than by its popular novels. These texts will be the focus of the next chapter's discussion of the theoretical dimension of Chinese religion.

5

theoretical expression in chinese religion

This and the next two chapters will elaborate on the brief introduction to the three forms of religious expression in China given in Chapter 1. Beginning with religious theory, discussion here focuses on such subjects as mythology and supramundane divinity. Yet two thirds of the present chapter deals with two thinkers often praised for their enlightened avoidance of the supernatural: Confucius and Lao Tzu (ignoring, for the moment, whether or not the latter is an identifiable historical figure). And although they clearly deserve such attention, having been claimed as the respective "founders" of the Confucian and Taoist traditions, we give them this special attention with some reservation. Because of their sophisticated theoretical perspectives, they represent a level of Chinese thought often far removed from religious practice, especially where Chinese folk religion is concerned.

Yet wherever one finds religion, there is bound to be disparity between the elite-level great tradition and the folk-level little tradition (as explained in Chapter 1). All one can aim to do, in any case, is reveal the continuity that exists between the two levels and thereby show how the religious system in question makes sense as a whole. For this reason, we begin with an overall view of Chinese religious theory, aiming to create a proper background for viewing Confucius and Lao Tzu as representing the highest level of theoretical expression in Chinese religion.

CHINESE RELIGIOUS THEORY: MYTH, SCRIPTURE, AND DIVINITY

The most basic form of theoretical expression in religion is the mythology of ancient and preliterate cultures, which exists orally before being recorded in writing—if it is ever written down. Being essentially *sacred histories*, myths explain how the world was created, became occupied by its current inhabitants, and came to have its present moral, spiritual, and physical characteristics. Therefore, myths deal with the same questions about the nature of existence as do even the most advanced forms of theology and philosophy. Now, in ancient China, we would expect to find, as most elsewhere, a set of myths that existed before the emergence of advanced religious and philosophical writings. But, although myths certainly existed in ancient China, it is rather difficult for us to know much about their original form and possible relations to one another. Perhaps the main reason for this lies in the fact that those who recorded these myths (or, in most cases, fragments of myths) seem to have had no interest in preserving the myths literally but, rather, chose to understand them according to their own ends as philosophers or historians. The result was a kind of "demythicization" by virtue of which myths, no longer able to be taken literally, were reinterpreted to fit into new, more sophisticated contexts. This process occurred within the formative period of China's classical tradition, during the Chou and Former Han eras.

"Demythicization" in Classical China

Although complete versions of ancient China's myths do not exist, we can get a rough idea of their content from what is preserved of them in classical sources. As would be expected, their content is similar to that of myths found elsewhere in the ancient world, while their particular flavor nevertheless conforms to the Chinese religious world view as described in previous chapters. Ancient Chinese mythology included stories concerned with creation, the separation of Heaven and Earth, a great flood, the invention of various elements of human culture, and so forth.

Since the flood myth seems to be such a widespread one, let us consider it as an example of both the universal and particular character of ancient Chinese mythology. The main heroes of China's flood myth are two ancient sages already familiar to us from Chapter 2: Emperor Yao and Yü the Great. Their opposites include Yü's father Kun (Gun) and a certain Kung Kung (Gung Gung), both of whom are presented in the *Book of History* as ministers who fail to carry out Yao's orders to control the flood—the feat later accomplished by Yü the Great. Even within this Confucianized tale of emperors and ministers, there remain vestiges of the key theme of most flood myths: a battle of order and chaos.[1]

---

[1] William G. Boltz, "Kung Kung and the Flood: Reverse Euhemerism in the Yao Tien," *T'oung Pao*, Vol. 67 (1981), pp. 141–153, presents this view in greater detail and with more attention to cross-cultural comparisons.

Whatever Yao and Yü were in the pre-Confucian version of the myth, if not emperors, they probably personified order, as they continue to in various Confucian versions, even though "order" is made into something more governmental than cosmological. In these versions, Yao is uniquely responsible for confronting the flood by virtue of his imperial office; and his successor, Shun, inherits this responsibility along with the office. But in earlier versions, the cosmological dimension was probably dominant. Yao, whose name connotes mountainlike loftiness, perhaps once represented an actual center of the cosmos (not of the state), just as Shun's cosmic powers can be seen behind his supposedly governmental acts of banishing such figures as Kun and Kung Kung to places outside the bounds of the then civilized world. And the cosmological dimension of Yü the Great's role is unmistakable even as described in a relatively late text, *Mencius*, where we read:

> In the time of Yao, the Empire was not yet settled. The Flood still raged unchecked, inundating the empire; plants grew thickly; birds and beasts multiplied; the five grains did not ripen; birds and beasts encroached upon men, and their trail criss-crossed even the Central Kingdoms. The lot fell on Yao to worry about this situation. He raised Shun to a position of authority to deal with it. . . . Yü dredged the Nine rivers, cleared the courses of the Chi [Ji] and the T'a [Ta] to channel the water into the Sea, deepened the beds of the Ju [Ru] and the Han, and raised the dykes of the Huai and the Ssu [Si] to empty them into the [Yangtse] River. Only then were the people of the Central Kingdoms able to find food for themselves . . . (3 A:4).
>
> . . . He led the flood water into the seas by cutting channels for it in the ground, and drove the reptiles into grassy marshes. The water, flowing through the channels, formed the Yangtse, the Huai, the Yellow River and the Han. Obstacles receded and the birds and beasts harmful to men were annihilated. Only then were the people able to level the ground and live on it (3B:9).[2]

Clearly indicated here is the symbolic nature of the flood as chaos, only after the control of which could a truly civilized order be established in the Central Kingdoms (i.e., ancient "China").

Less obvious is the connection of the so-called ministers Kun and Kung Kung with chaos. In a less Confucianized account of their role, they are more likely to have been the cause or even personification of the flood than merely ministers who failed to deal with it (which would better explain why Shun dealt so harshly with them).

Certain versions, in fact, accuse either one or the other of damming up rivers that Yü the Great had to dredge out later, although they consider this act to be bureaucratic mismanagement rather than cosmic mischief. Yet the diluvial, or at least aquatic, connotations of their names suggest an original association with chaotic floodwaters rather than orderly efforts

---

[2] D. C. Lau, trans., *Mencius* (Baltimore: Penguin Books, 1970), pp. 102 and 113; copyright © D. C. Lau 1970; reprinted by permission of Penguin Books Ltd.

to control them.[3] One can therefore conclude that Kun and Kung Kung were made imperial ministers by Chinese historians whose main concern was with the evolution of human (Confucian) culture rather than with cosmic battles between order and chaos. Just as the ancient Israelite authors of Genesis revealed their theological bias by offering a version of the ancient Near Eastern flood myth in which the flood was a calamity inflicted upon humanity as divine retribution for sin, so did the Confucians express their bias in turning mythical, spiritual beings into historical agents within the drama of human evolution.

Taking another case, we see that ancient China also had a myth about the separation of Heaven and Earth during some era long past. Myths of this type usually serve to explain why humanity can no longer easily communicate with Heaven, or how the paradisal age of free exchange between Heaven and Earth came to an end. While we have only a bare skeleton of such a Chinese myth, it can be said to conform to this general pattern. In the *Book of History,* we are told of an ancient era (unspecified) when the Miao people began to make excessive use of cruel punishments (a favorite target of Confucian writers, as was the Miao tribe, an ethnic group that they considered beyond the pale of civilization). When innocent victims complained to Heaven, Shang Ti took action. He exterminated the Miao and commanded two assistants, Ch'ung (Chong) and Li (otherwise unknown in Chinese myth and history), to cut off communication between Heaven and Earth, stopping the ascent and descent of spirits.

In another source, *Narratives of the States* (*Kuo-yü; Guo-yu*), a certain King Chao (Zhao) of Ch'u (515–489 B.C.E.) is described as questioning one of his ministers about the events of the *Book of History* passage. The minister sets the events in a degenerate time before the reigns of Yao and Shun and explains it as a case of a human ruler named Chuan-hsu (Zhuan-xu) taking action to end confusion in the handling of religious matters within his state. Because each household indiscriminately performed rites previously performed only by appropriately qualified shamans, he commanded two officials, Ch'ung and Li, to divide the affairs of Heaven and Earth between them, so as to determine the proper places of men and spirits. It was this, the minister said, which the text meant by "cutting the communication between Heaven and Earth."[4] Thus was China's myth of the separation of Heaven and Earth transformed into an occasion for properly dividing bureaucratic responsibilities.

---

[3] Boltz, pp. 148–151, points to the *Narratives of the States* (*Kuo-yü; Guo-yu*) as the source describing Kung Kung as the flood's cause, and he offers an ingenious philological analysis of his name as a symbol of the chaotic flood and perfect counterpart to Yao's name as the central cosmic mountain. Derk Bodde, "Myths of Ancient China," in *Mythologies of the Ancient World*, ed. S. N. Kramer (Garden City, N. Y.: Doubleday & Co., Inc., 1961), p. 399, refers to (unspecified) versions of the flood story in which Kun (whose name denotes a species of fish) steals a swelling mold from the Lord, uses it to dam up waters, and is executed, three years after which someone opens his belly so that his son Yü the Great may emerge.

[4] Bodde, pp. 389–391, in which he gives an account of this whole episode from the *Narratives of the States*. The *Book of History* version can be read in James Legge, trans., *The Chinese Classics*, Vol. 3, *Shoo King* (Oxford, 1865; rpt. Hong Kong: Hong Kong University Press, 1960), pp. 591–593.

Taking a final case, we must begin by noting that the most universal of all mythological types—creation mythology—is also one of the most difficult to find in classical Chinese sources. In fact, we must turn from Confucian to Taoist sources to see even its vestiges, for, as we have seen, the early Confucians were concerned more with human than natural evolution, more with politics than cosmology. Some parts of early Taoist texts, such as *Tao-te-ching* and *Chuang-tzu,* show an opposite concern. Taking them as our mode of access into ancient Chinese creation mythology, we must conclude that the original Chinese cosmogony (theory about the birth of the cosmos) was of the self-generative or so-called cosmic egg type. This cosmogony identified the "egg" from which the world came as a saclike entity called *hun-tun* (*hun-dun*), an onomatopoeic combination signifying "chaos" or, avoiding the negative tone of this word, "primordial formlessness." This meant that the ancient Chinese, or at least some of them, believed the world was not created by gods but evolved by itself.[5]

Of course, in Taoist sources, the important thing was not to discover the *origin in time* of the universe; it was to know primordial formlessness as the *ever present ground* of the existing universe. The change of emphasis in this kind of "demythicization" was from temporal priority to logical priority, meaning a change from viewing something as first in time to viewing it as first (i.e., most fundamental) in philosophical significance. As an equivalent for the great Tao itself, the significance of primordial formlessness remained high throughout later Chinese history, with great implications for Chinese conceptions of divinity. Yet before turning to these conceptions, something must be said of the place in Chinese religious history of canonical scriptures. For, as time passed, these scriptures increasingly served the functions of mythology as sacred history, source of exemplary models for human behavior, and repository of truth about the nature of the universe.

Canonical Scriptures

In each major civilization, the invention of writing has led inevitably to verbal formulations of religious theory that claim sacred status. The Judeo-Christian *Bible,* the Islamic *Quran,* and the Hindu *Upanishads,* to give but a few examples, are for their devotees a unique gift from the spiritual dimension. Moreover, their sacred status as "canon" usually has the backing of both popular tradition and elite religious authorities. In China, as pointed out in Chapter 1, each of the Three Teachings has an official canon to serve it as a standard of orthodoxy, a source of religious prestige, and a basis for those religious practices in which words have spiritual efficacy— written on protective charms, chanted in rituals, inscribed on monuments, and so forth. However, so far not much has been said about the nature

---

[5] A thorough and fascinating treatment of the cosmogonic dimension of early Taoist texts, including *Lao-tzu* and *Chuang-tzu,* is found in N. J. Girardot, *Myth and Meaning in Early Taoism: The Theme of Chaos (hun-tun)* (Berkeley: University of California Press, 1983).

of each tradition's canon, with the possible exception of Confucianism, whose Five Scriptures and Four Books have at least been mentioned.[6]

It was natural to have already mentioned the canon of the Confucians, for they were first to designate a certain group of works as their "scriptures" (*ching; jing*). These scriptures, already listed during the Former Han Dynasty as the five we know today, are key sources of information about religion and other aspects of culture in ancient China. In addition, Confucian scriptures became the basis of China's educational and examination systems, which meant that they were familiar to all educated Chinese, regardless of their personal, or even professional, interest in Buddhism or Taoism.

By stressing the longevity and importance of the Confucian Canon, however, we do not mean to slight the canon of Buddhism. It has also existed from very early times (though first in languages other than Chinese, such as Pali and Sanskrit) and has its own unique form of classification, which was adopted by Buddhists in China and elsewhere. This form of classification is called Tripitaka, meaning "three baskets," as noted in the discussion in Chapter 4 of the famous T'ang Dynasty monk by that name. In only one of the three baskets do we find actual "scriptures," defined as texts in which we have the inspired Dharma spoken by Buddha. Another contains the rules of discipline for Buddhist monks and nuns, while the remaining one has numerous doctrinal treatises by eminent Buddhists (not Buddha) *about* the Buddha's Dharma. Collections of Chinese texts in all three categories existed by the time Chinese Buddhism reached maturity (the T'ang Dynasty), but it was the founding emperor of the Sung (T'ai-tsu; Tai-zu) who in 972 ordered the first block printing of the entire Tripitaka. Eleven years and 130,000 blocks later, the printing was completed: 1,076 items stored in 480 cases. The modern Chinese Tripitaka, printed in Japan between 1922 and 1933, has 55 volumes of about 1,000 pages each in small Chinese type.[7]

More is contained in this canon, of course, than religious theory. Containing much history, biography, and other material only peripherally related to theory, it is more like the entire literary output of major Confucian scholars over the past two millenia than like the Five Scriptures and Four Books, more like an unabridged compendium of Judeo-Christian theology than like the Bible. Although average Buddhists could only hope to study a small part of it within a lifetime, its mere bulk serves them as a constant reminder of the depth and breadth of their tradition. That this would be important to the Chinese, who among all Asian peoples have by far the most complete version of the Tripitaka, should go without saying. Their dedication, indeed devotion, to literary pursuits has been a hallmark of their civilization, further exemplified by another encyclopedic scriptural collection: the Taoist Canon (*Tao-tsang; Dao-zang*), which was perhaps in-

---

[6] The complete Confucian Canon includes, in addition to these nine works, three commentaries on the *Spring and Autumn Annals*, a lexicon called the *Er-ya*, and sometimes the *Book of Filiality*.

[7] This and other information on the topic can be found in Kenneth Ch'en, *Buddhism in China: A Historical Survey* (Princeton: Princeton University Press, 1964), Chap. 13 ("The Chinese Tripitaka"), pp. 365–386.

spired by the example of the Buddhist Tripitaka but owed no similar debt to a core of foreign works translated into Chinese.

In the case of the Taoist Canon, not only would the average believer be prohibited from reading much of it because of its size, but even from seeing much of it because of its "top secret" status. In contrast to most of Buddhism's efforts to spread the Dharma and disseminate religious literature as widely as possible, Taoism couched its teachings in esoteric language and even kept the printed canon containing these teachings hidden away from the uninitiated. As reported by the Japanese scholar Yoshitoyo Yoshioka, for example, the famous Ming Dynasty edition of the Taoist Canon on which the modern study of Taoism depends was preserved by good historical fortune in one, and only one, place: Peking's famous White Cloud Monastery. At the beginning of his six-year stay there in 1940, Yoshioka witnessed the "Ceremony of the Airing of the Books," in which the Canon was taken from its sealed repository for the only time during the year, and over the course of three consecutive mornings Taoist monks briskly turned through all the pages of its 5,385 *chüan (juan;* lit. "scroll," but here more like "booklet").[8]

Key Buddhist scriptures were the words of Buddha, and the scriptures of the Confucians preserved the words and deeds of ancient sages from Yao and Shun to Mencius. Taoist scriptures, however, were generally said to come from the deities of an eternal celestial hierarchy rather than from any such historical figures. This was even the case with *Tao-te-ching,* whose author was deified by Taoist religion as The Supremely Exalted Lord Lao. Moreover, to a far greater extent than Buddhist and Confucian scriptures, Taoist ones were produced by ecstatic religious practices, such as visionary meditation and spirit writing. A brief look at the nature of the Taoist Canon, as follows, offers much evidence of this.[9]

The Taoist Canon is divided into Three Vaults and Four Supplements. The first Vault is based on texts of the Mao Shan school that were revealed to and transcribed by a certain Yang Hsi (Yang Xi) during the course of visionary experiences he had between 364 and 370. They were dictated to him by a group of Perfected Ones from the heaven of Shang-ch'ing ("exalted purity") and, therefore, became known as the Shang-ch'ing scriptures.[10] The second Vault features certain scriptures of the Ling Pao school that had as their source a triad of high-ranking deities called Celestial Reverences (T'ien-tsun; Tian-zun)—namely, The Celestial Reverence of the Original Beginning, The Supremely Exalted Lord of the Tao, and The Supremely Exalted Lord Lao. And the third Vault was built around

---

[8] Yoshitoyo Yoshioka, "Taoist Monastic Life," in *Facets of Taoism: Essays in Chinese Religion,* eds. Holmes Welch and Anna Seidel (New Haven: Yale University Press, 1979), pp. 247–248.

[9] More on the nature as well as history of this canon can be found in Ninji Ōfuchi, "The Formation of the Taoist Canon," in *Facets of Taoism* (cited earlier), pp. 253–268, on which this summary is largely based.

[10] Michel Strickmann, "The Mao Shan Revelations: Taoism and the Aristocracy," *T'oung Pao,* Vol. 63 (1977), pp. 1–64, well demonstrates the visionary nature and other features of the origin of the Shang-ch'ing scriptures.

the *Scripture of the Three Sovereigns,* a text of uncertain nature and origin but connected by its title with the Three Sovereigns of antiquity (see Chapter 2), who Taoism further identified as the lords of its three cosmic realms (celestial, earthly, and human).

As for the basic scriptures of the Four Supplements, they came into the emerging Taoist Canon rather late (sixth century) but, since they are historically the earliest scriptures, out of the apparent recognition that their omission was a grave oversight. In the first, the basic scripture is *Tao-te-ching.* In the second, it is the *Scripture of Supreme Peace (T'ai-p'ing-ching),* which is largely in the form of conversations between an unnamed "celestial master" and disciples called Perfected Ones, and which in part goes back to the Later Han period when the first Taoist movements were organizing themselves.[11] The third contains scriptures on alchemy; and the fourth, finally, contains those representing the oldest and most perseverent of all Taoist schools: the Way of Celestial Masters.

Now while the Taoist, Confucian, and Buddhist canons were being created, collected, and approved by the religious elite of the Three Teachings, popular mythology continued in its own evolution, borrowing its heroes from the celestial pantheon as well as earthly history of the great traditions. From the Han Dynasty's *Scripture of Seas and Mountains (Shan-hai-ching)* to the late imperial *Romance of the Investiture of the Gods (Feng-shen yen-yi; Feng-shen yan-yi),* there exist noncanonical works that have preserved for us the mythological divine world of Chinese folk religion, the world we have seen in surveying the popular novel *Journey to the West.*[12] As we turn to the topic of Chinese conceptions of divinity, an effort will be made to explain the particular nature and logic of that world.

Conceptions of Divinity

Stressing that Chinese religious theorists did not conceive of ultimate reality as a distinctly formed and empowered "Deity," the sinologist Laurence Thompson adds:

> But if the Ultimate Reality of the universe was not Deity, the Chinese, more than any other people, could not rest content with philosophical abstractions. In coping with the world, man requires at least the illusion that he can summon help, and hope requires the accessibility of help. A Lao Tzu or a Chuang Tzu might meet the vicissitudes of life with perfect equanimity, like leaves drifting resistlessly on the shifting currents; but for other men, life is a never-ending struggle. Fear of defeat, of loss, of disease, of death requires hope, which can only come from power stronger than that of mortals. In the world view of the Chinese, there was a level of reality above the mundane where such power existed and could be tapped. It is at this level that deity becomes

---

[11] Basic information on these movements was given in Chap. 2. As for the scripture itself, see Max Kaltenmark, "The Ideology of the T'ai-p'ing ching" in *Facets of Taoism* (cited earlier), pp. 19–52.

[12] A good survey of mythological data, well arranged according to various categories of deities, is found in Henri Maspero, "The Mythology of Modern China," in *Taoism and Chinese Religion,* trans. Frank A. Kierman, Jr. (Amherst, Mass.: University of Massachusetts Press, 1981), pp. 75–196.

> objectified in ways that are no different than those found in other cultures. That is to say, *divine power becomes anthropomorphized.*[13]

Put in other words, while the Tao and *ch'i*, for example, were specifically denied anthropomorphic attributes, such as will, purpose, compassion, anger, jealousy, and judgment of good and evil, these attributes were possessed in abundance by the gods of Chinese popular religion.

In fact, these gods were specifically *limited* to the possession of *human-like powers;* for even in Chinese popular religion, it was implicitly assumed that the universe was run by the indefinable power of the formless Tao. And this meant that nature ran itself, while the various creatures subordinate to it, including gods, had powers *qualitatively* no different from those of humans. Thus, as we saw in *Journey to the West,* various deities are conceived of as holding offices within a great divine-human bureaucracy. And in actual practice, Chinese deities have been given payments and bribes in the form of spirit money (which is burned on nearly every ceremonial occasion); they have been coerced into behaving in certain favorable ways by those, such as Taoist priests, who have knowledge of the appropriate ritual formulas; and their bureaucratic ranks and titles have been decided by human, albeit imperial, authority.

Moreover, in accord with bureaucratic practice, and also with the basic logic of *polytheism,* the belief that there are many gods rather than a single God, Chinese gods are thought to have a great variety of forms and functions. Thus, their conception quite logically reflects the actual diversity found in the natural and human worlds, just as the manner of dealing with them reflects ordinary ways of doing business. There is, in fact, something *contractual* about the manner in which a Chinese deity with a reputation for giving a certain kind of aid is asked to deliver a specific type of favor (the birth of a child, safety at sea, or improved commercial success). And such a request is usually accompanied by a promise that the aid will be repaid with an equally specific form of gratitude (spirit money, future faithfulness, or even a new temple for the god).

Another firm indication of the limited and anthropomorphic nature of Chinese popular gods lies in their frequently human origin. Yet for a human to become divine is not a simple matter. Chinese folk tradition recognizes that it is not normal for a person to become a god; and Chinese classical tradition stipulates that it is, in fact, wrong for someone to become worshiped by those other than his or her own descendants. In the words of Confucius: "To offer sacrifice to what is not one's own ancestor's spirit is improper adulation." (*Analects* 2:24). How, then, did such a large number of ancestral spirits become publicly worshiped gods? Chinese tradition gives its own answer: Extremely meritorious individuals become gods through outstanding service to the public, which can legitimately be repaid by communal, rather than familial, worship.

---

[13] Laurence G. Thompson, "Objectifying Divine Power: Some Chinese Modes," in *Deity and Death: Selected Symposium Papers,* ed. Spencer J. Palmer (Salt Lake City: Brigham Young University, 1978), p. 139. Emphasis added.

FIGURE 5.1. Appearing both human and divine, Chinese deities often have the demeanor and dress of royalty or high officials. Altar in the Hall of Sages and Worthies, Taichung, Taiwan.

The anthropologist Philip Baity has, however, shown this answer to be too simple and idealistic. He suggests that merit is *not* the primary criterion, which is instead the *bereaved status* in which a spirit is left when it dies unnaturally or suffers sacrificial neglect. He demonstrates that this was the case with several local deities in the area of his field work, northern Taiwan, and suggests that it was probably true of such major national deities as Kuan Kung and Ma-tsu.[14] Kuan Kung was a great military hero and celebrated Han Dynasty loyalist during the period of the Han's fall, while Ma-tsu, patroness of seafarers, was noted for her filial efforts to save her shipwrecked father and brothers during the Sung period. But, while traditional accounts would never connect the fact with their divinity, the key thing about both is that they died without leaving any descendants behind to sacrifice to them. Thus, if Kuan Kung and Ma-tsu had not passed through the volatile state of spirits having no place in the Chinese scheme of familial and social obligations, neither one would ever have become a national or even a community god. For a spirit initially becomes worshiped by the public out of necessity, because of its bereaved status. It is worshiped because it is feared and pitied as a spirit deprived of appropriate ancestral sacrifices. This is the way all bereaved spirits, popularly called "hungry

[14] Philip Chester Baity, *Religion in a Chinese Town* (Taipei: Orient Culture Service, 1975), Chap. 6, "The Genesis of Gods," pp. 238–269.

ghosts," are treated. To become further singled out and transformed into a god, something more is required—the reputation of having performed miraculous deeds, whether during life or after death. Spirits who gain and hold this kind of reputation are the ones who can ultimately join the popular pantheon as gods.

While it is probable that most deified humans in the Chinese pantheon had gained their divine status through the process just described, there were naturally exceptions. Some were, in fact, deified sheerly by virtue of their prominence as spiritual leaders, moral exemplars, and so forth. Confucius is a case in point. He was offered the proper sacrifices by his descendants, and only by them, for several centuries after his death. But when he became universally recognized as a Sage—first within the official state cult and then throughout the popular religion—he crossed the line separating human from divine. Of course, some still believed that, in becoming a Sage, Confucius had only become supremely *human*, not divine. In any case, as we now turn to Confucius' life and thought, the important thing is not to define his theological status as China's premier Sage. It is to understand why he merited that status.

CONFUCIUS ON MORALITY AND GOVERNMENT

Chinese historical tradition tells us that Confucius' forebears were nobles in the ancient state of Sung, in eastern central China, but that due to certain unfortunate events they were forced to flee to the state of Lu, in the area of modern China's northeastern seacoast province of Shantung. They were supposed to have fled after the murder in 710 B.C.E. of K'ung Fu Chia (Jia) and a child duke who had been put in his care by the former ruler of the state, Duke Mu (r. 728–720 B.C.E.). While it is possible that Confucius' connection with these events was invented to give him a noble background, the story as a whole fits well into the social and political pattern of the period. It was a period when the feudal order set up during the early part of the Chou Dynasty was turning into disorder, and many were seeking power through means that Confucius, among others, found deplorable.

Born in the state of Lu in 551 (or 552) B.C.E., Confucius was a man of humble station who made a name for himself through learning. K'ung was his family name, and his given name Ch'iu (Qiu); but he became known to posterity as K'ung Fu-tzu (Latinized as Confucius), or Master K'ung. According to his own assessment, he was not born smart but gained knowledge through his love of learning. In fact, his most famous autobiographical statement begins with an indication of his early commitment to learning:

At fifteen, I made up my mind to study. At thirty, I found my place to stand in the world. At forty, things no longer confused me. At fifty, I understood my Heavenly appointed destiny. At sixty, my ears were attuned (to the true meaning of other's words).

FIGURE 5.2. A statue of Confucius. Courtesy of Information and Communication Division, C.C.N.A.A., Republic of China.

And since seventy, I have been able to do what my heart desires without transgressing moral norms (*Analects* 2:4).[15]

Of course, as can be seen from this statement, study obviously had a moral rather than simply academic purpose for him. And he believed that life itself gave us an endless supply of moral learning situations, once saying that there would surely be his "teacher" among any three men walking together, for he could therein find something good to emulate and something bad to use as a lesson for self-correction (*Analects* 7:21).

Because Confucius loved learning, it should come as no surprise that he turned to teaching and gained the admiration of numerous disciples. Those whose words of admiration are recorded in the *Analects* leave no doubt about their absolute devotion to the Master. For example, when Tzu-kung (Zi-gong), one of the Master's politically most successful followers, heard that a certain high official said he was more worthy than Confucius himself, he responded as follows:

---

[15] Following custom, the *Analects* are cited by chapter and verse, using the most commonly employed divisions. Those of some other translations differ slightly, notably the recent and highly recommended one by D. C. Lau (Baltimore: Penguin Books, 1979). The reader may also wish to consult previous ones, such as those by Arthur Waley (London: Allen and Unwin, 1938) and James Legge, in *The Chinese Classics*, Vol. I (Oxford, 1861).

Using the analogy of buildings and their surrounding walls, my walls are only shoulder high, and one can look over them to see the good quality of the houses inside. But the Master's walls are several tens of feet high, so that if one cannot get in through the main gate, he will see neither the beauty of the ancestral temple nor the splendor of all the various officials within. And since perhaps few can enter that gate, was it not appropriate that His Excellency said what he did? (*Analects* 19:23).

On another occasion, upon hearing that this same official had slandered the Master, Tzu-kung compared Confucius to the sun and moon in order to demonstrate how far he was beyond the reach of common criticism (*Analects* 19:24).

For his own part, Master K'ung was not easy on his students; throughout the *Analects* we see him putting them in their place through the use of blunt wit and moral reprimand. He once said he would only teach a student who had already exhausted himself in trying to solve a problem; and he then added that when he reveals one corner of a square (i.e., one aspect of a problem) for a student, and the latter does not respond with the other three, he refuses to repeat the lesson (*Analects* 7:8). Moreover, it is hard to find cases where he heaps praise on any of his students, and only one of them received his unqualified approval. This was Yen Hui (Yan Hui), who exceeded Confucius in natural intelligence and was able, despite utter poverty, to maintain the moral standards of the Master in his affairs. Unfortunately, Yen Hui suffered an early death. This loss left the Master forlorn and was, in part, what led him to exclaim: "No one knows me!" When Tzu-kung asked him to explain this statement, he added: "I do not complain against Heaven nor find fault with other men; I learn from what is low but attain to what is high; perhaps it is but Heaven that knows me" (*Analects* 14:37).

The feeling that only Heaven knew him was, of course, confirmed in his mind by the lack of reception to his ideas during his own lifetime. He sought in his home state, as in all the others to which he journeyed, to exert an influence upon the rulers of his day; and his obvious lack of success did not deter him from seeking to carry on. For if there was anything religious about Confucius, it was his belief that he had a mission decreed by something with greater than human authority, which he called Heaven. Thus, when a certain Huan T'ui (Huan Tui), commander of the armed forces in the state of Sung, was apparently after him, Confucius said: "Heaven produced the virtue (*te; de*) in me. What can Huan T'ui do to me?" (*Analects* 7:22). Here, as elsewhere (*Analects* 9:5), he suggests that because his moral mission is Heavenly decreed, there is no point for him to be intimidated by earthly rulers. And as for the concept *te*, it denoted a moral endowment which, if fully cultivated, would make one worthy to rule the whole empire. Believing he had this Heavenly conferred virtue (*te*) and, also, knew his Heavenly appointed destiny, Confucius' sense of mission was quite extraordinary. Yet, as we will now see, it was matched by a sense of moral discipline so strict that the Master himself frankly confessed to his inability to maintain it in practice (*Analects* 7:32, 7:33, and 14:30).

Morality for Its Own Sake

Confucius put nothing, including personal survival, above doing what is right; and he argued that one must do what is right solely for its own sake. This meant, on the one hand, that his morality was not built upon the promise of future religious reward and, on the other, that it eschewed utilitarian considerations (that is, concerns about the actual or expectable *results* of one's acts). One could say he was the kind of person who simply believed in doing what he felt was right and letting the chips fall where they may.

As far as the connection of religious views with his ethics is concerned, the only positive connection has already been mentioned in discussing his sense of having a Heavenly decreed mission. All his other views on religious matters tend to point toward their irrelevance for the moral life. While he often speaks of rites and sacrifices, there is never a hint that he considers them to be valuable for the purpose of procuring either religious merit or material benefit from gods or ancestors. His attitude toward souls, spirits, and the afterlife (as quoted in Chapter 3 from *Analects* 6:20 and 11:11) was similarly agnostic. He also expresses the humanistic view that both the power and responsibility for moral development lies with the human being, his most famous expression of this view being the statement: "A person is able to enlarge the Way (*tao*); it is not the case that the Way can enlarge the person" (*Analects* 15:28). Here we confront the Confucian use of the word *tao* to mean the ideal moral path, with the indication that it must be created through human effort. In Confucius' view, then, since the Way must be humanly created, it is not a divine or otherwise preexistent model with which one may identify and thereby be saved, rectified, or enlightened.

Turning to the antiutilitarian dimension of Master K'ung's ethics, we must elaborate his concept of the ideal Moral Gentleman (*chün-tzu*; see Chapter 2) as well as his concept of its negative counterpart, the inferior man (*hsiao-jen; xiao-ren,* lit., "small person"). Of all the ways in which the Master contrasted the two, perhaps the most important was this: "The Moral Gentleman understands what is right; the inferior man understands what is profitable" (*Analects* 4:10). On one occasion, he defined cowardice as seeing what is right and not doing it (*Analects* 2:24). And on another occasion, he describ┤ the Moral Gentleman as one who takes rightness for his basic nature ⸌*Analects* 15:17). Thus was it possible that he was once described by someone else as a person who knows something cannot be done but still wants to do it (*Analects* 14:41).

Why, one may wonder, was Confucius so uncompromisingly opposed to utilitarian considerations in his ethics? An answer is suggested in yet another of his descriptions of the Moral Gentleman, where he culminates a list of nine ideal characteristics with the statement: "At the sight of gain, he thinks of what is right" (*Analects* 16:10). The talent to think only of moral rightness when one sees a chance for gain is special indeed, for nothing can make us fail to do what we know is right more surely than the thought of personal benefit. And, for Confucius, the only cure for this human weakness was to make a habit of disregarding *all* utilitarian considerations, personal and social. Thus, the Moral Gentleman must be unwavering in the face of hardships (*Analects* 15:1), know that the Moral Way may not be realized in the world despite his efforts (18:7), and yet be concerned about the Way and not about poverty (15:31). This is not to say that the Moral Gentleman must take a vow of poverty, for when the world exists in its proper state, he will hold a rightfully high station. Thus, the Master said: "When the Way prevails in a state and one is poor and lowly, this is shameful; when the Way does not prevail in a state and one has wealth and high station, that is shameful" (*Analects* 8:13). In following the moral life, then, one must be content to accept whatever happens. It has its own rewards, and one must not look beyond them to anything else, material or spiritual. One can perhaps do this, we may conclude, by holding to the attitude expressed in the following:

> The Master said: "To eat plain food and drink plain water and to make a pillow of one's bent arm—there is even joy in these. But as for wealth and high station acquired by what does not accord with rightness (*yi*), they are to me but passing clouds" (*Analects* 7:15).

On Being Humane

It is one thing to swear that one will always do what is right and quite another to *know* what is right. The reader is surely wondering by now: What *is* right for the Confucian Moral Gentleman? What is it with which he replaces the inferior man's undiscriminating desire for wealth and high station? It was with such a question in mind that Confucius made this statement:

> Wealth and high station are what people desire; but if one gets them by not complying with the Moral Way, he cannot remain in them. Poverty and low station are what people dislike; but if one ends up with them by not complying with the Moral Way, he cannot get rid of them. If the Moral Gentleman dispenses with *being humane,* how could he attain his proper disposition? He must not deviate from *being humane* even for the course of a meal. If he hurries, it must be to comply with it. If he gets into difficulties, it must be to comply with it (*Analects* 4:5).

Here we have the view that the content of the moral life, which one should not deviate from for a moment, is *jen* (*ren*) or "being humane." Interestingly, and certainly not by coincidence, the word for "person" in Chinese has the same pronunciation as this word. But even more about its essential meaning can be determined by considering its written form, which is a combination of the character for "person" and that for "two."

Jen, therefore, stands for the moral ideal in human relations; and, at the same time, it is found close to ordinary human life. Thus, Confucius could say: "Is *jen* far away? If I want *jen,* it is here" (*Analects* 7:29). It has its fully "human" quality, first, because it is *naturally* rooted in filiality (*Analects* 1:2). It has this quality, second, because it has nothing to do with superficial moral perfection or superhuman sageliness. This is born out by two important passages from the *Analects*. In one, the Master is asked whether refraining from ambition, boasting, resentment, and desire may be considered "being humane," and he replies: "It can be considered difficult, but I do not know whether it can be considered being humane" (*Analects* 14:2). The other is as follows:

> Tzu-kung asked: "Were there a certain one who was able to save the multitude through widely conferring benefits among the people, what would you say he was like? Could you say he was being humane"? The Master replied: "How could he just be described as 'being humane'; he must surely be a 'sage.' Even Yao and Shun would have been hard pressed to do as much. As for being humane, one should simply establish for others what one intends to establish for oneself and aid others to attain what one intends to attain for oneself. To be able to draw a parallel (for treating others) from the immediacy (of one's own moral life) may be said to lead in the direction of being humane" (*Analects* 6:28).

The final sentence of the latter passage is one way of stating the Confucian golden rule—do not do to others what you do not want them to do to you—which appears three times elsewhere in the *Analects* (5:12, 12:2, and 15:23). And each case suggests that being humane is largely a matter of moral empathy: experiencing others as having the same moral worth and capacities as oneself.

However, the practice of moral empathy was not so open to interpretation as all this may suggest. The traditional *li* (rules of ritual and social decorum), which were discussed in previous chapters, had a large role in defining how one related to others. And although Confucius stated that, without being humane, one's performance of *li* was of little value (*Analects* 3:3), we can be sure he wanted the two to work hand in hand. If fact, on one occasion he used the example of ritual behavior to define the content of *jen*, as follows:

> [The disciple] Chung-kung (Zhong-gong) asked about being humane. The Master said: "Always head out the door like one going out to meet an important guest. Always employ people's services like one officiating at an important sacrifice. Do not do to others what you do not want them to do to you" (*Analects* 12:2).

The fact that the Confucian golden rule is here mentioned in the same breath with two examples of ritual behavior indicates something already touched on in the previous chapter: Relating to others in compliance with *li* is a supremely appropriate way of treating them *as humans*—precisely the goal of *jen*.

Moral Charisma and the Way to Govern

Compliance with *li* was of special importance for the ideal Confucian ruler, for such compliance also had the goal of setting a moral example for others. And Confucian government was, above all, rulership by example. Confucius thus pointed to compliance with *li* as defining how a ruler should employ his ministers (*Analects* 3:19). And, in what appears to be a rather exaggerated claim, he also stated: "If for one day a person is able to truly subordinate himself in compliance with *li*, then all the world will turn to embrace the humaneness (thereby exhibited) in him" (*Analects* 12:1). Such a claim is not, however, out of place in the *Analects*, where leadership by moral example is given an almost magical power of ethico-political transformation. If fact, it is indicated to be far more effective than administrative measures and punishments:

> The Master said: "Lead them with administrative measures and straighten them out with punishments, and the people will avoid violation but have no sense of shame. Lead them by cultivating virtue (*te*) and straighten them out by complying with *li*, and they will not only have a sense of shame but also reform themselves" (*Analects* 2:3).

The term *te* ("virtue"), mentioned here together with *li*, referred to a moral quality received from Heaven. As we have already explained, it was considered sufficient to enable one to rule the whole empire—so long as one fully cultivated it. Moreover, it enabled one to do so without force and aggression, since the people would be willingly submissive toward a ruler who fully manifested his *te*. It might, therefore, be best described as a kind of charisma, that is, a *specifically moral charisma*.[16] This sort of meaning is certainly indicated in Confucius' proverbial comparison of ideal rulership with the role of the polestar in the heavens. The Master said: "Ruling by means of *te* can be compared to the North Polar Star—it remains in its place while the multitude of stars revolves in homage around it" (*Analects* 2:1).

How could one believe that someone might do so little to subjugate others and still gain their loyalty? One could hold such a conviction by having the faith that, under ideal circumstances, the members of society would automatically respond to someone who manifested moral charisma. For such a person would be beseeched by others to lead them; he would never have to take and hold power by means of force. Interestingly, despite their other differences, Lao Tzu shared with Confucius the belief that an ideal and lasting form of rulership could be established only by one who did not seek office but rather aimed simply to cultivate a kind of moral perfection that could inspire others to place him on the throne. In fact, another of Confucius' proverbial comments on rulership could have been written by Lao Tzu, mentioning as it does the Taoist concept of nonaction (*wu-wei*) in government:

> The Master said: "Without action yet ruling the state—was this not (the sage ruler) Shun? What did he do but reverently maintain himself (in his correct ritual posture) facing due south? (*Analects* 15:4)

---

[16] The term *charisma* is used here with reservations. On its dangers and other aspects of this important subject, see Herbert Fingarette, "How the Analects Portrays the Ideal of Efficacious Authority," *Journal of Chinese Philosophy* 8 (1981), pp. 29–50; along with Roger T. Ames' response on pp. 51–57. Fingarette himself rejects the term *charisma* because it connotes "an emphatically suprahuman power that intrudes and shatters the traditional and regularized forms of the human community" (p. 39); and Confucian authority is a human power shaped *according* to these forms.

The use of *wu-wei* is probably coincidental here, and were it a Taoist passage one could not interpret it as giving importance to correct ritual posture. For, as we shall see, Lao Tzu did not give human morality and ceremony the central role in his thought; he rejected them and gave this role, instead, to the Way of nature.

LAO TZU ON NATURE AND NONACTION

In the case of the *Analects*, we have a reliable representation of a particular historical figure. But it is difficult to say that *Lao-tzu* (to use the title of the *Tao-te-ching* most commonly used by Chinese) was written by any one particular individual, let alone the "historical" Lao Tzu whom Chinese tradition considers to be its author. Nevertheless, due to the intrinsic importance of tradition, we must be permitted to say who Lao Tzu ("Venerable Master") was supposed to have been and to continue to use the phrase "Lao Tzu said," when all we can mean by that is "in the book called *Lao-tzu* it says." In fact, the book's earliest title may simply have been *Tao-te-ching* ("Scripture on Tao and Te"), with no reference to an author.[17]

As for the traditional account of its alleged author and his writing of the work, this was recorded in China's first comprehensive history, *The Records of the Historian* (from the Former Han Dynasty), as follows:

Lao Tzu was a native of the Ch'u Jen [Chu Ren] Hamlet in the Li Village of Hu Hsien [Xian] in the state of Ch'u. His surname was Li, his personal name was Erh [Er] and he was styled Tan [Dan]. He was the Historian in charge of the archives in Chou.

When Confucius [believed to be Lao Tzu's junior by several years] went to Chou to ask to be instructed in the rites by him, Lao Tzu said, "What you are talking about concerns merely the words left by people who have rotted along with their bones. . . . Rid yourself of your arrogance and your lustfulness, your ingratiating manners and your excessive ambition. These are all detrimental to your person. This is all I have to say to you."

On leaving, Confucius told his disciples, "I know a bird can fly, a fish can swim, and an animal can run. For that which runs a net can be made; for that which swims a line can be made; for that which flies a corded arrow can be made. But the dragon's ascent into heaven on the wind and on the clouds is something which is beyond my knowledge. Today I have seen Lao Tzu, who is perhaps like a dragon."

Lao Tzu cultivated the way and virtue, and his teachings aimed at self-effacement. He lived in Chou for a long time, but seeing its decline he departed; when he reached the Pass, the Keeper there was pleased and said to him, "As you are about to leave

---

[17] Although it has been translated in English as *The Way and Its Power*, Arthur Waley, trans. (London: Allen and Unwin, 1935), the title need not be interpreted as logically connecting Tao with Te. However, due to recent archeological work on the Chinese mainland, we are now sure that these terms were applied to the respective halves of the work ("Tao" to Chaps. 1–37, and "Te" to Chaps. 38–81) as early as the beginning of the Han Dynasty. See D. C. Lau, *Chinese Classics: Tao Te Ching* (Hong Kong: The Chinese University Press, 1982) for a translation of the newly unearthed version as well as a reprint of his earlier translation of the traditional text (Baltimore: Penguin Books, 1963). As for other translations, it would be impossible to list them all here. It has been said that *Lao-tzu* is the most translated of all works next to the Bible.

FIGURE 5.3. A Sung Dynasty portrait of Lao Tzu riding his water buffalo away from civilization. Collection of National Palace Museum, Taipei, Taiwan, Republic of China.

the world behind, could you write a book for my sake? As a result Lao Tzu wrote a work in two books, setting out the meaning of the way [Tao] and virtue [Te] in some five thousand characters, and then departed. None knew where he went to in the end.[18]

Although, according to this, it sounds as though the work Lao Tzu left us is an organized explanation in two parts about Tao and Te, this is unfortunately not the case. It is a more poetical than logical work, whose ideas on these and other subjects are found dispersed throughout its eighty-one poemlike chapters. However, even assuming that it appeared relatively late (a century or more after Confucius) and was a compilation of ideas from (an) anonymous author(s), it contains a consistent and coherent view of life and the universe which, moreover, has had an influence upon Chinese religion and philosophy far out of proportion with its short length. Our discussion of it, divided into two sections, will focus on two aspects of its teachings: the metaphysical and the practical, that is, what it says about ultimate reality and about how to live in the world.

---

[18] Translated in Lau, *Lao Tzu: Tao Te Ching* (1963), "Introduction," pp. 8–9.

Nature and the Tao

The essential metaphysical stance of *Lao-tzu* is set forth in its opening chapter, as follows:

> *Though we can speak of taos, such are not the Constant Tao;*
> *Though we can name names, such are not Constant Names.*
> *Without name, [Tao] is the Beginning of Heaven and Earth;*
> *And with name, [it] is the Mother of the Myriad Things.*
> *Hence be ever without desires to observe its hidden subtleties;*
> *And ever have desires to observe its manifest tendencies.*
> *These two are one in origin but differ in name,*
> *So we must call their identity mysterious;*
> *Mystery of mysteries,*
> *Gateway to all hidden subtleties.*

Although we are at the outset told we cannot describe or name ultimate reality, this passage (like *Lao-tzu* as a whole) constitutes an admirable attempt to say what *can* be said about it. To say Tao without name is the "Beginning of Heaven and Earth" means it constitutes the primal substance or process that is at the root of all phenomena in the universe. As such, it is transcendent and defies being named; which is to say it has none of the characteristics of things that "exist" in the ordinary sense of the word. As later Taoists would argue more directly, this means ultimate reality is not Being but rather Nonbeing. Being is only the penultimate (next to final) reality, which is what Lao Tzu means by calling the Tao with name the "Mother of the Myriad Things." This reference to an immanent Tao lets us know that, in addition to its transcendent dimension as ultimate reality, Tao has another dimension by virtue of which it *participates* in the birth and nurture of every perceivable thing.

To understand Tao we are instructed to remain open to both dimensions (paradoxically being both with and without desires) and to find in the mysterious identity of the two the hidden subtleties of everything. Yet hidden they must ultimately remain. Not only here but throughout *Lao-tzu,* all the descriptions used to suggest Tao's nature—cloudy, formless, obscure, elusive, silent, void—serve to let us know how ungraspable it is. Turning to discuss some of these descriptions, let us begin where they may all have had their source: the previously mentioned theme of primordial formlessness found in Chinese "creation mythology."

In the twenty-first chapter of *Lao-tzu,* a series of comments on this theme are put to rhyme, as follows:

> *Now as phenomena Tao does endure,*
> *But always so elusive and obscure.*
> *Naught but obscurity, naught but elusiveness.*
> *Yet within a certain image is possessed.*

> *Oh how elusive and obscure,*
> *But within some "thing" exists for sure.*
> *Deep as a cave, and dark as night,*
> *Yet within an essence out of sight.*
> *This essence so extremely pure*
> *Holds evidence that also there does Tao endure.*

Here we meet the great paradox of Tao's mode of existence—elusive and obscure but indisputably present in every phenomenon. However, this passage does not refer directly to the formlessness of Tao in any cosmogonic sense. For that we must turn to *Lao-tzu*, Chapter 25:

> *Oh how silent, oh how void!*
> *Alone it stands and never suffers change;*
> *Goes round and round but never knows fatigue;*
> *Thus can it be called the Mother of all under Heaven.*
> *Not knowing its name, I style it "Tao";*
> *Forced to name it, I call it "great."*
> *Great means receding;*
> *Going far away means returning.*

Much of this can be understood in light of what has already been said, the main exception being the description of great as "receding," receding as "going far away," and going far away as "returning." In order to understand this, one must consider what *Lao-tzu* says elsewhere about cyclical return and the relativity of opposites.

In one place (Chapter 40) it says: "Returning is the motion of Tao, and being weak is the means it employs (to do so)." Thus, each thing in the universe eventually produces its opposite, and to fight this process (that is, to be strong rather than weak in response to it) would be to go against what is natural. Moreover, not only are opposites mutually causal, but they are of merely relative value in comparison with one another. Beauty has meaning only in relation to an opposing conception of ugliness; and the same is true of good and evil, difficult and easy, and so forth. And from the perspective of one who understands the nature and workings of Tao, there is no point in desiring any one of these over its seemingly less worthwhile counterpart. This perspective is most clearly stated in *Lao-tzu*, Chapter 2, as follows:

> *As soon as everyone in the world knows what makes "beauty" beautiful,*
>   *then "ugliness" already exists;*
> *And as soon as everyone knows what makes "goodness" good,*
>   *then "badness" already exists.*
> *Hence existing and not existing derive from one another;*
> *Difficult and easy complement one another;*
> *Long and short are mutually formed;*

High and low are relative to each other on an incline;
Sound and echo resonate with one another;
And before and after follow one another.
Therefore, the Sage rests content in affairs of nonaction (wu-wei);
And he carries out a teaching never spoken.

Here we finally arrive at Lao Tzu's conception of sagely behavior and are now ready to begin discussing the practical dimension of his thought.

Sagehood and Nonaction

While *Lao-tzu* is now most often read for spiritual insight, the concern of its author(s) was actually quite political. The "Sage" of which it speaks is thus one who would qualify as an ideal ruler, which does not mean that what it says is irrelevant for the rest of us. In fact, since it describes a path of casting things off rather than adding them on to oneself, anyone who aims to follow this path already has a surplus of "qualifications." Keeping in mind how Confucius felt about learning, consider this passage (Chapter 48) on the Taoist path:

Taking up learning, one increases daily;
Complying with the Tao, one decreases daily;
Decreasing and further decreasing, until at a state of nonaction;
Practicing nonaction, but nothing is left undone.
(The Sage) never takes any measures in order to gain sovereignty
over the empire;
As soon as he takes certain measures, he is no longer qualified
to have sovereignty.

Now, while Confucius also disapproved of meddlesome government, he would never have gone this far.

The passage just quoted only indicates a difference of degree between Lao Tzu and Confucius. There are also several places, however, where Lao Tzu makes a frontal assault upon Confucian moral values. For example, in Chapter 5 we have this comment about being humane (*jen*):

Heaven and Earth are not humane (jen); *they treat the myriad*
things as straw dogs.
The Sage is not humane; he treats all the people as straw dogs.

Because straw dogs had no real value (except perhaps as sacrificial items), to treat people and things like straw dogs meant to treat them with *indifference*, a key quality of the true Sage's attitude. Although being humane thus has no place among a true Sage's values, it is still closer to Tao than the other Confucian moral concepts discussed earlier. Consider this excerpt from an attack on Confucian values in *Lao-tzu*, Chapter 38:

> *Hence after Tao is lost, there is Te;*
> *After Te is lost, there is* jen *(humaneness);*
> *After* jen *is lost, there is* yi *(rightness);*
> *After* yi *is lost, there is* li *(ritual and social norms);*
> *These* li *are but a thin showing of loyalty and faithfulness,*
> *And they mark the beginning of disorder.*

This makes clear just how little use a Sage would have for such trappings of civilization and morality as are indicated by *jen, yi,* and *li.*

What values did Lao Tzu offer in place of these? As we have already seen, they were not values of the kind one holds in preferring the beautiful over the ugly or the good over the bad. Nor were they values of the kind normally associated with any human-centered ethics, such as the ethics of Confucius. Instead, they were moral values—if we can call them that without distorting their meaning—which ideally reflect a completely objective, naturalistic, and Tao-centered ethics. Risking the dangers inherent in putting such values into words, one could say they included spontaneity, humility, simplicity, noninterference, and contentment.

Spontaneity perhaps best captures in a positive value what Lao Tzu meant by nonaction (*wu-wei*). For since he did *not* mean never acting at all, he must be interpreted as opposing only purposeful action, which is why he advocated that a Sage's behavior should take nature as its model. And, as indicated earlier in this chapter, Chinese religious theory generally assumed that *only* a nonpurposeful force, rather than a willing Creator God, could be behind the infinite processes of nature. Thus, to be a Sage, you must cast off the attitude that you are an agent who must act to impose your will on everything and everyone around you. For the only reward for such action will be an early death.

Therefore, *humility* is the best attitude to have, even for a ruler. As argued in Chapter 17 of *Lao-tzu:*

> *The subjects of a supreme ruler just know he exists;*
> *The next best is one they love and praise;*
> *Still lower is one they fear;*
> *And lowest is one they feel contempt toward.*
> *Now since evidence of this seems insufficient,*
> *There are those who do not believe it.*
> *But (a supreme ruler) honors words enough to keep still.*
> *When accomplishments are made and tasks completed,*
> *All the people say "we became this way by ourselves."*

Here we meet the view that when things seem to get done by themselves— the one "doing" them humbly relinquishing all claim to merit—the doer has then mastered the *natural* way. Such person, regardless of social rank, understands *simplicity.* As indicated elsewhere in *Lao-tzu,* one most adept at the natural way is like water: the simplest of substances. For "Water is good at benefiting the myriad things and does not compete, dwells in places where the mass of people would hate to be, and, for these reasons, is close to Tao" (Chapter 8).

Water symbolizes the behavior of the Sage also because, as it does not compete but rather takes the path of least resistance, it stands for *noninterference*. Since interfering in the affairs of others or the operations of nature is the worst product of willful activity, Lao Tzu advises us to back away from all meddlesome behavior. Such behavior is not only harmful, but also pointless, for other than endangering oneself, it has little effect on the ever perseverant course of things. In *Lao-tzu*, Chapter 56, we read:

> *One who knows does not speak.*
> *One who speaks does not know.*
> *He blocks up his openings and shuts his doors.*
> *Files down his sharp edges and loosens his tangles,*
> *Dims his brightness and identifies with his dusty-plain surroundings.*
> *This is called being identified with the mystery of things.*

Some (such as later Taoist mystics) would interpret this passage as advocating a form of spiritual practice that included a meditative stilling of mental and sense activities (openings, doors, etc.). Whether or not such an interpretation is correct, the passage clearly reflects the view that success lies mysteriously at the end of a process of *not* seeking it. For there is no success in striving, not so long as success is defined as *contentment*.

Previously, we saw that Confucius envisioned a world in which, with the moral Way prevailing, one need not suffer the shame of violating what is right in order to avoid poverty. When Lao Tzu envisioned an ideal world, contentment was its defining characteristic. One example of this (Chapter 46) expresses it from a more or less negative point of view, as follows:

> *When Tao prevails in the empire,*
> *Riding horses return home to till the land;*
> *When Tao does not prevail there,*
> *War horses bear young out on the border.*
> *The gravest catastrophe is not being content;*
> *The most serious misfortune is being avaricious for gain.*
> *Hence, the sufficiency of being content is the only constant sufficiency.*

The same focus on contentment, described elsewhere (Chapter 80) from a thoroughly positive point of view, forms the substance of a hypothetical world where Tao fully prevails:

> *Where states are small and people few,*
> *One ensures that the various militia's weapons are not used,*
> *Sees that people, taking death seriously, venture not far from home,*

That though they have boats and carts, there is no cause to use them,
That though they have armor and weapons, there is no need to deploy them.
One ensures that they return to the (pre-writing) use of knotted rope,
Consider their food tasty,
Their garments beautiful,
Their homes secure,
And their customs joyful.
So that though neighboring states are within sight of one another,
Each with the other's chicken cackles and dog barks within earshot,
People grow old and die without going back and forth (between states).

Here is the Taoist utopia: a world of contentment achieved through noninterference. And just as the world of nature runs itself, such an ideal human world can be arrived at only by wielding a power unlike that of any ordinary ruler. This is the power of the Sage and of the Tao he emulates, the ineffable power by which the universe exists in harmony and through which human society, if given the chance, can live in peace. The belief that such a power can serve as the sole force in human affairs is an extreme, but characteristically Chinese, expression of the view that the natural and social worlds share the same operative principles. It is fitting that this chapter's treatment of the theoretical dimension of Chinese religion ends with an expression of this view, which perhaps lies at the heart of Chinese religious theory.

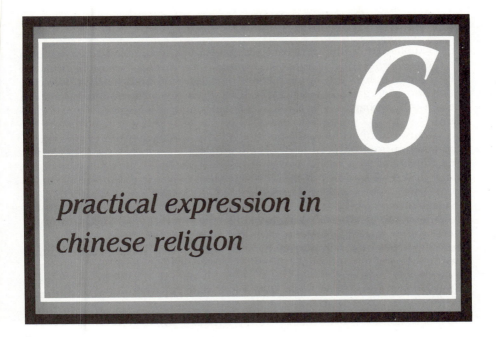

practical expression in chinese religion

When ultimate reality is defined as a single omniscient and omnipotent Creator God, who reveals himself to humanity as holy scripture, then we are bound to find *creedal religion,* that is, religion in which the emphasis is on firm belief in a *written form of truth,* one usually authorized by a church. As indicated in Chapter 1, this is what we find in the case of so-called religions of the book, such as Christianity, Judaism, and Islam. Moreover, these religions quite naturally stress not only belief in creeds but also theology: systematic reason concerning the divine. Now when the assumptions about ultimate reality held by these faiths are lacking, the role of belief and theology in religion changes. When ultimate reality is considered to be ineffable, as with Lao Tzu and many later Taoist as well as Chinese Buddhist thinkers, then we can hardly expect a similar emphasis on belief in statements said to issue from ultimate reality. And when divinity is not single but multiple, as in Chinese folk religion, then it becomes difficult for revelations from one particular deity to gain the kind of exclusive allegiance given to the Word of God in monotheistic faiths.

All this is meant to stress the relative importance in Chinese religion of practice over belief, not to completely deny the importance of the written word. The previous chapter made the importance of canonical scriptures in each of China's Three Teachings abundantly clear. Yet within traditional Chinese religion the written word had sacred status not only as a vehicle of religious theory. One could even say its sacredness was more relevant for practical than doctrinal purposes. Knowledge of it secured the Confucian literati their ruling position in society, and it enabled Taoist and Buddhist ritualists to administer services that the illiterate could not perform for themselves. To draw another comparison with the West, the situation was somewhat like the liturgical use of Latin in traditional Catholicism, which the average believer accepted as serving its sacred function, even though—or perhaps because—it was a language he or she did not understand.

Thus, although it would be utterly false to say that the Chinese have paid no attention to the content of religious creeds, rarely have they considered the belief in a certain one—to the exclusion of all others—to be a matter of life or death. For belief in a system of spiritual views has simply not been the main motivation for the religious acts of average Chinese. Instead, in performing these acts, they have been driven from behind by the *force of past tradition* and drawn ahead by the *attraction of future benefits*. Lacking any systematic theology, they would perform religious duties because such duties are required by tradition; and if forced to give other reasons, they would be more likely to offer practical than doctrinal ones, stressing the expected results for personal or social well-being. This is unfortunate for the researcher, since it makes Chinese religious life as a whole appear to be riddled with inconsistencies. But this is a problem only for the researcher, not for the average practitioner. From the latter's point of view, the demands of tradition and the possibility of beneficial results have been reasons sufficient unto themselves.

A SURVEY OF CHINESE RELIGIOUS PRACTICES

Having stated how the practices of Chinese religion are rooted in the theoretical considerations of the previous chapter, the time has now come to offer a representative survey of these practices, beginning with commonplace seasonal observances and moving toward the specialized activities for which the services of religious professionals are needed. Following this survey, a detailed description will be offered of two examples from opposing dimensions of Chinese religious life: official and popular.

Seasonal Observances

As one would expect for a society in which nature has had great religious significance and life has, until recently, been dominated by agriculture, most religious festivals in China are connected with the seasonal round as determined by the movements of the sun and moon. For example, its three great annual festivals are the Lunar New Year; the Dragon Boat, or Double Fifth, Festival (fifth day of the fifth lunar month); and the Mid-Autumn (lunar 8/15), or Moon, Festival. While not nearly to the same extent as in the past, these are still the year's three main occasions for whole families to get together and for gifts to be presented to appropriate relatives, associates, and friends. All three mark special points on the agricultural calendar. Chinese New Year, for example, is fixed according to a lunar calendar, which always beings within fifteen days (in either direction) of February 5, a fixed solar date that the Chinese call Spring's Beginning (as it falls halfway between the winter solstice and the spring equinox). Therefore, the New Year season, which was traditionally about a month in length, is meant to be a great period of rest and celebration before the start of spring planting. Just as nature is at rest during this time of year, waiting for its spring renewal, human society should be also.

Since, as in other cultures, the theme of the New Year season in China is *renewal*, the season begins early in the last month of the preceding year with house cleaning. Later, about a week before New Year's Eve, the Lord of the Stove (see Chapter 1) is sent off to Heaven to report on the behavior of family members during the past year. Traditionally, his printed image was taken down from the wall behind the stove, had its lips smeared with syrup (to assure that he would speak only sweet words to the Jade Emperor in Heaven), and was burned. And his return home on New Year's Eve, marked by pasting up a new print of him, assured his presence for the main event of the season: the New Year's Eve family feast.

The New Year's Eve feast is preceded by worship of the family ancestors and those various gods who may share their altar. In recognition of the ancestors' status, food is symbolically given to them before the family eats. Afterward, to honor the living elders, each family member kowtows ("knocks the head" to the floor) before the family head and his wife. At midnight and at sunrise, and possibly without cessation in between, firecrackers are set off. On New Year's Day, and for several days afterward, courtesy visits are made to important friends, relatives, and associates outside one's main household. The season ends on the evening of the first full moon (1/15) with what may be interpreted as a celebration of light. This celebration takes place during the year's darkest season, as it does in many other parts of the world. In China, it is called the Lantern Festival, when major temples hold lantern-making competitions and children run about with small hand-held lanterns.

As for the Dragon Boat and Mid-Autumn festivals, while also fixed by lunar reckoning, the first usually falls just before the summer solstice and signals the oncoming summer heat; the second comes at autumn harvest time, shortly before or after the autumn equinox.

The Dragon Boat Festival was most popular in South China, where summer's heat arrives earlier and where the custom of dragon boat races originated. It was a time for wearing, eating, and displaying by one's doorway items that help to ward off disease and misfortune. Since rivers were among the chief sources of misfortune, both dragon boat racing and the festival's distinctive delicacy, triangular-shaped rice dumplings wrapped in bamboo leaves, probably had their origin in rites performed for river spirits. However, tradition connects these rites, on the one hand, with boatmens' efforts to find the body of Ch'ü Yuan (Qu Yuan), a third century B.C.E. poet and official who committed suicide in a river because a corrupt king would not accept his advice. On the other hand, it connects them with subsequent efforts to feed his spirit by throwing rice in the river.

The Mid-Autumn, or Moon, Festival also has its distinctive food, round and sweetly filled pastries called "moon cakes." And, of course, it has its stories about figures from Chinese history and legend who are connected with the moon. Aside from giving and eating moon cakes, the festival's main activity is simply "to enjoy the moon," which means going outdoors at night in pairs or larger groups to gaze at the moon, which is full on the fifteenth of any lunar month and appears especially large at autumn harvest time.

Although offerings for ancestors are set out on the family altar on each of the three days just discussed, they are so-called festivals of the living and may be contrasted with three other festivals of the dead. The first of these is called Ch'ing Ming ("clear and bright"), since it falls on one of the twenty-four seasonal divisions of the solar year that has this name. These divisions are literally called "nodes of the life force" (*chieh-ch'i; jie-qi*), and they refer to different configurations of *ch'i* and their climatic results. They occur on twenty-four evenly spaced dates throughout the solar year, the most fundamental of which are the winter and summer solstices and the two equinoxes. The date of Ch'ing Ming is April 5 or 6 and, while it has roots in a lively ancient spring festival, it now consists mainly of grave-sweeping activities. These include, in addition to cleaning and renovating ancestral tombs, setting out offerings and burning spirit money for the ancestors as well as placing objects of good omen near the grave. Depending on local custom, such objects may include willow branches (which ward off evil) or egg shells (which symbolize sending off the old and welcoming the new). While thus devoted to ancestral worship, this day remains a celebration of spring in that going to visit gravesites, which are usually located in wooded, hilly areas, gives the family an opportunity for a spring outing together.

The next festival, taking up the entire seventh lunar month during late summer, is in no uncertain terms dedicated solely to deceased spirits, not only of one's own family but especially of those who have no known family ties: bereaved spirits, or "hungry ghosts." This month of ghosts demonstrates the concern in Chinese religion about the pitiable existence of souls uncared for by the living. This concern has been greatly enhanced by Buddhist views of souls wandering through various "hells" (more accurately called purgatories, since they are not usually one's permanent abode), working off the bad karma of former misdeeds and waiting to be reborn. While the festival nevertheless includes familial ancestral offerings, made on the fifteenth of the month, it is dedicated to the "hungry ghosts" who are released from their hellish abode on the first of the month and sent back there on its last day. During the time they are believed to be invisibly in our midst, offerings are everywhere set out for them in compassion for their plight, on the one hand, and in fear of their desperate behavior, on the other. If fact, this is a month during which no tradition-honoring Chinese would think of opening a business, buying a house, scheduling surgery, or getting married—for it is without qualification the most inauspicious time of year.

The third festival of the dead is similar to the first in that it gives the family another chance to go out to the suburban hills and visit ancestral tombs. This is perhaps their last chance to do so before the onset of winter cold, as it occurs on the first of the tenth lunar month, just more than one month before the winter solstice. In this case, in addition to the usual offerings, cold weather clothes made from paper are sent (that is, ritually burned) to the ancestors. It is quite a minor festival, which is not even observed in some parts of China, such as Taiwan (where it may seem unnecessary to send winter clothes for climatic reasons).

Although the six festivals just discussed are the most widespread and obligatory, they are primarily centered around the family and close friends. They do not bring the whole community together for large-scale public ceremonies. This usually happens on the occasion of a god's birthday celebration, when every temple dedicated to the god will have its annual festival. Moreover, if the temple is a major center for the god's worship, the festival will draw participants not only from throughout the community but also from distant places. A case of this will be considered later in this chapter, when the annual birthday celebration held for Ma-tsu in Taiwan will be described in detail. Therefore, rather than now consider the activities of birthday celebrations for gods, let us just give an idea of how they fit into the festival calendar by listing the birthdays of some major Chinese deities already mentioned in this book (all dates are lunar): the Jade Emperor, ninth of the first month; Lao Tzu, fifteenth of the second month; Kuan-yin Bodhisattva, nineteenth of the second month; Ma-tsu, twenty-third of the third month; Śākyamuni Buddha, eighth of the fourth month; Kuan Kung, twenty-fourth of the sixth month; and Confucius, twenty-seventh of the eighth month (but now celebrated as a national holiday, which is called Teacher's Day, on solar September 28 in Taiwan, Republic of China).

These dates and those of many lesser deities' birthdays (along with seasonal observances above and beyond those just mentioned) are listed in a yearly almanac, without which no traditional home would be complete. In addition to listing major and minor festivals, the almanac describes what kind of activities may be undertaken on any given day. For example, according to an almanac published in Taiwan for 1983, on December 31 (lunar 11/28) you may perform sacrifices (e.g., for ancestors), undertake repairs or construction, break ground, gather with family and friends, frame a door, raise a roofbeam, set up a bed or stove, or dig a well. However, you should not on that day marry out your daughter, choose a bride for your son, or move into a new home. The same almanac also gives you an abundance of information, if you want to be a do-it-yourself diviner or desire simply to know more about fate and how to become its master. Of course, it describes what the year has in store for persons born during previous years linked with each of the twelve Chinese astrological animals (rat, tiger, hare, dragon, snake, horse, sheep, monkey, cock, dog, pig). It also includes charts for calculating your fate according to exact time of birth, for determining what mates are suitable for you on the basis of their and your own astrological animals, and for knowing how often to have sexual relations according to your age. Finally, it contains articles on such subjects as the existence of gods and ghosts, spiritual mediumship, setting up spirit tablets on an altar, calling back a child's frightened soul, conceiving a child of determinate (male or female) sex, and selecting lucky days for yourself by a "simple, accurate method."

As you can see from all this, carrying out regular seasonal observances is only one part of the religious activities in which traditional Chinese engage in order to remain in accord with nature's pattern of operations, to know the direction of its destined course, and, when possible, to improve individual or family fate. Moreover, since activities performed by the average believer are not always sufficient in such matters, there exists a multiplicity of spiritual specialists: spirit mediums, palmists, fortunetellers, geomancers, Taoist priests, Buddhist monks and nuns, and so forth. The next half of our survey of Chinese religious practices will deal with those in which these specialists had a necessary role.

Services of Religious Professionals

When speaking of imperial China (before 1911), one must include Confucian state officials among the religious specialists who performed services for the Chinese populace. For these officials had a hand in state ritual sacrifices offered to supramundane powers on behalf of the whole empire. Yet since Chinese state religion will be focused on later in this chapter, no more need be said of it now. We should point out, however, that members of the Confucian literati, whether they held official posts or not, had a special, even sacred, status by virtue of their having mastered the Chinese written language and gained a classical education. In fact, it was among the lower echelon of the literati that one found most religious specialists— first, because they were educated enough to learn the necessary skills and, second, because they needed the extra income that one could earn by performing desired services. However, in addition to being more literate than their clientele, such specialists were also likely to have a specifically religious disposition and course of training. And this remains true at present, at least where practitioners of traditional Chinese religious arts are able to pass their skills on to their descendants or chosen disciples.

As in every society, there are among the Chinese those considered to be more spiritually sensitive than average. And there are a plethora of methods for practicing spiritual cultivation and gaining knowledge in ritual matters. Rather than discuss all these spiritual methods and specialists, we aim to consider only the general functions of these methods and to make detailed comments about only the full-time religious professionals of Buddhism and Taoism.

One sometimes gets the impression that those hired by Chinese to render spiritual assistance are viewed no differently than those hired to perform medical, constructional, or other technical services. Of course, they are often called in only after ordinary means have failed. And the difference in function between spiritual and nonspiritual services is clear to everyone. They all know, for example, that a geomancer who chooses the site for a house deals with different problems and forces than the carpenter who builds it. And a geomancer is one of the most technicianlike

FIGURE 6.1. Taoist priest in Taiwan performing "ghost month" services for his clients.

of spiritual practitioners. At the other end of the scale are those whose ability to render aid depends directly upon their spiritual state, not upon any technical knowledge. Spirit mediums are a case in point, since they must become possessed by gods and spirits of the deceased, which is considered possible only for one in an other-than-ordinary state.

However, whether an ecstatic spirit medium or a sober geomantic technician is employed, the reason is bound to be a practical one (disease, poor business, family disharmony, barrenness, etc.); and the choice is usually made for functional reasons, that is, according to the skills possessed by a certain spiritual practitioner rather than on the basis of what religious organization he or she represents. This is why it is difficult, if not impossible, to specify an exact religious affiliation for average lay Chinese, except, of course, in the case of Chinese Muslims, Jews, Christians, and devout Buddhist laypersons. However, the matter is clearer in the case of Buddhist as well as Taoist religious professionals, whose lives revolve around religious cultivation and service.

Here we must focus on ritual services rather than spiritual cultivation. (The reader is referred back to the discussion in Chapter 2 of Taoist mysticism and ahead to the discussion in Chapter 7 of Buddhist monastic life for information about the methods of Taoist and Buddhist cultivation.) Yet it must be pointed out that the state of spiritual power or purity attained through religious cultivation was an important factor leading to the ritual use of Taoist priests and Buddhist monks (or nuns). For example, should anyone but an attained Taoist master undertake the battle to exorcise a demon from its unwilling host, it is believed, the person would not only fail in their task but also risk great danger. Likewise, the purity and lack of family ties of morally disciplined and celibate Buddhist mendicants renders them capable of providing services for *other* people's deceased ancestors, including so-called soul masses, which transfer merit from Buddhas and Bodhisattvas to the souls of those trying to make their way through purgatory. Moreover, as in so many societies, there are those, such as the elderly monks popularly called "living Buddhas," whose spiritual state is considered to be so pure and advanced that a mere touch of their hand can cure disease or alter destiny.

The key prerequisite for most services performed by Buddhist and Taoist religious professionals, however, is training in ritual matters. For the spiritual powers of the individual monk or priest are nothing compared to the powers of the supramundane beings they may call upon through the proper ritual motions and liturgical language. Thus, for example, the soul masses just mentioned consist of chanting scriptures which, in the proper ritual context, can summon the aid of the appropriate Buddha or Bodhisattva. And a Taoist priest's efforts at exorcism are linked to his knowledge about secret names and qualities of heavenly deities that he can use to call upon their support. Of course, in each case, what underlies belief in the efficacy of a rite is the principle of associative magic, by virtue of which appropriate words uttered or acts performed by those in the visible world are taken to have their automatic consequences in the unseen spiritual dimension. Of course, within the Chinese religious world view, with its emphasis on the interconnectedness of all things, material and spiritual, this principle was taken for granted.

As to the differences between Buddhist and Taoist ritual services, a widely held view specifies that the former are connected mainly with death, and the latter with life. But there are many exceptions to this. For instance, in one area of Taiwan a whole group of Taoist priests are known as specialists in funeral rites and, for this reason, must forego the opportunity to perform life rituals (since their association with rituals for the dead is polluting, and therefore dangerous, from the spiritual point of view).[1] Such an exception naturally calls into question the absoluteness of any association of Taoists with life rituals and Buddhists with death rituals. Yet it also reveals the basic logic underlying the division of ritual labor between them. Because death and spirits of the deceased are considered to be polluting, Buddhists are most naturally suited to handle such matters as funerals, soul masses, and the storage of ashes for those who choose to have their forebears cremated. For Buddhists have, in theory, committed themselves to facing the problem of human death and suffering; and they have, in practice, chosen a life free of family ties, which means their contact with

---

[1] See Philip Chesly Baity, *Religion in a Chinese Town* (Taipei: Orient Cultural Service, 1975), pp. 172–173.

death's polluting influence will not affect any kinsmen. By contrast, a Taoist priest will marry and be involved in securing peace and prosperity for his family and, moreover, for his clients. Therefore, it is most reasonable and convenient for him to avoid death rites and to specialize in rituals for the living. These include rites serving to "request peace and calm" (*ch'iu p'ing-an; qiu ping-an*), "improve one's destiny" (*pu-yun; bu-yun*), "open the eye" (*k'ai-yen; kai-yan*) of a wooden image by invoking the deity to inhabit it, and the *chiao* (*jiao*) ritual of renewal, which similarly invokes deities for the purpose of consecration, but on the scale of an entire temple and its surrounding neighborhood or village.

With some idea of the ritual practices in which Buddhist and Taoist religious professionals are involved, it is now appropriate that we move on to the state ceremonies usually connected with the name Confucianism and describe them in somewhat greater detail. As we do so, the reader should know that these ceremonies are no longer practiced today. Yet we nevertheless dedicate a whole section to their description, first, because of the importance they had in traditional times and, second, because they constitute a solemn and systematic expression of Chinese religious views— one that stands in direct contrast to the ecstatic and uncontrolled expression of religious sentiment found at a popular festival.

IMPERIAL CULT RITUALS—SOLEMN AND SYSTEMATIC

The idea of an official state religion is foreign to most modern nations, where consitutional guarantees of the separation of church and state, and of religious freedom, often exist. Most premodern states, however, had political systems either linked to one of the major world religions or headed by a sacred ruler who performed rituals that were central in holding sway over the state's subjects. Moreover, even modern nations have some form of civil religion, with mythicized versions of the nation's history, the worship of national heroes, sanctified state ideologies, and official ceremonies celebrating such events as the founding of the nation.[2] Thus, wherever political power is exercised, it seems necessary to place it within some context of ultimate meaning, that is, to ground it in a set of myths and symbols with greater-than-human significance. This is well expressed in the following definition of *civil religion* by Dunbar Moodie:

> Civil religion, as I define it, denotes the religious dimension of the state. As such it is invariably related with the exercise of power and with the constant regeneration of the social order; it provides a transcendent referent for sovereignty within a given territory. The ultimate nature and destiny of political power is thus connoted in the symbols of the civil faith and reenacted by civil ritual. The origins, the extent and limits, and the

---

[2] On civil religion in America, see: Russell E. Richey and Donald G. Jones, eds., *American Civil Religion* (New York: Harper & Row Publishers, Inc., 1974).

final purpose of political sovereignty are all thereby set within the context of ultimate meaning; aspirations to sovereign power and the exercise of sovereignty are given transcendent justification.[3]

This definition, while conceived for the study of a modern case, is well suited for discussing traditional Chinese state religion. For Confucianism was, from the Han Dynasty onward, an integral part of the state itself rather than an independent faith, such as the Roman Catholic Church or even the Church of England. The Confucian scriptures provided the basis for both the nation's civil faith and civil ritual; and Confucian scholar-officials guided developments in both spheres through their interpretation of these scriptures.

Despite this, however, it was not this class but rather their titular leader, the Chinese emperor, who was the focus of the state cult. Reflecting ideas about divine kingship throughout the premodern world, he was believed uniquely to represent for all humanity the sacred cosmic forces upon which their lives depended. Here will be discussed the rituals of the imperial cult by virtue of which he fulfilled this unique role. (Information about the civil faith underlying traditional Chinese government can be found in other parts of this book where Confucian thought and related matters are discussed, such as the section in Chapter 2 on Han Confucianism and the section in Chapter 5 on Confucius.) More specifically, the rituals to be discussed in the sections that follow will be based on the imperial cult of the Ch'ing Dynasty. Although this was a foreign (Manchu) dynasty, its cult was based on ancient Chinese models and closely resembled that of preceding dynasties, especially the native Ming Dynasty.

Chinese Sacred Kingship

From early times, the Chinese ruler was said to be appointed by Heaven, but this appointment was conditional. He and his royal line held Heaven's Mandate only so long as they served faithfully and successfully in their duties. A significant part of what a Chinese emperor did to fulfill his obligations, and to show that he was indeed the Son of Heaven, was to perform state rituals. As we already know, gods of nature and royal ancestors were the respective objects of state rituals all the way back to Shang times. On the one side, the worship of agricultural deities and a complex state ceremonial calendar based on the natural cycle had been added by Ch'ing times. On the other side, the deification of national heroes and the evolution of imperial audiences, accession ceremonies, and birthday celebrations had occurred. One can thus see that the imperial cult grew along two major lines: one associated with nature and the cosmos, and the other with human society and history.

[3] Dunbar T. Moodie, *The Rise of Afrikanerdom: Power, Apartheid, and the Afrikaner Civil Religion* (Berkeley: University of California Press, 1975), p. 296.

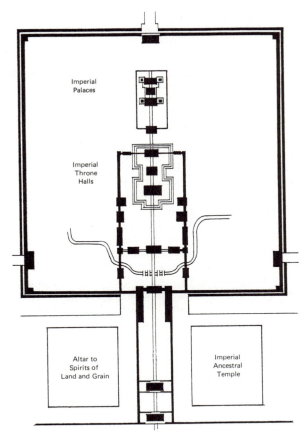

FIGURE 6.2. Plan of Peking's Forbidden City, featuring the main structures along its north-south axis.

Sacred Pattern of the Chinese Capital

Such a division was, in fact, indicated by the most consistent feature in the design of Chinese capitals back to the early Chou period, namely, the construction of two ceremonial sites just to the south of the royal palace, the Ancestral Temple (on the east) and the Altar to the Spirits of Land and Grain (on the west).[4] This is only one of many indications that the Chinese capital was a ceremonial center as well as a seat of government. Looking at Ming-Ch'ing Peking, it was, first of all, constructed according to the principle of north-south axiality. All of its palaces, throne halls, and main gates faced south along a single axis, thereby remaining open to beneficent *yang* forces and protected from baleful *yin* influences.

Secondly, the whole city had a concentric pattern, with the most sacred

---

[4] Arthur F. Wright, "The Cosmology of the Chinese City," in *The City in Late Imperial China*, ed. William G. Skinner (Stanford: Stanford University Press, 1977), pp. 39–40.

and important structures in the center. In *Peking as a Sacred City,* Jeffrey Meyer describes this pattern as follows:

> First, there are the outer walls enclosing the city itself, within, near the center, is another walled area, square except for the southwest corner, which marks the limits of what is called the Imperial City; which in turn surrounds another walled city called the Forbidden City, the seat of imperial government and home of the Emperor. Finally, in the center of the Forbidden City is a group of three halls built on a three-tiered platform which is the true center of the whole ensemble.[5]

The Forbidden City, Peking's "holy of holies," contained three imperial palaces to balance the three throne halls mentioned by Meyer. The former were located in the back (northern) part of the city, where only the emperor, empress, imperial concubines, and eunuchs who served them were permitted to go. The throne halls were located in the front half, and only the highest ranking members of nobility and officialdom could enter these halls to participate in the civil rituals associated with imperial audiences, military victories, the appointment of new officials, and so forth. Nowhere within the entire complex could the common individual set foot.

Finally, throughout Peking's ceremonial sites and overall layout, we see the influence of the philosophy of *yin, yang,* and the five phases. Not only the location and design of the ceremonial sites used for imperial rituals, but also their timing and manner of performance conformed to the principles of this philosophy. As we saw in Chapter 2, this feature of the state cult system owed its existence to the incorporation of *yin-yang* cosmology into state ideology by the Han Confucianists. According to their theories, the emperor's ritual activities needed to adhere closely to a complex set of numerical, directional, calendrical, and color correspondences that were all connected with *yin, yang,* and the five phases. This is most amply demonstrated by examining the Ch'ing imperial sacrificial system.

System of Imperial Sacrifices

The Ch'ing imperial sacrifices were divided into three categories: Great, Medium, and Lesser sacrifices.[6] In the first, one finds Heaven, Earth, the imperial ancestors, and the Spirits of Land and Grain. Looking just at sacrifices to the former two, one sees precisely the kinds of symbolic correspondences that dominated the whole system. Heaven (or more specifically, Huang T'ien Shang Ti: "August Heaven, Supreme Ruler") was worshiped on the day of the winter solstice at Peking's southern suburban altar, which was round in shape and exclusively featured *yang* (odd) numbers in its construction. The ceremony began in the predawn hours of this shortest day of the year, when *yang* forces were believed to begin increasing in

---

[5] Jeffrey F. Meyer, *Peking as a Sacred City* (Taipei: Orient Cultural Service, 1976), p. 42.

[6] This and other aspects of the Ch'ing Dynasty state cult are described in E. T. Williams, "The State Religion of China During the Manchu Dynasty," *Journal of the North China Branch of the Royal Asiatic Society,* 44 (1913), pp. 11–45.

strength, and *yin* forces correspondingly to decline. Because this day marked the critical point in the annual cycle, sacrifices were made not only to Heaven but also to all its subordinates, including imperial ancestors, celestial deities representing planets and constellations, the spirits of famous mountains and rivers in China, and so forth. The place that each of these divinites occupied on one of the three tiers of the Altar to Heaven, and the sacrificial offerings that each received, corresponded to its rank in relation to August Heaven; and the ceremony itself occurred in nine stages, nine being the supremely *yang* number.

By contrast, the sacrifice to Earth took place on the summer solstice day at a square altar to the north of Peking, and it included offerings to a significantly smaller entourage of cosmic deities. For Earth was far less important than Heaven, as indicated by the limitations of its square territory when compared to the boundless expanse of Heaven, whose "roundness" symbolized harmony and perfection for the Chinese.

Sacrifices at the Imperial Ancestral Temple, although directed to the emperor's human antecedents, not to natural divinities, were nevertheless scheduled for the beginnings of the four seasons and the end of the year—dates important for cosmological rather than historical reasons. Those to the Spirits of Land and Grain were, quite logically, also linked to the natural cycle. They occurred during the second and eighth lunar months—the times of spring planting and fall harvesting.

In the Altar to the Spirits of Land and Grain, we find an expression of the full range of directional and color correspondences connected with the five elemental phases. Perhaps because the ancient kings simply used a square mound of pounded earth for their altar, even in late imperial times, the very center of the altar had only bare earth instead of bricks. However, indicating the general trend of later developments, on the day before a sacrifice this plain earth was covered with five-colored soil, symbolizing the five directions: east (blue), west (white), north (black), south (red), and the center (yellow). As for the rest of the altar, consider the following description by E. T. Williams:

> The core of the altar was of earth. This was faced with glazed bricks of various colors. On the east the bricks were blue, on the south, red, on the west, white, on the north, black, while the top of the altar was colored yellow. . . . The altar was about forty feet square and raised three or four feet above the level of the court. The walls of the court were of glazed bricks in colors corresponding to the four sides of the altar.[7]

Similar correspondences were indicated on a larger scale in the general layout of Peking's ceremonial sites, as will be seen in turning to consider the various Medium Sacrifices.

While Great Sacrifices were offered to Heaven and Earth in the northern and southern suburbs, medium-grade ones were offered to the Sun and the Moon at altars to the east and the west of Peking. The sacrifice

---

[7] E. T. Williams, "Agricultural Rites in the Religion of Old China," *Journal of the North China Branch of the Royal Asiatic Society,* 67 (1936), p. 46.

to the Sun took place on the morning of the spring equinox and featured the use of red silk, a red gem, and music in seven pieces. The one to the Moon occurred on the evening of the autumn equinox, its gem and silk were white, and its music had six pieces. At the Temple of Agriculture, located in Peking's southern suburbs to the west of the Altar to Heaven, there were altars for Medium Sacrifices to Heavenly and Earthly Spirits, the Year Star (Jupiter), and Shen Nung (the "Divine Farmer" listed among the ancient Three Sovereigns in Chapter 2). The Heavenly and Earthly Spirits were worshiped as needed in response to severe climatic problems, the Year Star received sacrifices during the first and last months of the year, and Shen Nung was worshiped in conjunction with the emperor's spring plowing ceremony. The last of these events ceremoniously opened the growing season for all Chinese farmers, and it had its counterpart in another spring ceremony performed for the First Sericulturist by the empress (sericulture being the art of raising mulberry trees and silkworms for silk production). Also in the spring, and again in the fall, other Medium Sacrifices were offered at temples to the Emperors and Kings of Former Dynasties as well as to Confucius (at least up to 1906, when an imperial edict pronounced that the Master receive Great Sacrifices as an equal of Heaven and Earth).

Lesser Sacrifices were offered to a host of miscellaneous deities, (thirty by the end of the Ch'ing era), including some of leading importance within Chinese religion generally, such as Kuan Kung, Wen Ch'ang (Wen Chang, the God of Literature), and Ch'eng Huang. The emperor did not attend these sacrifices himself without some strong personal reason, such as there was for his going to worship at the Palace of the Polestar on his own birthday; for the Polestar fulfilled a role in the Heavens that the emperor sought to fulfill on earth. Precisely what this means can be grasped from Master K'ung's previously quoted statement:

Ruling by means of *te* can be compared to the North Polar Star—it remains in its place while the multitude of stars revolves in homage around it (*Analects* 2:1).

This statement helps us not only to understand why the emperor paid special attention to the Polestar, but also to understand why he personally led most of the sacrifices discussed and, in many other ways, lived an existence seemingly overburdened with time-consuming rituals.

By performing rituals that kept human society in tune with the cosmos, the Chinese emperor established himself as a moral exemplar rather than a tyrant, one who could reign, like the Polestar, without using the heavy hand of force. He also thereby showed that he was the Son of Heaven—the legitimate representative of forces that ruled the cosmos. As the Son of Heaven, however, he was the responsible agent of Heaven, empowered to rule over humanity only so long as he was a just and satisfactory sovereign. He was not a god himself, but rather a human conduit through whom powers of rulership passed, ultimately ending up in the hands of the Confucian scholar-officials that staffed the Chinese bureaucracy.

Now, as his representatives, these officials were empowered not only to enforce imperial orders at lower levels of government but also to perform the necessary state rituals at those levels. And in both spheres, political and religious, it was their contact with the common people that was significant. Official religion, in particular, only impinged upon the life of the common people at the local level, since it was forbidden for their eyes to gaze upon any imperial sacrifice. Indeed, at the local level, the government *sought* involvement in the people's religion (some would even say it did so with a zeal that betrayed the desire to use and manipulate popular beliefs for its own political ends). When the people credited one of their gods with some "miracle" that saved the community, the imperially appointed local magistrate would make an appearance to personally thank the god. When such a god performed numerous miracles over a long period, the emperor would send a plaque for its temple bearing his personal words of gratitude. He might even grant the deity an official title and, thereby, include it in the official pantheon.

An outstanding case of this is evident with the goddess Ma-tsu. Not only did she become honored by imperial decree with the title Consort of Heaven (T'ien-hou), but she also came to have officially supported temples connected with her cult, usually called Palaces for the Consort of Heaven, where formal state rites were performed. In fact, in the Ma-tsu temple in Peikang (Beigang), Taiwan, whose annual festival will soon be described, these rites are still held by civic leaders every spring and autumn. However, the solemn and formal performance of these rites on the day of her birthday (lunar 3/23) stands in remarkable contrast to the activities of the preceding days, during which the largest and liveliest of Taiwan's annual religious festivals occurs.[8] Let us now have a look at this example of Chinese popular religious fervor.

A POPULAR FESTIVAL—ECSTATIC AND INFORMAL

At the same time that European pioneers were crossing the Atlantic to make a home in the New World, thousands of Chinese were crossing the western Pacific straits that separate the island of Taiwan from the Asian continent. While the latter journey was far shorter than the former, it was no less hazardous. Known as rough seas frequented by typhoons and pirates, the Taiwan Straits were not easily crossed in a sixteenth- or seventeenth-century Chinese junk. And just as European pioneers, many of them devout members of minority faiths (French Huegenots, Quakers, Puritans, etc.), overcame the fears and challenges of their ocean voyage holding faith in their hearts and Bibles close to their breasts, the Chinese settlers of Taiwan also made their ocean crossing under the comfort of spiritual protection. For on board with them were images of gods from altars and temples located in their former home towns on the Chinese mainland.

---

[8] Laurence G. Thompson, "Popular and Classical Modes of Ritual in a Taiwanese Temple," *Bulletin: Society for the Study of Chinese Religions*, No. 9 (1981), pp. 106–122, analyzes this contrast.

Ma-tsu and Taiwan

Most of these settlers were from the coastal communities of South China, where Ma-tsu was a favorite deity. For she was closely connected with the protection of those who went out to sea, whether fisherman, traders, naval men, or pioneers. This accounted for the fact that it was often a Ma-tsu image that the settlers took with them and, after a successful crossing, set up on an altar or, if they became properous enough, in a temple. And her protection was believed to continue after their settlement in the new land, as they engaged in battle with human enemies, such as Taiwanese aborigines, European colonialists, gangs of bandits, and even immigrants from other areas of their Chinese homeland, not to mention natural ones—floods, droughts, earthquakes, and typhoons. For this reason, Ma-tsu achieved a general appeal throughout Taiwan that she never had on the mainland, where she was popular primarily among coastal fishing and trading households. She even had a role in Taiwan's formal history, in connection with which she performed some of the deeds that enhanced her position in the official state religion.

When, in 1662, Taiwanese history's greatest hero, Cheng Ch'eng-kung (Zheng Cheng-gong), ousted the last of the foreign colonialists (the Dutch), he attributed his naval victories to Ma-tsu's aid and renovated her temple at the port near Taiwan's early capital (a city now called Tainan). In 1683, when the forces of the Ch'ing Dynasty finally took Taiwan, where Cheng had established rule under the last scion of the Ming Dynasty, Ma-tsu was again thanked for the victory. In fact, it was on this occasion that she received the title Consort of Heaven from the K'ang-hsi (Kang-xi) Emperor (r. 1662–1722). Later, during the reign of the Chia-ch'ing (Jia-ching) Emperor (1796–1820), the famous naval commander Wang Te-lu (Wang De-lu, 1771–1842), after defeating a notorious pirate fleet off the South China coast, expressed his gratitude to Ma-tsu by dedicating a bell to her temple at Peikang; and the emperor himself ordered the performance there of spring and autumn rites (which probably marked the start of those official ceremonies that are still performed today). Moreover, Ma-tsu, as represented in this same temple, first established in 1694, was still later credited with making it possible to suppress a major rebellion (1862) and with ending two of the most severe droughts in Taiwan's history (1852 and 1887). After the second drought ended, the Kuang-hsu (Guang-xu) Emperor (r. 1875–1908) donated a plaque to the temple that displayed his personal words of praise: "Your compassionate clouds sprinkle down (rain) to enrich (the land)."[9] And today, at least in Taiwan, her prowess still grows. But who was she? Let us now try to answer this question.

---

[9] The details of this paragraph have been checked against several sources: *Pei-kang Ch'ao-t'ien Kung chien-chieh* ("Brief introduction to Peikang's Palace of Audience") (Peikang, Taiwan: Ch'ao-t'ien Kung Management Committee, 1973); Suzuki Seiichirou, *Tai-wan chiu-kuan hsi-su hsin-yang* ("Old customs, traditions, and beliefs of Taiwan"), trans. P'eng Tso-min (Taipei: Chung-wen, 1981; orig. publ. 1934), pp. 385–386; and Lin Heng-tao, gen. ed., *Tai-wan ku-chi ch'uan-chi* ("Complete collectania of Taiwan's old relics"), Vol. 4 (Taipei: Hu-wai sheng-huo, 1980), pp. 41–42.

Ma-tsu's Human Existence

Across the straits from Taiwan, off the coast of Fukien (Fujian) Province on a small island called Meichou (Meizhou), early in the Sung Dynasty, a daughter was born into a family named Lin. When she grew up, she became well versed in telling fortunes; and after she died, people began to worship her. This is all that early sources tell us about the person who would become Ma-tsu.[10] But we also know that, whoever she was when alive, her popularity spread swiftly after her death and deification. For between 1122 and the end of the Sung in 1279, she had already been bestowed a dozen official titles in recognition of her miraculous deeds. Thus, those who had faith in her miracles embellished the simple facts of her earthly existence with correspondingly miraculous details.

For example, a typical biography appears in the pamphlet introducing Ma-tsu's temple in Peikang (the Palace of Audience), prepared by its managing committee, which includes the following particulars.[11] In 960, the year the Sung Dynasty was established, on the twenty-third of the third (lunar) month, the Lin family's prayers for another child were answered and a daughter was born, with a red glow from the northwest coming to fill the room where the birth occurred. Although the couple had prayed for a son, since they already had five daughters, they knew this child was special and treated her "like a brilliant pearl in the palm of one's hand." Because she was larger than most babies and did not cry, she was given the name Silent Maiden. She was also extremely intelligent and different in temperament from her brothers and sisters, all of whom kept away from her. At thirteen, an old Taoist master saw her hidden spiritual talent and offered to transmit his secret teachings to her. Her ability to give spiritual aid and advice was again enhanced at sixteen, when she was playing in a courtyard with several girlfriends, and a deity suddenly emerged from a nearby well. While all the others ran in terror, Lin the Silent Maiden remained calm and was able to receive a sacred copper charm as a gift from the god. Afterward, her success as a spiritual guide to others continued to grow, but she never became close to her sisters, nor did she marry.

Then, finally, one day during her twenty-eighth year, she told her family that she loved purity and calm more than the hustle and bustle of this mortal world. Therefore, she had come to announce her intention to go climbing high into the mountains the next day. Since the next day was the ninth of the ninth month, the day of the Double Yang Festival and a time for all to go hiking in the hills, her intention seemed perhaps not so unusual. But alas it was, for upon reaching the top of the highest peak, she continued to ascend and disappeared into the sky.

Precisely when and why the spirit of the deceased Miss Lin was first worshiped is impossible to say; but we have seen how a large-scale cult

---

[10] That only these few basic facts can be confirmed has been demonstrated by the research of Mr. Li Hsien-chang, as cited in Laurence Thompson, "The Cult of Ma-tsu," *The Chinese Way in Religion* (Encino, Calif.: Dickenson Publishing Co., Inc., 1973), pp. 200–201.

[11] *Pei-kang Ch'ao-t'ien Kung chien-chieh*, pp. 3–4.

FIGURE 6.3. Chinese pilgrims see their goal—Ma-tsu's Palace of Audience—at the end of the main street in Peikang, Taiwan.

developed around her, as the goddess Ma-tsu, which still thrives today in places like Taiwan and Hong Kong. We have also seen how centers of her cult, such as Peikang, Taiwan, provide lively illustration of her involvement in history. Now let us see how her birthday is celebrated in present-day Peikang at the Palace of Audience, which has clearly become the leading Ma-tsu cult center in Taiwan.[12]

The Peikang Ma-tsu Festival

Every year in early spring, between the time of the Lantern Festival (lunar 1/15) and Ma-tsu's birthday (lunar 3/23), the small city of Peikang, Taiwan, becomes the host for between a half million and a million visitors. If one accepts the latter figure, this would constitute more than five percent of the island's entire population. Most of these visitors belong to what are called "incense-offering groups" (*chin-hsiang-t'uan; jin-xiang-tuan*), the majority of which are connected with Ma-tsu temples in other parts of Taiwan. For example, over sixty percent of the more than six hundred such groups formally registered with Peikang's Palace of Audience in 1973 were from Ma-tsu temples.[13] Because of their importance for both the size and significance of the festival, let us look first at their activities.

---

[12] The following description is based, for the most part, on the author's visits to Peikang during the Ma-tsu Festival in 1981, 1982, and 1983.

[13] *Pei-kang Ch'ao-t'ien Kung chien-chieh*, p. 18.

FIGURE 6.4. An incense-offering group parades down the street toward Peikang's Ma-tsu temple, with a spirit medium leading.

An incense-offering group is formed at the home temple, composed of those in its vicinity, from the deeply devout to the merely curious, who want to take advantage of an opportunity to join in a religious pilgrimage. Arriving by bus, as is most common, a group finds itself in a huge parking lot about one kilometer away from the temple in Peikang, which is kept out of sight by a high embankment. Climbing over the embankment, the group's members enter the world of a Chinese popular festival played out on the grandest scale. Standing at one end of a main street, at the other end of which towers Ma-tsu's Palace of Audience, they are ready to pass into a scene that literally millions of other religious pilgrims have beheld during the past century and before. The air is scented with incense and clouded by the incessant explosion of firecrackers. Before them the street is filled with other visitors moving slowly toward the temple off in the distance. To the right and left along the street, stands are set up for selling all imaginable kinds of food and souvenirs; and back from the street's edge, inside the doorways of local households, preparations of feasts for out-of-town guests add further color. A few Buddhist monks and nuns stand silently at roadside, their begging bowls held forth for donations. Others, far less silent in their approach, descend upon members of the incense-offering group aiming to sell them items, such as incense sticks and spirit money, that will be needed for worship in the temple.

FIGURE 6.5. Activities in the crowded courtyard at the Palace of Audience during Peikang's Ma-tsu festival.

Yet for the average bystander, the arriving members of an incense-offering group are themselves even more interesting than the local scene. Their progress down the main street is often marked by repeated kneelings and prostrations, all made in the direction of Ma-tsu's image in the temple that stands before them as their goal. They proudly bear the Ma-tsu image(s), identifying flags, and portable brazier of their home temple. And those among them who are spirit mediums brandish swords, spiked balls, and other weapons for self-mutilation, representing a somewhat gruesome but essential dimension of the festival. Falling into trance and striking themselves with their weapons, usually to make superficial but nevertheless bloody wounds on their backs, they verify that the god's spirit is present and, moreover, protecting them from the pain of their self-inflicted wounds. Possessed by gods and thus able to drive away evil influences, the spirit mediums lead the group toward the temple.

Arriving at the temple, an attempt is made to announce their presence and clear the way for their business, which is to pass their sacred images and other ritual paraphernalia into the main hall of the temple to be placed upon the altar of the powerful Peikang Ma-tsu. As the temple bell rings out on one side, and the drum resounds on the other, the sacred items are passed hand to hand up to the altar in a careful but less than formal manner. In fact, perhaps the only key requirement of this rite is that the items be passed over the large incense brazier that is the temple's sacred portal and a prime manifestation of Ma-tsu's spiritual power. This is where all visitors place sticks of incense to carry upwardly the sweet scent of their gratitude toward Ma-tsu. It is also where they can activate their flags and charms with her spiritual power, later taking them home to serve as protective talismans.

Just as individual visitors "charge" such spiritual souvenirs by ceremoniously dousing them in the smoke rising from incense braziers at Peikang's Palace of Audience, the ostensible purpose of every incense-offering group is also to engage in a ritual that will recharge the sacred items from its home temple, as if they were batteries being connected with a central power source. However, there is a special brazier, called the "ten thousand years brazier," that is used exclusively for this purpose. There is also an appointed time, chosen by divination, for the ritual culminating this process, which was initiated when the branch temple's Ma-tsu image(s), brazier, and other items were first placed on the altar. The ritual itself is too complex to describe in detail, but it is easy enough to indicate its essential feature—taking some ash and flaming spirit money from the "ten thousand years brazier" of the Peikang Ma-tsu and placing it in the small portable brazier brought from the branch temple. It is believed that this simple act, within its proper ritual context, will guarantee Ma-tsu's continued spiritual protection of the home community.

Now, while incense-offering groups may come anytime during the period between the Lantern Festival and Ma-tsu's birthday, the days just preceding the birthday itself are the most popular with visitors of all types. This is especially true of the nineteenth and twentieth of the third lunar month. On each of these days the local Ma-tsu and her entourage of secondary deities from the Palace of Audience are taken out to make a circuit of the city of Peikang. This is a typical god's birthday ritual for major community temples, made special in Peikang mainly by its nighttime occurrence and exhorbitant use of firecrackers. Departing from the temple at dusk, and led by the Peikang Ma-tsu in her royal palanquin, the procession includes other deities carried in palanquins or, as in the case of Ma-tsu's two spiritual assistants, Thousand-league Eyes and Downwind Ears, worn over the body and operated from within like a giant-sized puppet. As each palanquin progresses a few meters, it stops to perform the rite of "treading on cannon." Coils of several hundred firecrackers each are piled beneath the palanquin and set off as its young male bearers race back and forth directly over them, demonstrating their faith in the god's protection. In addition to allowing the community's young males to demonstrate their bravery, the continuous volleys of firecrackers serve *to drive evil forces from the community*. And this, in fact, is the main function of the procession as a whole, also manifesting itself in the antics of those who act as Thousand-league Eyes and Downwind Ears. As one might guess from their names, these deities (found on opposite sides of the main altar in every Ma-tsu temple) are unfailing in their perception of evil deeds. And on the night in question, they roam in and out of people's homes driving out the evildoers of the unseen world and adding to the halloweenlike character of Ma-tsu's annual parade through darkness.

After the festivities of the nineteenth and twentieth, Peikang begins to settle down and is comparatively calm by the actual anniversary of

Ma-tsu's birth. It is therefore perhaps appropriate that on this day the formal rites are held that date back to the official state religion of the Ch'ing Dynasty. Unlike the festive and ecstatic ambiance created in celebrating the birthday of a popular deity, official religious ceremonies exclude public participation, give little role to displays of emotion, and lack the stunning sights and sometimes deafening sounds of the common people's festivals. For in state rituals the important thing is to conform to the system of *yin, yang,* and the five elemental phases and, thereby, to maintain human society's smooth cooperation with the forces and patterns of nature. By contrast, the main thing in a popular festival is to experience and be assured of the concrete presence of divine power, which can intervene on one's behalf when something goes wrong in the normally smooth functioning of the social or natural world. In the case of traditional China, at least, such differences in religious style can be traced to more fundamental differences between social groups. This, however, is an issue that falls within the domain of the next chapter.

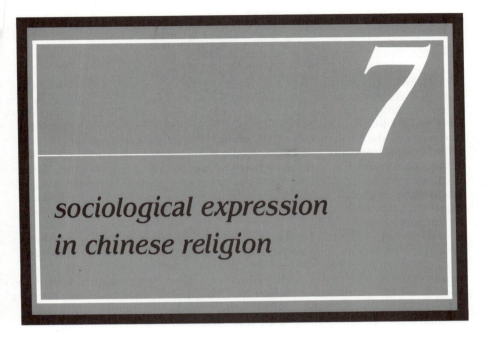

*sociological expression
in chinese religion*

The social form of a religion says just as much about its essential character as do its beliefs and practices. In every case, religious social organization reflects the nature of the beliefs and practices of those whom it joins together. We can therefore assume, for example, that those who participated in the Chinese state cult were socially organized in a way that reflected its formal ideology and systematic ceremonies, and that a similar correlation between sociological and other dimensions of religious expression existed for those who took part in aspects of Chinese folk religion, such as popular festivals. Beginning with these two cases, this chapter will present a brief sociological analysis of Chinese religion, followed by detailed descriptions of two key examples of Chinese religious social organization.

A SOCIOLOGICAL VIEW OF CHINESE RELIGION

In what follows, the first aim will be to take a look at social and religious factors important for understanding traditional China's literati elite. The second will be to consider those factors important for understanding its average folk believers. The third will involve considering the influence of the family factor in Chinese religious social life. And the fourth will concern the development in China of specifically religious (voluntary and nonfamilial) groups.

Religious Social Organization of the Literati Elite

We have seen that the Chinese emperor reigned as well as ruled, being both the sacred king at the head of an imperial cult and the leading authority of all secular administration. Similarly, there were two dimensions to the nature of traditional China's Confucian literati. In addition to being secular bureaucrats, they had a sacred status, first, as representatives of the Son of Heaven and, second, as living symbols of an ancient tradition maintained in their own state cult commemorating Confucius, their patron saint. Their existence as a social class thus had its religious dimension, which we will discuss in considering them as an example of religious social organization. To begin with, however, we must say something of their social existence as such.

Traditional China's literati class was not an unchanging and self-perpetuating aristocracy. Its membership was drawn from society at large through a system of civil service examinations, and few families could continue to provide successful examination candidates generation after generation. Sometimes this was because they lost the financial means to give their sons the best education, and sometimes because their sons just could not make the grade regardless of how much was spent educating them. Even those who successfully entered society's ruling stratum could suddenly fall from power due to some purge, scandal, or court intrigue, taking their families with them into a downward spin. It is for this reason that a leading historian of Chinese bureaucracy, Etienne Balazs, once commented: "The first thing that strikes one about this stratum is the precarious position of its members individually, contrasted with their continuous existence as a social class."[1] Thus, this class was not characterized so much by the influence of its individual members as by (1) their collective role as public figures in an impersonal bureaucratic structure and (2) their identification as a group with the sacred traditions maintained through the Chinese state cult.

Any individual's rank within this bureaucratic structure was indicated by his official dress, which set him apart from the rest of society. For wearing the so-called Mandarin Robe automatically meant that one had not only the personal fortitude but also the Heavenly conferred fate that led to success in the examinations. From a religious point of view, this made successful examinees more than qualified civil servants. In the words of Max Weber, an early pioneer in the sociological study of Chinese religion:

If the technique and substance of the examinations were purely mundane in nature and represented a sort of "cultural examination for the literati," the popular view of them was very different: it gave them a magical-charismatic meaning. In the eyes of the Chinese masses, a successfully examined candidate and official was by no means a mere applicant for office qualified by knowledge. He was a proved holder of magical qualities, which, as we shall see, were attached to the certified mandarin just as much

---

[1] Etienne Balazs, *Chinese Civilization and Bureaucracy,* trans. H. M. Wright and ed. A. F. Wright (New Haven: Yale University Press, 1964), p. 6.

FIGURE 7.1. Tablet of Confucius on the altar inside the Temple of Confucius, Taichung, Taiwan. The words on the tablet identify Confucius as "Most Sagely Former Master K'ung Tzu."

as to an examined and ordained priest of an ecclesiastic institution of grace, or to a magician tried and proved by his guild.[2]

Moreover, all certified mandarins were *ex officio* state cult ritualists, whether they served as such in some part of the imperial cult or in their own cult of Confucius.

At every administrative center in the empire down to the district level, there was a Temple of Confucius for holding spring and autumn sacrifices to the Master. These temples usually surpassed all other structures in the local landscape in size and grandeur. But their decor was dignified, not ornate; and during most of Chinese history (see Chapter 2), they had commemorative tablets, rather than religious images, to represent "Most Sagely Former Master K'ung Tzu" (using his official title) and other illustrious Confucians. In addition, as we would expect for the cult of a bureaucratic class, all the tablets were carefully arranged according to rank, from those who faced south alongside Confucius on the altar of the main hall to the great majority whose tablets were set up in the supplementary, eastern and western halls.

Deriving their authority from sacred institutions of this kind, local officials had powers at their disposal that transcended their bureaucratic role; or, if viewed through the eyes of Chinese folk religion, powers that were part and parcel of their role as representatives of otherworldly administrators within a divine-human bureaucracy headed by the Jade Emperor

---

[2] Max Weber, *The Religion of China*, trans. Hans H. Gerth (Glencoe, Ill.: The Free Press, 1951), p. 128.

in Heaven. What this meant for the social status and administrative efficiency of local officials has been well described by John Watt in *The District Magistrate in Late Imperial China:*

> As representative of the local city god, or as counterpart of the judge of the underworld, magistrates were able to use these relationships to secure confessions or compliance resistant to purely terrestrial authority. As imperial delegate, the magistrate represented the local symbol of the unitary power of the Son of Heaven, and as such the district's legitimate source of authority. On arrival at their districts, magistrates were accordingly treated to elaborate ceremonials of welcome and similarly revered at the end of a successful tenure. While in office they constituted the sole "father and mother official" and could expect great respect whenever making a formal appearance.[3]

Therefore, although the sources of the literati's sacred authority matched their social existence as examined, rational, and hierarchically ranked bureaucrats, their use of this authority brought them into contact with the rather different world of Chinese popular religion. As we will now see, this was a socio-religious world in which sacred authority was not highly organized but rather diffusely distributed among an almost infinite variety of deities, temples, and religious figures.

Diffuse Popular Religion

Of all that Chinese popular religion includes—seasonal observances, visits to fortunetellers, syncretic lay associations, ceremonies at the home altar— here we will focus on only its most visible public dimension: the system of community folk temples. And, as we must admit at the outset, this was in fact no system at all. C. K. Yang, perhaps the first sociologist of religion to stress adequately the diffuse rather than organized nature of this "system," painted an interesting picture of its unique form among religious institutions:

> If the well-known facts of religious life in China are analyzed, the first striking characteristic is the lack of any membership requirement for worshiping in a temple or convent. With the exception of a few convents which were closed to the public, anyone could enter temple or convent to pray, to make a vow, to seek divine guidance, or to conduct any other type of worship without restriction. There was no special identification marking him as a member who worshiped in a certain temple. The priest in the temple might or might not know him. After performing the religious rituals, the worshiper generally paid the attending priest for the incense and for oil for the sacred lamp; the making of this payment discharged any further obligation between the worshiper and the priest. The worshipers enjoyed no stable, binding tie with the temple or the priest. An important factor in this connection was the absence of priests in most temples and convents, and thus the absence of any agent uniting the worshipers into an organized body.[4]

---

[3] John R. Watt, *The District Magistrate in Late Imperial China* (New York: Columbia University Press, 1972), p. 17.
[4] C. K. Yang, *Religion in Chinese Society* (Berkeley and Los Angeles: University of California Press, 1970), pp. 327–328.

To a certain extent, the reason Chinese popular religion thus lacked social organization lay in its polytheistic theory of divinity and its functionalistic method of practice. Choosing where to worship on the basis of current need and a god's reputed ability to respond to such need, worshipers were unlikely to group themselves into permanent religious institutions.

This does not mean community temples have functioned in Chinese society without any organization whatever. Such would be impossible. Yet it does mean their significant organizational structures have been shared with other elements of Chinese society (state, family, and community). For the "system" of community temples has had *no independent organization of its own*. The state has superimposed its structure on them, for example, by registering them, aiming to control their activities, and honoring them with special acts of recognition, such as the granting of official titles to their gods. And they have also come inevitably under the all-pervasive influence of the Chinese family system. Yet their most essential connection has been with the neighborhoods and communities in which they exist, which is why we choose to call them "community temples."

The temples to popular gods found within easy access of every Chinese neighborhood, regardless of who possesses them as real estate, are *public* from both the religious and social points of view. As observed in our discussion of religious theory in Chapter 5, the gods in many such temples are former ancestral spirits that have paradoxically become the property as well as the responsibility of the general public. As a result, the material and spiritual support of the gods' temples has fallen upon the communities in which they are located. While individual wealthy benefactors and occasional visitors are a factor in their support, those linked with community temples by location are usually their most regular supporters. And the reverse is also true: these temples serve their communities in innumerable ways.

In addition to being where traditional Chinese communities have turned for spiritual aid in times of distress, local temples have also been places in which their members meet for all kinds of other social purposes. A local temple could, for example, (1) satisfy commercial needs by serving as a marketplace (if not regularly, at least at festival time), (2) meet political needs by becoming the location of a god-witnessed communal agreement, (3) answer military needs by being the site of a strategy planning session for a town beseiged by bandits, and (4) fulfill recreational needs by serving the community as everything from a children's playground to an old folk's home. Yet despite their extreme importance, one could not say that the activities of a local Chinese temple have been truly matters of religious obligation for *all* community members. For in Chinese religious life, when we wish to see what is obligatory rather than optional, we must turn to look at the family.

The Family Factor

Many take the proverb "blood is thicker than water" to be self-evident, for they see something that cannot be matched by other kinds of relationships in the biological bonds between parents and their offspring, or among siblings from the same parents. In China, reverence for such natural bonds has extended well beyond the nuclear family, producing the fundamental unit of Chinese social and political order—the patrilineal clan or lineage. Traditionally, its rules and the word of its male leader provided the guidelines for all behavior. Entrance into a clan by birth or marriage gave each member the most essential set of obligations, religious and otherwise, that he or she would ever have in life. Because of its size and importance, the Chinese family developed a necessarily complex and well-defined structure, as reflected, for example, in its system of mourning and ancestral practices. These will be discussed later in this chapter, in a section specifically concerning family religion. Here we aim to indicate only the influence of family structure and values on *other* social forms of Chinese religion.

The lineal relation between parent and child, expressed in the moral concept of filiality, became the basic building block of Chinese social institutions. This is why such institutions tended to be hierarchically structured. Religious institutions were no exception to this; and they also borrowed much from the religious product of filiality: ancestral worship. As we have seen, the genesis of popular gods in China owed much to the ancestral cult. With the exception of specifically natural divinities, such as Sun and Moon, the same was true of official state cult deities. In both cases, the basic means of worship—offering a sacrificial banquet—had its model in ceremonies held for the dead as well as the living within Chinese family life.

Even in the case of specifically religious groups, which we are about to discuss, one can detect the influence of the values and structure of the Chinese family system. Syncretic lay religions, whether worshiping Buddhist or Taoist deities, rarely failed to sanction the code of familial morals found in classical Confucian sources; and they often featured a hierarchy of leaders with titles borrowed from Chinese kinship terminology. Even more noteworthy, despite Buddhism's demand for celebacy and its ostensible abandonment of family life, it evolved in China by making similar compromises with the family system (as will be seen later in this chapter).

Specifically Religious Groups

Although religion has nearly always and everywhere sanctified the family, one of its key historical functions has been to draw people together into voluntary, nonfamilial groups that can transcend the interests of individuals, families, clans, and even nations. These groups are able to transcend such interests precisely because they have *independent* forms of religious social organization. This makes it possible for them, as more or less free-standing social units, to have a variety of relations with society at large and to serve certain functions for religious believers better than natural social groups like the family.

In Chapter 3, Buddhist monasticism and the White Lotus Religion were introduced as cases of specifically religious groups that manifested, respectively, indifference and opposition toward the traditional Chinese state. Other specifically religious groups have existed in China that have also been relatively independent from Chinese governmental and familial institutions, independent enough at least to become sources of social and religious innovation. Following the laws governing the emergence of specifically religious groups throughout the world, they have for the most part grown in the environment of social change and mobility provided by Chinese cities, where many residents have been cut off from the secure network of the clan relationships of their native homes.

From their point of view, the specifically religious group could meet a variety of important socio-religious needs. First, it could serve as a *surrogate kin group and mutual aid association*. Second, it could offer methods for seeking not only social but also *individual salvation*, borrowing, for example, upon the ritual and meditative traditions of Buddhism. And, to a far greater extent than family religion or even monastic Buddhism, it could provide *opportunities for innovation* in matters of religious belief and practice. For in China such groups have been characteristically *syncretic*, building their doctrinal and ritual systems with features borrowed from Confucian, Taoist, Buddhist, and, in recent times, Christian, Islamic, and other religious traditions. Because of the generally diffuse nature of religion in China, religious groups there rarely drew fixed boundaries between themselves or demanded exclusive allegiance from their members. And with the exception of certain groups firmly rooted in Western traditions, such as Christianity, they never considered taking precedence over the most essential and obligatory form of all Chinese religious life—the family ancestral cult.

RELIGION AND THE CHINESE FAMILY

A social institution as important as the family is everywhere bound to receive religious support and sanctification. Thus, most cultures require the performance of holy rites of matrimony before a new family may begin to evolve. And when family unity is threatened by death, funeral rites are needed to bring consolation and the message that remaining members can bear the loss, carry on, and perhaps even rejoice in the lost member's new existence in a better world. Examples of these and similar practices will emerge as we look at the family as one social form of religion in China. But let us begin by saying something about Chinese family organization itself.

The family lineage of traditional China has been described as a closely unified patrilineal group, with a well-defined structure, that determined the complex mutual obligations between lineage members. The group's unity was guaranteed, at least as an ideal, because its members had a common surname and shared descent from common ancestors. These ties were usually supported by written proof in the form of family historical and geneological records, kept perhaps for centuries, and by the possession of common property. Therefore, they usually assured that all lineage members would cooperate, even if sometimes reluctantly, when an individual household within their ranks faced a crisis. An individual household normally consisted of those related by blood, marriage, or adoption to one male of the older generation *who shared the same stove*. As indicated in the previous chapter, this group was the subject of the stove god's annual New Year's report to the Jade Emperor in Heaven. When the group became too large or developed internal tensions too strong to resolve, it could be divided to form new households by means of a ceremony called "splitting the stove."

This and other aspects of Chinese lineages will be further exemplified as we proceed to discuss the religious rituals connected with Chinese family life, beginning with marriage, turning second to funerals and mourning customs, and concluding with the topic of ancestral worship.

The Rites of Marriage

A traditional Chinese marriage is best conceived of as a contractual transfer of personnel (the bride) from one patrilineal group to another. It was not arranged by the bride and groom but rather by their respective families, who themselves turned the responsibility of matching mates over to a hired go-between and, ultimately, to Heaven. This becomes clear as one begins to examine the six rites that constituted the major steps in the traditional marriage procedure. Whether or not the families knew one another, as a first step, the groom's family would hire a go-between to make formal inquiries about the prospective bride. Assuming both families were still interested, the second step was to send the go-between once again in order to request certain astrological data based on the girl's date of birth. Her family's formal consent to provide this information showed approval for continuing with the steps leading to a wedding, the third of which was to assure the match was truly made in Heaven. This was done by having a fortuneteller compare the girl's astrological data with that based on the boy's date of birth.

If no problem emerged here, the families could prepare to take the fourth and most difficult step—the engagement. It was difficult because it involved an exchange of gifts which, rather than being merely ceremonial, was an integral part of the contract being made between the two families. This was especially so because the girl's family, losing her to another lineage forever, sought compensation that included a cash bride's price. Whatever arrangements were finally negotiated therefore reflected the worth of the girl and her family. So important was this step that, to all intents and purposes, its completion constituted the *de facto* completion of the marriage. Even if death intervened during the engagement period, which might last a year or longer, it would probably be necessary for the girl, if she survived her fiancé, to join the lineage that had contracted for her services. Conversely, the boy would probably need to complete the ceremony so that his deceased partner's soul could have a secure place within his family's ancestral cult, though this would not prevent him from marrying a second, living bride.

As for a living couple's ceremony, an auspicious date for it was chosen and formally fixed in the fifth of the six rites. Last, of course, was the ceremony itself, in which the bride was finally taken from her natal home and officially transferred to the home of the groom's family. While there was much joy in the event, especially during the unavoidably lavish feast held after her arrival at the groom's home, its primary symbolic message was one of radical separation between the bride and her natal family. Consider the following passage from Margery Wolf's *Women and the Family in Rural Taiwan:*

> The arrival of the groom and his party to claim the bride quickens the pace of activity. The party is served a sweet rice-ball soup that the bride's attendants have been drinking unenthusiastically. The groom's soupbowl has a soft-boiled egg in it, and he is expected to break the yolk, symbolically breaking his bride's ties with her family. . . . The go-between then calls the couple to the family altar to bow first to the gods and then to the girl's father's ancestors. At this point the sedan chair . . . is carried into the living room, and parents and daughter begin to exchange the ritual formulas of farewell, wishing each other long life, wealth, happiness, and for the bride, many sons. By this time mother and daughter are weeping uncontrollably. The father or his representative hands the sedan chair bearers an *ang pau* ["red envelope" containing money], and the bearers lower the handles of the chair so the bride may enter. The chair is closed, and the bearers carry it out of the house. The house doors are quickly slammed behind the bride's chair to prevent the wealth of the family from following the bride. Her brother spits or throws water on the departing chair to indicate that just as spilt water cannot be returned to the container, so the bride cannot return to her natal home. . . .[5]

It was destined to be this way when the bride first came into the world, for she was born into one male descent line solely for the purpose of being transferred into another for perpetuity.

As another anthropologist, Maurice Freedman, has astutely observed, the significance of this critical, one-time transfer between agnatic (i.e., male descent) groups lies in the fact that its essential ritual feature is the physical movement of the bride. Freedman's point is made in a passage contrasting the symbolic significance of marital and ancestral ritual:

> The main dimension through which the ancestor rites move is time. Agnation is, so to say, a vertical extension; the rites look backward and forward in time, and with respect to place stress immobility. Families and lineages are conceptually anchored in space; they move forward along time. In the rites of marriage time recedes, for what is crucial is physical movement, symbolized above all in the transfer of the bride but realized also in the many comings and goings between the two houses that both precede and follow the central event. Space is now of the essence. It is no wonder, then, that in the People's Republic, in the face of fierce attacks against superstitious ceremonialism, people persist in practicing the central rite of the traditional wedding (the transfer of the bride in her sedan chair) by conveying her on a bicycle. Walking, even when practical, is just not good enough; a dramatic movement must be made.[6]

[5] Margery Wolf, *Women and the Family in Rural Taiwan* (Stanford: Stanford University Press, 1970), pp. 180–181.

[6] Maurice Freedman, "Ritual Aspects of Chinese Kinship and Marriage," *Family and Kinship in Chinese Society,* ed. Maurice Freedman (Stanford: Stanford University Press, 1970), pp. 180–181; reprinted by permission of Stanford University Press.

Freedman's contrast between the lateral nature of marital ceremonies and the linear, time-oriented nature of ancestral rites also concerns us now as we prepare to discuss funerals, mourning, and, finally, ancestor worship. For Chinese concern over unity within the patrilineal family, which made marriage such a critical event, was also the factor that caused such stress to be placed on a family's symbolic links with its ancestral past in all rituals dealing with the dead.

Funerals and Mourning

Because elderly Chinese have a rather healthy attitude toward death, and a keen awareness of the high cost of tombs and funerals, they begin to prepare for the inevitable event at an early stage. Retiring and returning to their native home—had they ever left it in pursuit of a career—they resign themselves to a passive role in society, are cared for by their off-spring, and in many cases devote themselves to religious matters to a far greater extent than ever before. The one thing they may have an active interest in is the preparation of the coffin and tomb that will soon become their final resting place. The actual burden of preparation, however, falls upon their son(s), whose filial duty it is to provide the best for them that the family can afford. When it becomes apparent that an elderly person is dying, he or she is moved to the main hall of the home, thus joining (at least symbolically) the ancestors represented there by tablets on the family altar. Unless the move is premature, this sets in motion a series of familial religious practices that may last for months.

At least in those ideal situations in which a person lives to a normal age and suffers a natural death, the process of dying is gradual rather than abrupt, incorporated into the course of ordinary life rather than handled quickly and kept out of sight. However, this does not mean that the Chinese fail to consider death a highly polluting event from the religious point of view. Although the ultimate aim of Chinese funeral rites is to guarantee the safe passage of the deceased's soul into the spirit world and assure its comfort there, these rites must also see that the contagious misfortune of death does not spread to any relatives, friends, or neighbors of the deceased. Belief in the contagiousness of death is perhaps most clearly manifest in the custom of "double-death day" rituals. When someone dies on what is indicated in the almanac as a "double-death day," in order to prevent another occurrence of death in the family, a special rite must be performed—a rite which, in part, employs the sacrifice of a cock to counteract the omen of a second death.[7] Even more common than this is the practice of having red cloth or paper put up above neighbors' doorways to make sure their families are safe from the contagious miasma of death. For, in China, the color red not only serves to express joy but also, in cases like this, to ward off evil influences.

---

[7] See, for example, Francis L. K. Hsu, *Under the Ancestors' Shadow: Kinship, Personality, and Social Mobility in China* (New York: Anchor Books, 1967), pp. 155–156.

FIGURE 7.2. Funeral procession with pallbearers carrying a traditional-style coffin. Lukang, Taiwan.

As for those rites meant to guarantee the safe passage and future comfort of the deceased's soul, they are too numerous and complex to describe fully. But the most important ones will now be discussed, in order of their normal occurrence.[8] After the death of a person who has already been moved to the family's main hall, it is washed there by family members. White cards are sent out to announce the death to relatives and friends, for white is considered to be the opposite of red and is used to express sorrow. A temporary ancestral tablet (about a foot tall, made of paper, and identifying the deceased along with his or her death date) is set up to facilitate the receipt of prayers and offerings by the soul of the deceased. Guests arrive to pay respects and present gifts, such as incense and spirit money, elegiac phrases written on white scrolls, and (real) money to help defray funeral expenses. Next come the steps that lead up to the encoffining, such as putting "longevity clothes" on the corpse, placing jade or other jewels in its mouth, and performing other acts to protect the deceased from evil influences. Then the encoffining occurs, shortly after death; but the family may have to wait weeks or months for the auspicious day chosen for the actual funeral rites, which include "sealing the coffin," transporting it to the gravesite, and burying it.

On this day, the main event is the grand procession in which the

[8] It should be pointed out that what follows is based entirely on data concerning traditional Taiwanese customs, especially as described in Emily Ahern, *The Cult of the Dead in a Chinese Village* (Stanford: Stanford University Press, 1973) and Laurence G. Thompson, "Funeral Rites in Taiwan," *The Chinese Way in Religion* (Encino, Calif.: Dickenson Publishing Co., Inc., 1973), pp. 160–169.

coffin is taken to its final destination. Traditionally carried by four or more pallbearers—the richer the family, the larger the number—it is now more likely to be loaded on a large truck lavishly decorated with flowers. Right in front of the coffin is a sedan chair (or truck) for the soul of the deceased, with lanterns to illumine the way to the grave, the temporary ancestral tablet, and a container holding rice. This container is called "dipper" (*tou; dou*); and, since the Chinese consider the constellation with this name to be a source of cosmic destiny, it symbolizes the person's and his family's fate. Further in front proceeds an assortment of musicians, priests, and people carrying banners, elegiac scrolls, parasols, the deceased's picture, and so forth. Behind the coffin there finally trails a long stream of mourners, led by the "filial son" (eldest living son) and others who are close to the deceased in their blood relationship and, for this reason, physically close to the corpse in ritual order.

At the gravesite, the coffin is lowered into the grave to the doleful tones of mortuary music, the somber chanting of priests, and the grief-stricken wailing of mourners. Once it is safely in its final resting place, which has been carefully selected according to the principles of geomancy, there occurs perhaps the most symbolically significant rite of the entire funeral: "dotting the *chu*" (*zhu*: the Chinese character meaning "host" or "master"). Laurence Thompson has described this rite as follows:

The filial son again sacrifices to the local earth god, and then, bearing the [paper ancestral] spirit-tablet, kneels in front of the grave, where some dignitary (according to one source this would be the head of the clan) has been invited to "dot the *chu*" (i.e. with a brush dipped in vermillion ink, to place the final dot on the character *chu*, which signifies that the tablet is now the actual residence of the soul of the deceased). The spirit tablet is then set on a rice measure in front of the grave, where it receives the libation of the one who has dotted the *chu*, accompanied by the burning of incense, kneeling of all parties, and the din of music from the band. Led by the Buddhist and Taoist priests the funeral party circumambulates the grave wailing, and then they return home.[9]

One may say that at this point funeral services end and ancestral worship begins. But before discussing the latter, something must be said of the way funerary sentiments extend into ordinary life through the practice of mourning.

In his article "Chinese Kinship and Mourning Dress," anthropologist Arthur Wolf has tried to show what a clear and complete accounting of Chinese kinship structures and obligations can be found by looking at mourning clothes. He begins the article as follows:

Seen from a distance, from the top of a building or one of the hills on which most graves are sited, the procession following a Chinese coffin is a colorful sight. The mourners wear long robelike gowns, some of rough dirty-brown sackcloth, others of gray flax or grass cloth, and still others of unbleached white linen or muslin; scattered

[9] Thompson, "Funeral Rites in Taiwan," p. 166.

among these are blue gowns, red gowns, and, on the rare occasion, a yellow gown. Female mourners cover their heads with a hood that almost hides the face and hangs down the back to the waist; men wear a hempen "helmet" over a short hood or one of two kinds of baglike hats of unbleached or dyed muslin. . . . I have never tried to count the number of mourning costumes in the Chinese repertoire, but there must be at least a hundred recognizable variants. A funeral procession of fifty mourners usually includes twenty or more different combinations of textiles and colors.

Later he explains this variety in mourning apparel by reference to the various degrees of joy and sorrow (based, in turn, on degrees of obligation) that are appropriate for various relatives of the deceased. He states:

Contrary as it is to Western ideas of mourning, the expression of degrees of joy and sorrow at a funeral is entirely appropriate in China. A Chinese line of descent is essentially a chain of obligation in which every man's first duty is to perpetuate the chain. Each person receives from his father and grandfather a name, education, and property; in return for these he is obligated to respect and obey his parents and bear children to continue the line. There are therefore two emotions that are appropriate when a man dies. There must be grief and sorrow on the part of those who are most indebted to the deceased, but there can also be joy. If the man has lived to witness the birth of great-grandsons or even great-great-grandsons, he has repaid his parents and grandparents in full measure. His sons and grandsons must wear mua:-po (sackcloth) and te-a-po (gray flax) to express their grief, but his great- and great-great-grandsons should wear joyful colors to announce this accomplishment to the world. The mournful degrees of our scale express the obligations of junior to senior; the joyful degrees, the happy fulfillment of these obligations.[10]

The basis for all this behavior is the classical conception of five degrees of mourning, which are calculated not only lineally, as in Wolf's example, but also laterally, so that mourning obligations theoretically extend to all the descendants of a common great-great-grandfather.

Moreover, differences between heavy and light mourning obligations are expressed not only in the type of dress worn at a funeral but also in the nature and length of the mourning period that follows. For example, first-degree mourning (observed by the sons, daughters, and wife of a deceased man) traditionally lasted for from two to three years, divided into phases of progressively less strict observance so that mourners could gradually return to normal life. During the first phase, one had to disregard all concern for personal comfort and appearance by eating simple food, wearing coarse clothing, not shaving or cutting one's hair, and so forth; and throughout the entire period, one's status had to be reflected in both appearance and behavior by avoiding colorful clothes as well as joyful activities. All this was meant to preserve the most essential religious sentiment underlying the entire Chinese family system—remembrance of one's ancestors.

[10] Arthur P. Wolf, "Chinese Kinship and Mourning Dress," *Family and Kinship in Chinese Society*, ed. Maurice Freedman (Stanford: Stanford University Press, 1970), p. 189 and p. 192; reprinted by permission of Stanford University Press. As with the funeral rites just discussed, Wolf's analysis is based on Taiwanese data.

Ancestral Practices

For many modern educated Chinese, as perhaps for the Confucian elite of former times, "worship" of ancestors is a matter of remembrance or commemoration and nothing more. Yet for the great majority of other Chinese, ancestor worship is part and parcel of humanity's religious relations with the spirit world. For them, just as the stove god represents the family to the Jade Emperor in Heaven and thereby links it to the universal divine-human bureaucracy, the home ancestral altar ties the family to another religious system that transcends the household. This is the system of the lineage ancestral cult, which roots every family in past history and, at the same time, ties it to all other families of common ancestry.

The sons of a family must remain united in their common obligation to serve their progenitor after death according to the demands of filiality. This is understood to be the necessary repayment for the gift of life and many years of nurturing. Reciprocal obligation, then, is the essential feature of relations between the living and the dead, as expressed by Emily Ahern in her enlightening study *The Cult of the Dead in a Chinese Village:*

> In studying the reciprocity that is at the heart of ancestor worship, we shall find that the living are expected to care for the dead in payment of the debts they owe them. Beyond this, in the act of meeting this obligation, the living hope to inspire a further reciprocal response from the ancestors, to obtain through them the good life as they perceive it: wealth, rich harvests, and offspring who will ensure undying memory and sustenance in the afterlife.[11]

Now, to understand the conditions of reciprocal relations between the living and the dead, one must first answer the question: Who merits treatment in the cult of a particular family altar? The ideal candidate is an adult male of the family, with sons, who has maintained or added to the family's property and bequeathed it to his sons; and the same is true of the wife who helps him to accomplish this. On the other hand, a woman born into the family would not be a candidate at all, for, as we saw in discussing marriage, she was born to join another family's ancestral cult.

Of course, what is ideal and normal does not always prevail, and it is often from exceptions that we can best understand the rule. By now it should be obvious that Chinese popular religion demands a close accounting of all souls of the deceased, for any bereaved spirit can become a problem; and if the spirit was your former relative, the problem is likely to be yours. Of course the best way for a soul to be accounted for—before it becomes bereaved and problematic—is to incorporate it into the appropriate ancestral cult. If a family has an unmarried daughter, for example, a husband can be brought in (perhaps I should say "bought in," as he would not normally agree to do it for free) to help her maintain family property and bear sons who will someday carry on the family name. More-

---

[11] Ahern, p. 91.

over, if the man is willing to be adopted by his wife's family and take its surname, he will be in the same position as she. Both will have met the conditions for being included, upon death, in the ancestral cult of the wife's natal family. Considering a slightly different situation, if one's son or daughter dies after reaching adulthood but before marrying (those who die in childhood not normally requiring a place in any ancestral cult), one may need to solve the problem through ritual marriage. A ceremony is held to wed the deceased person to a living one, who may already have a spouse, solely for the purpose of legitimizing his or her inclusion in an ancestral cult.

Manipulations of this kind seem to indicate that fears about bereaved spirits becoming vengeful ghosts dictate who becomes responsible for the care of a certain ancestral soul. However, this is not typically the case, as will be seen in answering our next question: Who normally has the obligation to worship a particular ancestral soul? When a man inherits life and family property from his father (or, if adopted, only property), he becomes obliged to make an ancestral tablet and perform sacrifices for the father. While this obligation falls first and foremost on a father's eldest son, his brothers are not entirely free of it; for, due to lack of primogeniture in Chinese society, they also inherit and thus have a debt to repay.

Usually within a year of the funeral, a permanent ancestral tablet is made to replace the paper tablet used on that occasion. It is a tall, thin piece of wood (perhaps a foot tall and less than one third as wide), and the name, title(s), and death date of the deceased are often inscribed on it. It will join the tablets of other ancestors on a high altar in the most honored place of a family residence. This altar may be a large, hand-carved heirloom displayed in the upper floor of the central structure on a vast estate or simply a board fixed high upon one wall of a single-room dwelling. Here, among candles, flowers, incense pots, and food offerings, there may also be a general tablet for family ancestors who have passed from memory as well as the images of one or more deities from the Chinese pantheon.

Now the question arises: What occurs in front of this altar? A variety of things, and each seems to have its own distinct logic. For example, there normally are two small incense pots on the altar so that the worship of gods can be kept separate from that of ancestors. The two can be worshiped at the same time, however, as in the case of daily incense offerings or the offerings of incense, food, and perhaps other items that are made at the beginning and middle of the month. These may be made by the woman of the house, which is not usually the case with formal rites specifically for family ancestors. These rites, at which the male head of the household officiates, must be further divided into two kinds. First, there are rites for individual ancestors who are still within memory. These rites are held on death-date anniversaries and distinguished by the offering of a particular ancestor's favorite foods, wine, cigarettes, and so forth. Second, there are rites for all the family ancestors, which are held on regular calendrical holidays. These are occasions, like the New Year celebration described previously, for the whole family to be together and have a feast. Even the ancestors are therefore provided with cups, bowls, and chopsticks and invited to eat. And the living members of the family take this opportunity to kneel before the altar and kowtow in order of their relative status— elder before younger, male before female.

A mental image of such an occasion, with three, four, or, when the ideal is realized, five generations of the living gathered and countless more of their deceased predecessors present in spirit, gives one a feeling for the essence of family religion in China. Yet this is only part of the picture, for in addition to being revered at the *domestic altar,* ancestors are also worshiped at *their gravesites* and in *clan ancestral halls.* In describing these last two cases, our main purpose will be simply to show the way in which each differs from worship at the domestic altar. We cannot describe them in detail.

Because the grave contains the ancestor's body and is located at a place believed to border on the spirit world, the ancestor is quite differently conceptualized and treated there. Some Chinese even go so far as to say that the soul hovering above the grave is different in kind from that residing in the ancestral tablet, the former being a semimaterial *yin* soul and the latter a fully spiritual *yang* soul (see Chapter 2). While anthropological research has cast doubt on the universality of this two-soul theory, it has verified and clarified the idea that the ancestral soul at the grave is approached in a quite distinct way. Referring again to Emily Ahern's study, it characterizes the attitude toward ancestors at the grave as lacking the usual sense of certainty and familiarity. This is why they are offered only a standard variety of dry food rather than specially prepared favorites. Ahern says this can be explained by the foreboding environment in which the soul is believed to exist at the grave, adding the following insight:

> Accordingly, many of the activities at the grave are directed against any uninvited ghosts who might be on hand. To ensure that the ancestor receives the offerings made to him, for example, the smoldering ashes of the paper money burnt for him are doused with a cup of wine to "mark" this and all the rest of the offerings as his alone and to prevent other ghosts from taking them. The living who are present also need to be protected. The most common measure taken to this end is to pass out red steamed cakes to everyone who comes to the grave, the red color acting as a prophylactic to ward off any danger from lingering contact with ghosts.[12]

These facts further underline the unavoidable role of fear about bereaved spirits ("ghosts," roughly speaking) within Chinese ancestral practices. Here, of course, the concern is not with the possibility of one's own ancestor's soul becoming bereaved but only with what mischief might be caused by other souls who have already suffered this fate. Yet from the point of view of Chinese familial ideals, the message is the same: The worst possible fate for anyone, living or dead, is to be cut off from the network of support and obligations that constitutes the Chinese family system.

In contrast to the comparatively large role that fear of this dire fate has in worship at the grave, the establishment and use of clan ancestral

---

[12] Ahern, pp. 173–174.

halls emphasizes the celebration of an opposite and desirable fate: familial
fame and prosperity. In fact, mere possession of such halls is a sign of
success. For unlike graves and domestic altars, they are optional, luxury
items that only the wealthy can afford. Large structures built separately
from the living quarters of all family branches, they might be mistaken
for temples were it not for the fact that they feature, behind their altars,
tiers of ancestral tablets rather than images of deities. And more impor-
tantly, they emphasize yet another kind of ritual attitude toward family
ancestors, the distinctive nature of which has been described by Maurice
Freedman as follows:

> Shifting our attention [from domestic worship] to the rites conducted in ancestral halls
> we see at once that we are dealing with a different kind of ancestor. There is a sense
> in which there are now no individual ancestors but rather a sort of ancestral collectivity,
> the common spiritual property of a corporate group. . . . The twice-yearly [spring and
> autumn] rites and festivities are a manifestation, to both the worshippers and those
> from whom they are differentiated by their acts, of a claim to a special standing and
> distinction bound up with the reciprocal relationship of honor between living and dead.
> Men glorify their ancestors and parade them as the source of their being. For their
> part the ancestors bask in the glow of the solidarity and achievements of their
> descendants.[13]

Thus, whereas the ritual posture of domestic ancestor worship was characterized as familiar and relaxed, and that of grave worship as cautious,
ancestral hall rituals might be said to emphasize *formal distance* from ancestors with whom one may be unfamiliar and *joyous pride* in their legacy.

Now, the picture of ancestral practices, mourning customs, funeral
rites, and marriage ceremonies just given is a composite one containing
many generalizations. It is offered with the aim of presenting the major
themes upon which traditional Chinese communities have created countless
local variations. These are themes that have shaped Chinese family religion
wherever it has existed and that have colored many other dimensions of
Chinese religious life. That they have even influenced Chinese monastic
Buddhism, the religion of those who "leave the family" (*ch'u-chia; chu-jia*),
will become clear in the section that follows.

THE BUDDHIST MONASTIC COMMUNITY IN CHINA

Regardless of age or social status, any man in China who makes the decision
to become a Buddhist monk must go through the same simple ceremony
to express his renunciation of ordinary life.[14] This is the tonsure ceremony,

---

[13] Freedman, "Ritual Aspects of Chinese Kinship and Marriage," p. 176; reprinted by permission
of Stanford University Press.

[14] While there has certainly been no lack of nuns in Chinese Buddhism, their presence being more
obvious to the observer than the presence of monks in contemporary Taiwan, to give one example,
the unfortunate fact is that virtually all the sources from which one can paint a picture of Chinese
monastic life emphasize monks rather than nuns. The picture offered here thus focuses throughout
on the monk and leaves the reader to imagine how things may have been for his female counterpart.

in which a monk shaves the head of a Buddhist layman, as the latter re-
nounces his concern for lay life and states his sincere intention to take
refuge in the Three Jewels: Buddha, Dharma, and Sangha (the Buddhist
monastic community). This only makes him a "novice," which means he
can still easily return to lay life before taking ordination as a monk. But
in all probability, he will never again let his hair grow, wear anything but
monkly apparel, eat anything but vegetarian food, or live anywhere but
within the regimented confines of monasteries. In almost every way, then,
he becomes marked as one who has chosen to live outside the Chinese
family system and in renunciation of its ideals, which is clearly indicated
by the fact that he gives up his family surname and takes on a new, religious
name. This is as true today as it was in the traditional monastic system
to be described in the pages that follow.

The great irony for a traditional Chinese man who underwent tonsure
was that he had actually joined a *new* family. This was the tonsure family,
headed by the monk who had shaved the novice's head and including all
others who had ever received tonsure from him. As a matter of fact, in
China, one who left his family (*ch'u-chia*) to become a monk entered a
situation resembling, in many ways, the one he left behind. This ironic
fact has been well stated by Holmes Welch in his admirable study *The
Practice of Chinese Buddhism 1900–1950:*

> The Chinese term *ch'u-chia* is derived from the Sanskrit *pravrajya,* "going forth." It
> means "to leave the home," "to renounce lay life." Since the word *chia* means "family"
> as well as "home," there is also the idea of renouncing the family. In a civilization
> that was based on family relationships, it is hard to imagine a greater offense to public
> decency, as the enemies of Buddhism were always ready to point out. Yet what really
> happened was that a new family was acquired as the old was renounced. A Chinese
> could only "leave the home" by accepting a monk as his master. That monk became
> his "father." Fellow disciples became his "brothers." Not only were all the kinship
> terms borrowed from lay life, but family institutions and attitudes were borrowed too.
> A disciple often inherited his "father's" temple and was expected to look after his
> grave and soul tablet like a filial son.[15]

Furthermore, the dually familial and nonfamilial status of a monk in Chinese
society was paralleled by another paradoxical fact: He was in a sense both
the most and the least free of all individuals within that society. In joining
the Buddhist Sangha, on the one hand, he freed himself of ordinary obligations to the state and family, gained material security, and could look forward to a life with more than the average amount of leisure to spend in
study and personal cultivation. Yet, on the other hand, his new religious
family—and the society that allowed him to exist as an exception in their
midst—demanded that he follow the narrow spiritual path on which he

---

[15] Holmes Welch, *The Practice of Chinese Buddhism 1900–1950* (Cambridge, Mass.: Harvard University Press, 1967), p. 247; reprinted by permission. Copyright © 1967 by the President and Fellows
of Harvard College.

set foot when he received tonsure. Where that path would lead, at least in the case of those who remained true to its ideals, will now be indicated.

Ordination

Theoretically, training for ordination began as soon as one entered the Sangha as a novice, but whether or not one actually received such training depended on the quality of one's home temple, that is, the temple of the monk from whom one received tonsure. Traditionally, because the imperial government only allowed a limited number of large public monasteries to offer ordination, thereby controlling the number of those who could escape conscription and/or avoid taxes, these institutions came to specialize in that service. And smaller, private temples were the places at which monks were trained before ordination and to which many afterward returned to live out their days. Because private temples (*tzu-sun miao; zi-sun miao,* lit. "son and grandson temples") belonged to the religious families that ran them, not to the Sangha as a whole, they varied greatly in quality. At a good one, novices would spend most of their time learning about the rituals, chanting and meditative procedures, sacred texts, and monastic etiquette that would later be their stock in trade. At a bad one, they were likely to learn only how to do the menial tasks necessary to keep up the temple property and the ritual methods necessary to help earn money for their master. Even recently, although the original reasons for keeping the two kinds of monastic institutions separate disappeared in 1911 with the end of imperial rule, it has remained the case that the largest and most reputable monasteries have carried out the great majority of ordinations.

Thus, leaving his home temple, a novice headed for a major monastery at which he would join dozens or even hundreds of others for ordination rites carried out over a period of several weeks. Where these rites were taken seriously, they would constitute quite an initiatory ordeal for the novice. This meant, first of all, that his monkly behavior would have to be brought up to the standards of the ordaining monastery in every respect. What this involved earlier in this century at the famous Pao-hua Shan (Bao-hua Shan) monastery of Nanking has been described by Holmes Welch as follows:

> During the first two weeks, those who were becoming monks and nuns—the clerical ordinands—studied how to eat, how to dress, how to lie when sleeping, how to make their beds, how to pack their belongings for a journey, how to stand and walk, how to enter the great shrine-hall, how to make a prostration to the buddha image, how to receive guests, how to hand over the duty (as a duty monk in the meditation hall, for example), and so on. Most of them had already learned most of this from their tonsure master while being trained in their small temple. But Pao-hua Shan put a high polish on the perfection of their deportment. . . . Besides deportment the ordinands during these first two weeks studied certain texts, in particular the fifty-three gathas and mantras. These were sentences that a monk was supposed to recite mentally on various occasions each day (when getting out of bed, drinking water, hearing the large bell, and so on).

> After deportment and texts had been mastered, there came a night of repentance and purification during which all the ordinands—lay as well as clerical—prostrated themselves in the great shrine-hall. On the following day the first ordination was held.[16]

With the first ordination, the status of the clerical ordinands did not actually change, for they simply reiterated their taking refuge in the Three Jewels and formally accepted their vows of abstinence as novice monks.[17] At the second ordination, after another couple of weeks of intensive study, they gathered again to take the more advanced vows of the Pratimoksa (two-hundred and fifty rules of Hinayāna discipline), the entire content of which was read to them as they knelt for hours. Yet it was the third ordination, involving the acceptance of the Bodhisattva Vows (promising in every way to secure the enlightenment of all other sentient beings before oneself), that seems to have taken the most courage. For on the day before these vows were taken, all the ordinands knelt to have their heads marked with the scars by which one may so easily identify any ordained monk or nun in China. The marks (usually totaling nine or twelve) are made by small cones of incense placed horizontally in lines of three between the forehead and the crown. These incense cones are allowed to burn to the scalp as the ordinand tries valiantly to chant sacred verses in an effort to overcome the pain.

Monastic Study and Service

Having completed this ordeal and taken his final set of vows, the novice was given his ordination certificate and could set out in a variety of different directions in beginning his monastic career. Going back to his home temple and tonsure master was a common option. There he would be welcome and secure, could gradually make progress toward the goals of Buddhist religious life, and even be able to earn some personal funds by performing rites for the dead on behalf of the temple's lay clientele. Money earned could be used for travel, books, and personal items, or it might be saved for future investment in a temple of his own. The ambitious monk who took the latter course, saving personal funds as well as seeking donations from the lay community, would be in a position to have his own base for spreading the Dharma and establishing his own family of tonsure disciples.

He could earn a similar kind of career security and reputation, by other means, within a large public monastery. There he could work his way up from the lowest rank of monk doing menial tasks to the position of abbot leading the whole monastery. Of course, this would take talent and hard work, since only one well advanced in his knowledge and experi-

---

[16] Welch, pp. 287–289; reprinted by permission. Copyright © 1967 by the President and Fellows of Harvard College.

[17] The vows of a Buddhist monk, the first five of which formal lay Buddhists also accept, consist of abstinence from (1) killing, (2) stealing, (3) adultery, (4) lying, (5) drinking alcohol, (6) perfumes and flowers, (7) singing and dancing, (8) using a large (comfortable) bed, (9) taking regular meals, and (10) acquiring personal valuables.

FIGURE 7.3. Buddhist monks in ceremonial robes reciting scriptures for client's ancestors during the week of Ch'ing Ming. Charity Monastery, Taichung, Taiwan.

ence of scriptures, rituals, meditation, and administrative procedures had a chance to reach high office. Yet anyone who made normal progress up the administrative ladder would be comfortable and well established by the time he reached his declining years. Thus, without taking the more entrepreneurial route of the monk who owned a private temple, he too could be assured of material security. However, in neither case was this understood to be a monk's goal in life, which was rather to spread the Dharma and gain release from the torments of material existence.

Now, to spread the Dharma, one first had to learn it well, and this meant studying it with the best masters. Thus, despite the fact that a monk had become the tonsure disciple of a certain master, he could study the Dharma under any more renowned master who would accept him as a Dharma disciple (by virtue of which he also entered another religious family). In fact, since many masters became experts in only one part of the voluminous Buddhist canon and store of practical exercises, it was advisable for a monk to learn from more than one master. And, of course, this also meant traveling to different parts of China and experiencing life in other monasteries, which had its own appeal.

Travel and Asceticism

A monk who was not a pilgrim relinquished one of the great opportunities of religious life in China. For any ordained monk with enough money saved to make it between large public monasteries, in which he was given free lodging, could do more traveling in his lifetime than the average Chinese would have dreamed of doing. Such wandering was, in fact, a legitimate part of the Buddhist religious quest: an adventure symbolic of nonattachment.

But traveling between monasteries was hardly the ultimate in Buddhist spiritual detachment. A monk seeking further detachment could go to shut himself off from the world as a hermit. Ideally, this meant putting up with the most meager and lonely possible existence, dwelling in a mountain cave or hut and living on what could be foraged from the surrounding environment. Actually, it usually included visits from supporters bearing both food and spiritual encouragement. Therefore, roughly the same result could be achieved by the more common practice of "sealed confinement" (*pi-kuan; bi-guan*) in a room on the monastery grounds. This usually began with a formal ceremony to which friends and lay supporters were invited to hear a declaration concerning the period of confinement's nature and length (commonly three years) and to witness the sealing of the door to the confinement room.[18] Such a declaration would indicate the purpose of the confinement by stating specifically what religious exercises would be performed during its course.

What were some of these exercises? Whether during sealed confinements or the course of daily monastic life, the most characteristic ones were study, chanting, and meditation. Study was previously discussed in connection with a monk's search for Dharma masters after ordination. As for chanting and meditation, they complemented study by allowing the monk to turn off his discriminating mind, to go beyond a superficial intellectual grasp of the Buddhist Dharma, and to experience directly the spiritual aims of which the Dharma spoke. While both chanting and meditation could thus lead to the same result, it is meditation that was widely recognized as the most efficacious exercise for spiritual cultivation.

Meditation

Of course, it was the Ch'an (Meditation) School that has become most closely identified with meditative practice in China, as in Japan (where it is called Zen), and now in the West. In one form of Ch'an practice, efforts to experience directly what the texts refer to as one's "Buddha-nature" were facilitated by the use of a meditative aid called the *hua-t'ou* (lit. "head of the words"). *Hua-t'ou* are key statements from the "public cases" (*kung-an; gong-an*) that concern famous exchanges between former masters and their disciples. Now, from one point of view, a *hua-t'ou* is actually an obstruction rather than an aid. That is to say, its aim is to obstruct one's faith in false intellectual security and drive one to behold something more fundamental, an indescribable feeling of doubt out of which may arise a direct experience of Buddha-nature. Master Hsu-yun (Xu-yun, d. 1959), modern China's most renowned Ch'an teacher, once used the example

---

[18] See Welch, pp. 321–322, for a more complete description.

of the *hua-t'ou* "Who is repeating Buddha's name" (when one recites sacred verses)? He then offered the following instructions concerning its use:

> When one looks into hua-t'ou, the most important thing is to give rise to a doubt. Doubt is the crutch of hua-t'ou. For instance, when one is asked: "Who is repeating Buddha's name?" everybody knows that he himself repeats it, but is it repeated by the mouth or by the mind? If the mouth repeats it why does not it do so when one sleeps? If the mind repeats it, what does the mind look like? As mind is intangible, one is not clear about it. Consequently some slight feeling of doubt arises about "WHO." The doubt should not be coarse; the finer it is, the better. At all times and in all places, this doubt alone should be looked into unremittingly, like an ever-flowing stream, without giving rise to a second thought. If this doubt persists, do not try to shake it; if it ceases to exist, one should gently give rise to it again. Beginners will find the hua-t'ou more effective in some still place than amidst disturbance. However, one should not give rise to a discriminating mind; one should remain indifferent to either the effectiveness or ineffectiveness (of the hua-t'ou) and should take no notice of either stillness or disturbance. Thus, one should work at the training with singleness of mind.[19]

Two things of special note in this passage are its admonition to look into the doubt arising in meditation "at all times and in all places" and its reference to one's need to "work" at this.

Ch'an Buddhism takes seriously the need for continual meditative concentration, regardless of whether one is actually sitting in meditation or doing one's other daily activities. It does not conceive of meditation as a kind of comfortable mental bliss, but rather as "work." Paradoxically, however, this is a kind of work adversely affected by intellectual effort or even the desire to experience Buddha-nature, which is one's ostensible goal. Reminiscent of the way of Lao Tzu, it is more a matter of casting things off than adding them on to oneself, as is suggested by another of Master Hsu-yun's instructions, as follows, on "laying down (the burden of) thinking":

> We only have to lay down everything, day or night, no matter whether we walk, stand, sit or recline, in the midst of either stillness or disturbance, and whether busy or not; throughout our bodies, within and without, there should be only a doubt, a uniform, harmonizing, and continuous doubt, unmixed with any other thought. . . . If there be fear of false thinking, this fear will increase false thinking. If there be awareness of purity, this purity will immediately be impure. If there be fear of falling into non-existence, there will immediately be a fall into existence. If there be desire to attain Buddhahood, there will immediately be a fall into the way of demons. (For this reason) it is said: "The carrying of water and fetching of firewood are nothing but the wonderful Truth. The hoeing of fields and the cultivation of soil are entirely Ch'an potentialities." This does not mean that only the crossing of legs for sitting in meditation can be regarded as Ch'an training in the performance of one's religious duty.[20]

[19] Quoted in Charles Luk (Lu K'uan Yu), *Ch'an and Zen Teaching: First Series* (Berkeley: Shambala, 1970), p. 38; reprinted by permission of Shambala Publications, Inc., P.O. Box 271, Boulder, Colo. 80305. All rights reserved.

[20] Luk, p. 45; reprinted by permission of Shambala Publications, Inc.

Now much of the distinctiveness of Chinese Buddhism lies precisely in this attitude that the quest for spiritual enlightenment must occur within the context of ordinary life rather than in any effort to escape from it. Having its source in the world-affirming nature of China's native traditions—Confucianism and Taoism—this same attitude is probably also responsible for the familylike character of Chinese monastic life. As we saw previously, its familylike character was immediately evident to a young novice monk just entering the Sangha, and, as we will now see, this was also evident to a senior monk nearing the end of his days in the Sangha.

Old Age and Death

Coming to the end of our description of a Buddhist monk's career in China, and thus to the topic of old age and death, we will see even more clearly how the monastic community there mirrored familial institutions. For just as the elders of a Chinese family were supported by their offspring in old age and received offerings from them as ancestors, so did senior monks depend on the pre- and post-death care of the following generation. While members of lay society were honored in old age and given the most comfortable retirement a family could afford, old monks had perhaps an even more enviable status. Not only did a monk's advanced years give him a right to the standard measure of care and honor, but it also gave evidence of his sanctity and, when supplemented by a truly successful religious career, could make him a "living Buddha" in the eyes of Buddhist laypersons. For as ironic as it may seem against the background of Buddhist doctrine about the emptiness of material success, reaching an old age and building a large "family" around oneself were in China considered just as worthy of worship within Buddhism as outside it. And as in life, so in death. Consider the following remarks by Holmes Welch concerning the death of a Chinese Buddhist monk:

> It was the hope of the monk, as of the layman, to die "at home" surrounded by his "family" of brothers and disciples. If so, it was they who arranged for the mortuary rites and for the disposition of his effects. If a monk fell ill at a public monastery with none of his "family" at hand, the guest department would obtain medical treatment and have a penance cited to assist his recovery. If death came it made all the necessary arrangements. . . . If a monk died in a small temple, as most monks did, he would be as solicitously provided for by his disciples as the father of a family in lay life. If he died at a large public monastery where he served in a high office, his associates made sure that his obsequies were duly performed, regardless of his personal wealth. That is, his soul tablet would be placed on an altar in the great shrine-hall with offerings of fruit, rice, and vegetarian dishes. All the monks of the monastery would recite the Maitreya Penance, the Maitreya Hymn, and the name of Amitabha. The merit created thereby would serve to speed the deceased to the Western Paradise.[21]

---

[21] Welch, pp. 340–341; reprinted by permission. Copyright © 1967 by the President and Fellows of Harvard College.

All these details again remind us that, after "leaving the family" to become a monk in China, one found oneself in what was in many ways a familiar environment. But we should never overlook the fact that, despite its compromises with Chinese familism, monasticism has been a reluctantly granted and skeptically viewed exception within the fabric of China's social life, far less accepted there than, for example, in India—the land of Buddhism's birth.

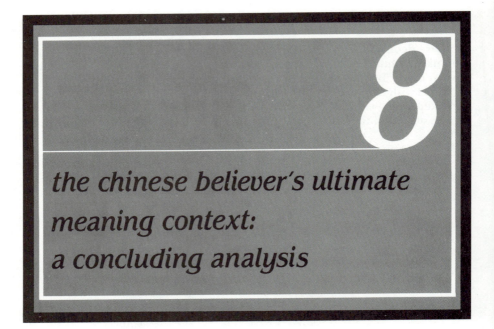

the chinese believer's ultimate meaning context: a concluding analysis

This book began with the image of a woman standing before the altar in a neighborhood temple, preparing to ask the god for some personal advice. Now we should have a better idea of what she, as an average believer within Chinese religion, may have thought or felt at that moment. At least, we should have a better understanding of the *context* within which her thoughts and feelings would occur. For her, as for any devout religious believer, this is a context of ultimate meaning: a system of beliefs, values, and behavioral guidelines with which she can understand her world and know how to act within it (see Chapter 1). What, finally, do we know about the system of ultimate meaning that shapes the thoughts and feelings of an average religious believer in China? To answer this question will be the purpose of our concluding analysis.

First of all, we know we can call it a "system" only with great hesitation. Not rooted in a systematic theology carefully worked out by church leaders and disseminated to rank and file members, it is a mixture of beliefs and practices that seems even to lack logical consistency. But balancing this fault, it does not easily engender doctrinal disputes or the inter-religious strife that might result from such disputes. For it does not insist on a single, verbal formulation of religious truth. While this virtue may be the result of omission rather than design in the case of Chinese folk religion, a number of Chinese philosophers have explicitly stressed that, while words may help point toward the truth, they should never be mistaken for the thing itself. Among the first to do so was the early Taoist thinker Chuang Tzu, who once made the following remark:

FIGURE 8.1. Woman preparing to worship at the Palace of Guidance, Taipei County, Taiwan.

The fish trap exists because of the fish; once you've gotten the fish, you can forget the trap. The rabbit snare exists because of the rabbit; once you've gotten the rabbit, you can forget the snare. Words exist because of meaning; once you've gotten the meaning, you can forget the words. Where can I find a man who has forgotten words so I can have a word with him?[1]

While Chuang Tzu may have thus wished to "converse" with someone who was beyond words, our hypothetical average believer would have to take a more practical approach in avoiding the trap of fixed doctrinal "truths," being allowed to do so by the multiplicity of religious alternatives in her environment.

Therefore, *secondly*, we must again stress the pluralistic nature of the world of Chinese religious life, with its relative lack of systematic doctrine at the theoretical level and its extremely pragmatic attitude at the behavioral level. Assuming, for example, that our hypothetical believer was standing in a Buddhist temple for the Boddhisattva Kuan-yin, we know this would not keep her from visiting a Ma-tsu or Kuan Kung temple on another occasion or, when she has a different type of spiritual problem, attending the séance of a medium who speaks the voice of yet another god. *Thirdly*, however, we can be sure that, whatever she does outside the home, she will observe the required religious obligations at the domestic altar in her home. For worship at this altar is the common denominator within the Chinese believer's ultimate meaning context—a symbol of the faith in familial ideals that permeates all Chinese religious life.

---

[1] Burton Watson, trans., *The Complete Works of Chuang Tzu* (New York: Columbia University Press, 1968), p. 302.

A CONTEMPORARY CASE

Assuming for the moment that the woman whom we have taken as our average Chinese religious believer lives in contemporary Taiwan, her religious environment is as alive, pluralistic, and changing as that of anyone living anywhere at any previous point in Chinese history. The same gods that were thanked by Taiwan's pioneers for safe passage across the sea now receive gratitude for the island's new found prosperity through industrialization. This can be seen, for example, in the virtual boom in temple construction over the past few decades. Moreover, the methods once used to assure divine protection from bandit raids and natural disasters are now used to maintain spiritual safety in the face of new ills.

For example, when the worst aviation disaster in Taiwan's history occurred, on August 22, 1981, its religious implications became a concern not only for relatives of those who died but also for airline and government officials. The plane having come apart in midair, its occupants were strewn over a lightly populated area of northwestern Taiwan. This created great concern about the location and identity of particular individuals' bodies, and as anyone who understands Chinese religion would expect, even greater concern about the status of their souls. Although a Buddhist "Dharma meeting for the salvation of (the victims') souls" was held at the disaster site, the officials responsible were severely criticized for the way it was handled and publicized. In the words of an irate relative of one of the victims: "If I hadn't gotten the information from the news, I would have missed this Dharma meeting for the salvation of souls. This Far Eastern Airlines disaster has already killed over a hundred people, must it still cause the deceased to go and become orphaned spirits or lost ghosts?"[2] Complaints such as this arose because people were at least as concerned about the spiritual consequences of the disaster as they were about its material causes, apparently somewhat to the surprise of officials.

On a happier subject, religious festivals continue to be as popular as before, although they too have conformed to the modern world in many ways. Invoking the gods to descend and honoring them with offerings and entertainment remains their key feature. Yet since it is believed they are pleased by essentially the same things that please people, the gods are now given the latest imported foods alongside more traditional dishes and entertained in startlingly modern fashion. This means, for example, that a religious procession is likely to contain floats with rock-and-roll bands, sparsely clad beauty queens, automatic fire-breathing dragons, or even a life-size figure of President Chiang Ching-kuo (Jiang Jing-guo) smiling and waving its mechanical hand at parade watchers. Such attractions are not only modern but also expensive. Their use is therefore further testimony to the fact that community temple activities continue to enjoy widespread support despite rapid industrialization and social change in Taiwan.

---

[2] *Chung-kuo shih-pao* ("China Times"), Taipei, August 27, 1981.

However, as in any era of social change, community religion must give way to other social forms of religion or, especially in the modern world, nonreligion. Those who leave their families and native villages to work or study in growing urban areas such as that of Taipei, for example, may find their religious interests best met by joining an organized religious group. Contemporary Taiwan certainly has an abundance of such groups, including not only ones representing Buddhism and other world religions (Islam, Hinduism, Protestantism, Catholicism) but also a plethora of lay sects which, as in prior Chinese history, form their doctrine by synthesizing a variety of native as well as foreign religious teachings. These lay sects may be Buddhist in name, such as the Red Swastika Society, first established in Peking in 1922, or have historical links to Buddhism, as with the Way of Pervading Unity, founded on the mainland during the mid-nineteenth century. Or they might appear at first sight to be Taoist, as in the case of the Religion of the Yellow Emperor, founded in Taiwan in 1957, which claims to represent this ancient sage and putative founder of many Taoist practices.[3] However, they seem to accept spiritual insight that comes from any source, as indicated by the fact that those among them who practice spirit writing are willing to receive messages not only from Kuan-yin or Kuan Kung but also from Jesus or Muhammad.

If asked why these lay sects hold to such an attitude, their members may respond with the Chinese proverb (adopted from a passage in the *Book of Changes*): "There are various paths but only one common goal" (*shu-t'u t'ung-kuei; shu-tu tong-guei*). If further questioned, they would be glad to explain that this is the goal of proper social behavior and individual spiritual growth toward which all religions aim. While the syncretic sects of contemporary Taiwan thus reveal a spiritual diversity unprecedented even within the Chinese religious environment, the continued strength of organized Buddhism there is equally impressive—if, indeed, "continued strength" is not an understatement. For Buddhism is now undergoing a major revival in the hands of many monks and nuns who left mainland China in the wake of the communist revolution, being helped by a highly educated young clergy and striving for a kind of unity and standardization in practice that was perhaps never before possible. At the same time, it is reaching out to potential lay converts through a whole new array of publications, lectures, and other activities.[4]

Thus, there is no lack of organizations to which the religious seeker in modern Taiwan may belong, although belonging seems to have a different meaning there than in most Western religious contexts. That is, belonging lacks the kind of exclusive identification with a religion that exists for a Westerner who says, for example, "I am a Catholic," a "Jew," a "Baptist," or even a "Zen Buddhist." Moreover, as in the West, there

---

[3] The reader with further interest in these groups may refer, among other sources, to the Index in Daniel L. Overmyer, *Folk Buddhist Religion: Dissenting Sects in Late Traditional China* (Cambridge, Mass.: Harvard University Press, 1976).

[4] On this, see, for example, Hsing Fu-ch'üan, *A Survey of Public and Popular Buddhism and Buddhist Temples in Taiwan* (Taipei: Pacific Cultural Foundation, 1983).

are now many secular agnostics in Taiwan who reject all forms of religion. Yet they are more likely than their Western counterparts to maintain traditional marriage, funeral, and related rituals in some form. They are willing to participate in these rituals, and perhaps others that they consider plainly superstitious (especially if pressed by family members), first, because of the time-honored status of such activities and, second, because they consider it better to do so than to cause dissention or hurt others' feelings. Does this, along with other facts already mentioned, indicate a lack of discrimination and seriousness in matters of religion among the Chinese? Or is it as simple as this?

A LASTING IDEAL

In 1895, after twenty-three years in Taiwan, George Leslie Mackay, the "missionary hero of the Presbyterian Church in Canada," in whose name is now dedicated one of Taipei's finest modern hospitals, recorded his experiences for posterity under the title *From Far Formosa*. A careful observer, Mackay recorded details about religion not too different from those presented in this text, yet he concluded from those details precisely that the Chinese lack discrimination and seriousness in their religion. Some of his views are worth quoting here, if only to indicate that the world of Chinese religion can appear confused and incomprehensible even to a seasoned (albeit biased) observer. Beginning with an observation about how China's "three systems" (Confucianism, Buddhism, and Taoism) coexist, these views are as follows:

> These three systems existed side by side until the dividing-walls began to crumble, and now the three are run together, a commingling of conflicting creeds, defiling life, and destroying all religious sentiment. . . . The Chinese in Formosa have innumerable gods and goddesses, many religious festivals, and countless superstitions that burden their life. The names of their idols would fill pages, and the details of their beliefs and worship volumes. There are gods having authority over each of the various powers of nature, departments of industry, relationships of life, states of feeling, physical conditions, and moral sentiments. . . . Many of the Chinese, especially the women, are devout worshipers; many others are skeptical, and the majority are careless. Idolatry has a powerful hold on their minds, but it is only when reverses and troubles come that the average man will resort to the temple. They believe the gods have power to help or to injure them, but so long as things go well they are careless about their devotions.[5]

Mackay thus saw the pluralistic, all-inclusive, and sometimes perfunctory nature of Chinese religious life as merely indicating inconsistency, insincerity, and lack of piety. But these views can be interpreted otherwise.

Outward behavior is easily misunderstood when one is unaware of its motivating ideal. When one looks for intellectual consistency, devotional intensity, sectarian loyalty, or an unwavering will in religious matters, Chi-

---

[5] George Leslie Mackay, *From Far Formosa*, 4th ed., J. A. Macdonald, ed. (New York: Fleming H. Revell Co., 1895), pp. 125–129.

nese spiritual life may in fact seem deficient. Without saying these are completely lacking in the Chinese case, none could be considered its root value. Instead, this role has been given to the *ideal of harmony*. Why, one may now ask, should an emphasis on harmony prevent a society from also esteeming any of the other values just mentioned? While it is true enough that, as an ideal, harmony would not necessarily come into conflict with such other values, the practical search for an actual state of harmony may well require their frequent sacrifice. In other words, the *practice* of harmony means *reconciliation*—in family life, in business, in personal affairs, and also in matters of religious belief. And the last of these may be the least important, since it can be taken to involve giving up only one's preference for a certain way of formulating truths that are, in the final analysis, beyond words. At a more important level, reconciliation also involves a certain attitude toward existence (as suggested by the phrase "reconciled to his lot in life"), which has often been misinterpreted as an "oriental spirit of resignation."

Now, in reconciling themselves to the natural order as a kind of universal destiny, and also to the demands of family and society, the Chinese have not all been living in hopeless resignation. Their attitude of reconciliation has been coupled with the faith that the world can and will be brought to its proper state of harmony. The most famous vision of this goal, an inspiration for both traditional philosophical commentaries and modern political slogans, is the following passage on the age of Grand Unity (*ta-t'ung; da-tong*) from the *Ritual Records:*

Once Confucius was taking part in the winter sacrifice. After the ceremony was over, he went for a stroll along the top of the city gate and sighed mournfully. He sighed for the state of Lu.

His disciple . . . asked: "Why should the gentleman sigh?"

Confucius replied: "The practice of the Great Way, the illustrious men of the Three Dynasties—these I shall never know in person. And yet they inspire my ambition! When the Great Way was practiced, the world was shared by all alike. The worthy and the able were promoted to office and men practiced good faith and lived in affection. Therefore they did not regard as parents only their own parents, or as sons only their own sons. The aged found a fitting close to their lives, the robust their proper employment; the young were provided with an upbringing and the widow and widower, the orphaned and the sick, with proper care. Men had their tasks and women their hearths. They hated to see goods lying about in waste, yet they did not hoard them for themselves; they disliked the thought that their energies were not fully used, yet they used them not for private ends. Therefore all evil plotting was prevented and thieves and rebels did not arise, so that people could leave their outer gates unbolted. This was the age of Grand Unity.[6]

It is most interesting and informative that Confucius is depicted as being moved to speak these words by taking part in a major state ceremony. For it is quite reasonable to suggest that a well-performed ceremony is a

[6] Wm. Theodore de Bary, et al., *Sources of Chinese Tradition*, Vol. 1 (New York: Columbia University Press, 1960), pp. 175–176.

perfect model of social harmony. Chinese society, often in actuality as well as in ideal form, brings to mind an image of a large-scale ceremony in which each participant relates to others according to his or her proper role, "acting" courteously so as to achieve a successful performance, whether or not inner emotions are in agreement. For society must maintain at least an apparent harmony, as if performing a dress rehearsal for the awaited future ideal.

In traditional China, there were also more immediate models of an ideal state of harmonious cooperation—the human body and the natural universe. And an important symbolic relationship was established between these two as microcosm and macrocosm. Therefore, it was an *organicistic world view* that shaped various forms of the Chinese understanding of the natural as well as social order. One of the first Western writers to fully appreciate this fact, the historian of science Joseph Needham, has particularly stressed two features of this "philosophy of organism," to use his phrase. The first, related to the concept of reconciliation just discussed, he states as follows:

> Not in human society only but throughout the world of Nature, there was a give and take, a kind of mutual courtesy rather than strife among inanimate powers and processes, a finding of solutions by compromise, of avoidance of mechanical force, and an acceptance of the inevitability of the birth and doom of every natural thing.

The second, related to the lack of a transcendent Creator God in Chinese conceptions of the universe, he explains in this description of the Chinese view of natural harmony:

> The harmonious cooperation of all beings arose, not from the orders of a superior authority external to themselves, but from the fact that they were all parts in a hierarchy of wholes forming a cosmic pattern, and what they obeyed were the internal dictates of their own natures.[7]

These passages, moreover, make it clear that the philosophy of organism is directly related to the harmony ideal. In fact, the former accounts for the possibility of the latter by positing that many diverse and dissimilar entities are capable of harmonious cooperation precisely because they *are* different in nature and function.

This is, then, the basis for an ideal that could most accurately be called *organismic harmony:* a multiplicity of parts, each making its unique and specific contribution to the functioning of a single whole. Of course, while a metaphysician like Lao Tzu could see the parts of this whole as all having equal status, they were more commonly viewed as having a hierarchical and concentric arrangement: some higher, some lower; some central, some peripheral. Like the human organism, each of the larger and more complex entities in the social and natural worlds had its "head,"

---

[7] Joseph Needham, *Science and Civilization in China*, Vol. II (Cambridge: Cambridge University Press, 1956), pp. 283–284 and 582.

essential "organs," and "appendages." Each part had its place within some larger whole, a microcosm within a macrocosm, the former functioning according to principles also operative at the level of the latter. Hence, the individual was located within the organism of the family, itself one unit in the clan organism, which was in turn one small part of the social body constituted by all Chinese. And this social body existed, or at least aimed to exist, in accordance with the ideal of harmonious cooperation that was perceived as prevailing in nature.

Glossary

(The two systems of Romanized Chinese terms used below are the Wade-Giles and the Pin-yin, as explained in the Preface. Here, for students of spoken Chinese, the numerals indicating the four tones of modern Mandarin are added to the Wade-Giles terms.)

Bodhisattva ideal of Mahāyāna (q.v.); a spiritual being of great power and merit who has voluntarily delayed attainment of Buddhahood so as better to give others compassionate aid.

Buddha one of Buddhism's Three Jewels (q.v.); a spiritual being who has attained total enlightenment and liberation (Buddhahood).

Ch'an²/Chan Buddhism the Meditation School; dominant form of monastic Buddhism in East Asia.

chieh²-ch'i⁴/jie-qi (lit. "nodes of the life force") dates of the Chinese farmer's almanac which divide the solar year into 24 equal parts.

ch'i⁴/qi nature's spiritual life force, permeating the physical universe and, with special significance for Chinese medicine and martial arts, the human body.

ching⁴-tso⁴/jing-zuo (lit. "quiet sitting") Neo-Confucian term for meditative practice.

Ch'ing¹ Ming²/Ching Ming (lit. "clear and bright") spring festival of grave cleaning and ancestral worship; fifth of the *chieh-ch'i* (q.v.).

ch'ing¹-t'an²/ching-tan (lit. "pure conversation") discussions untainted by worldly concerns and delving into abstruse problems, especially popular among nonconformists of the Period of Disunity.

ch'u¹-chia¹/chu-jia (lit. "leaving home") becoming a Buddhist monk or nun.

chün¹-tzu³/jun-zi the ideal Moral Gentleman within Confucian thought.

Dharma one of Buddhism's Three Jewels (q.v.); the Buddhist "law" or doctrine.

Dragon Boat Festival held on lunar 5/5, near the summer solstice, to celebrate and take precautions concerning summer's arrival; also called Double Fifth.

fang¹-shih⁴/fang-shi ritual specialists who served as doctors and magicians in ancient China; among predecessors of the later Taoist priesthood.

feng¹-shui³ (lit. "wind and water") geomancy; a system used to locate the best spiritual/physical site for building a home, tomb, temple, etc.

Hinayāna (lit. "lesser vehicle") the older and, according to Mahāyāna (q.v.), more conservative branch of Buddhism; dominant in much of South and Southeast Asia, where it is called Theravāda ("Way of the Elders").

hsiao⁴/xiao filiality; attitude of respect and concern toward parents and superiors.

hsien¹/xian someone who has become an immortal spiritual being (especially a Taoist Immortal).

jen²/ren (lit. "being humane") for Confucius, moral perfection in one's behavior toward others.

karma the moral law of cause and effect by which one reaps what one sows.

kuei³/guei (lit. "ghosts") pitiable and potentially malevolent spiritual beings.

k'ung¹/kong (lit. "empty"; *śunya* in Sanskrit) in Mahāyāna metaphysics, concept of the nonsubstantiality of all phenomena.

li³ (lit. "ritual") originally religious, the code of ceremonial behavior designated by this term was extended to every area of social life.

Mahāyāna (lit. "greater vehicle") in opposition to schools of Buddhism that it called Hinayāna (q.v.), it called for a broader definition of and greater lay involvement in the quest for salvation; dominant in Tibet, East Asia, and parts of Southeast Asia.

Mid-Autumn Festival held on lunar 8/15, at autumn harvest time, to "enjoy" and/or worship the moon; also called the Moon Festival.

nei⁴-tan¹/nei-dan (lit. "inner elixir") Taoist meditative practice in which "alchemical" processes are conceived as occurring inside the body at certain *tan-t'ien* (q.v.); contrasted with *wai-tan* (q.v.).

pai⁴-pai⁴/bai-bai (lit. "worship") offering incense, food, etc., to a god and bowing or making the appropriate prayerlike hand motions.

Pure Land Buddhism branch of East Asian Buddhism that emphasizes faith in the saving grace of Amitābha Buddha (who reigns over the Pure Land, a Buddhist "heaven") and stresses chanting such phrases as *na-mo a-mi-t'o-fo* ("praise to Amitābha Buddha") as a means to salvation.

p'u³ tu⁴/pu-du (lit. "universal crossing-over") a ceremony performed by Buddhist or Taoist ritualists during the seventh lunar month ("ghost month") to aid in the salvation of all helpless, bereaved spirits.

Sangha one of Buddhism's Three Jewels (q.v.); the Buddhist monastic community.

shen² (lit. "gods") honored and benevolent spiritual beings.

tan¹-t'ien²/dan-tian (lit. "alchemical fields") energy centers within the body that have a key role in Taoist meditative and martial art exercises.

Tao⁴/Dao (lit. "way") the metaphysical Way (Tao) of Nature (especially in Taoism); or the correct way to follow in human moral behavior (especially in Confucianism).

Te²/De (lit. "virtue") the conferment of Heaven (Confucian view) or Tao (Taoist view) which should be nurtured as the basis of one's ultimate potential.

Three Jewels "Buddha, Dharma, Sangha" (q.v.); three things in which one "takes refuge" in becoming a Buddhist layperson, monk, or nun.

T'ien¹/Tian (lit. "heaven"; "sky") supreme power or principle in the cosmos, sometimes with anthropomorphic qualities.

t'ien¹-shih¹/tian-shi (lit. "Celestial Master") highest office in the main branch of the Taoist priesthood; kept within the Chang family line since its inception with Chang Tao-ling of the Later Han Dynasty.

wai⁴-tan¹/wai-dan (lit. "external elixir") physical substance for the preservation of life sought by Taoist alchemists in their quest for immortality; contrasted with *nei-tan* (q.v.).

White Lotus Buddhism a syncretic lay religion which, a century or so after its Sung Dynasty beginnings, developed millenarian tendencies in connection with belief in the imminent arrival of the future Buddha, Maitreya.

wu³-hsing²/wu-xing (lit. "five phases") the elemental phases of all natural processes represented by the five terms wood, fire, earth, metal, and water.

wu²-wei² (lit. "without action") the Taoist ideal of nonaction; completely spontaneous behavior, devoid of all purposeful acts.

yang² the active, incipient, transforming phase of any natural cycle; associated with Heaven, sun, light, heat, male, dry, daytime, etc.

yin¹ the passive, quiescent, settling phase of any natural cycle; associated with Earth, moon, dark, cold, female, wet, nighttime, etc.

Bibliography

INTRODUCTORY STUDIES

Bauer, Wolfang. *China and the Search for Happiness*. Trans. Michael Shaw. New York: Seabury Press, 1976.

Smith, D. Howard. *Chinese Religions from 1000 b.c. to the Present Day*. New York: Holt, Rinehart & Winston, 1968.

Thompson, Laurence G. *Chinese Religion: An Introduction*. 3rd ed. Belmont, Calif.: Wadsworth Publishing Co., Inc., 1979.

Yang, C. K. *Religion in Chinese Society*. Berkeley and Los Angeles: University of California Press, 1961.

SOURCEBOOKS AND REFERENCE WORKS

Chan, Wing-tsit. *A Sourcebook in Chinese Philosophy*. Princeton: Princeton University Press, 1963.

DeBary, W. T., et al. *Sources of Chinese Tradition*, 2 vols. New York: Columbia University Press, 1960.

Doré, Henri. *Researches into Chinese Superstitions*, 11 vols. (of 18 vols. in French original). Shanghai, 1914–1933; rpt. Taipei: Ch'eng Wen Publ., 1966–1967.

Fung Yu-lan. *A History of Chinese Philosophy*. Trans. Derk Bodde, 2 vols. Princeton: Princeton University Press, 1952–1953.

Groot, J. J. M. de. *The Religious System of China*, 6 vols. Leiden: E. J. Brill, 1892–1910; rpt. Taipei: Nan T'ien Book Co., 1982.

Needham, Joseph. *Science and Civilization in China*, 5 vols. Cambridge: Cambridge University Press, 1954– (in progress).

Thompson, Laurence G. *The Chinese Way in Religion*. Encino, Calif.: Dickenson Publishing Co., Inc., 1973.

_____. *Chinese Religion in Western Languages: A Comprehensive and Classified Bibliography of Publications in English, French, and German Through 1980*. Tucson: University of Arizona Press, 1985.

CONFUCIANISM: CLASSICAL SCRIPTURES

(Also see Chan, DeBary, and Fung as listed above.)

Karlgren, Bernhard, trans. "The Book of Documents." *Bulletin of The Museum of Far Eastern Antiquities*, 1950.

_____, trans. *The Book of Odes*. Stockholm: Museum of Far Eastern Antiquities, 1950.

Lau, D. C., trans. *Confucius: The Analects*. Baltimore: Penguin Books, 1979.

_____, trans. *Mencius*. Baltimore: Penguin Books, 1970.

Legge, James, trans. *The Chinese Classics*, 5 vols. Hong Kong: Hong Kong University Press, 1960. The contents and original publ. dates of each volume follow.

Vol. 1 (1861, revised 1893): *Confucian Analects, The Great Learning,* and *The Doctrine of the Mean;* Vol. 2 (1861, revised 1895): *The Works of Mencius;* Vol. 3 (1865): *The Book of Historical Documents;* Vol. 4 (1871): *The Book of Poetry;* Vol. 5 (1872): *The Ch'un Ts'ew with the Tso Chuen* ["Spring and Autumn Annals with the Commentary of Tso"].

——————————, trans. *Li Chi: Book of Rites.* Ed. Ch'u Chai and Winberg Chai. New Hyde Park, N. Y.: University Books, 1967; first publ. 1885.

STEELE, JOHN, trans. *The I-Li or Book of Etiquette and Ceremonial,* 2 vols. London: Probsthain, 1917.

WILHELM, RICHARD, trans. *The I Ching or Book of Changes.* Bollingen Series 19, 2nd ed. New York: Pantheon, 1964.

CONFUCIANISM: STATE RELIGION AND POST-CLASSICAL THOUGHT

BILSKY, LESTER JAMES. *The State Religion of Ancient China,* 2 vols. Taipei: Orient Culture Service, 1976.

CHAN WING-TSIT, trans. *Reflections on Things at Hand: The Neo-Confucian Anthology Compiled by Chu Hsi and Lü Tsu-ch'ien.* New York: Columbia University Press, 1967.

CHANG, CARSON. *The Development of Neo-Confucian Thought,* 2 vols. New York: Book-man Associates, 1957 and 1962.

CHING, JULIA. *To Acquire Wisdom: The Way of Wang Yang-ming.* New York: Columbia University Press, 1976.

DEBARY, WM. THEODORE. *Neo-Confucian Orthodoxy and the Learning of the Heart-and-Mind.* New York: Columbia University Press, 1981.

MEYER, JEFFREY F. *Peking as a Sacred City.* Taipei: Orient Culture Service, 1976.

SHRYOCK, JOHN K. *The Origin and Development of the State Cult of Confucius.* New York and London: Century, 1932; rpt. New York: Paragon, 1966.

WILLIAMS, E. T. "The State Religion of China During the Manchu Dynasty." *Journal of the North China Branch of the Royal Asiatic Society,* 44 (1913), pp. 11–45.

TAOISM

GRAHAM, A. C., trans. *Chuang-tzu: The Seven Inner Chapters and Other Writings from the Book Chuang-tzu.* London: Allen and Unwin, 1981.

LAU, D. C., trans. *Lau Tzu: Tao Te Ching.* Baltimore: Penguin Books, 1963.

MASPERO, HENRI. *Taoism and Chinese Religion.* Trans. Frank A. Kierman, Jr. Amherst, Mass.: University of Massachusetts Press, 1981.

RAWSON, PHILLIP AND LASZLO LEGEZA. *Tao, The Eastern Philosophy of Time and Change.* New York: Avon Books, 1973.

SASO, MICHAEL R. *Taoism and the Rite of Cosmic Renewal.* Pullman, Wa.: Washington State University Press, 1972.

SEIDEL, ANNA AND HOLMES WELCH, eds. *Facets of Taoism: Essays in Chinese Religion.* New Haven: Yale University Press, 1979.

WELCH, HOLMES. *Taoism: The Parting of the Way.* Boston: Beacon Press, 1965.

BUDDHISM

BLOFELD, JOHN. *The Jewel in the Lotus: An Outline of Present Day Buddhism in China.* London: The Buddhist Society, 1948.

CHANG CHENG-CHI. *The Practice of Zen.* London: Rider and Co., 1960.

CH'EN, KENNETH K. S. *Buddhism in China: A Historical Survey.* Princeton: Princeton University Press, 1964.

LAI, WHALEN AND LEWIS R. LANCASTER. *Early Ch'an in China and Tibet.* Berkeley: Asian Humanities Press, 1983.

PRIP-MØller, J. *Chinese Buddhist Monasteries: Their Plan and Its Function as a Setting for Buddhist Monastic Life.* New York: Oxford University Press, 1937; rpt. Hong Kong, 1967.

WELCH, HOLMES. *The Practice of Chinese Buddhism,* 1900–1950. Cambridge, Mass.: Harvard University Press, 1967.

WRIGHT, ARTHUR F. *Buddhism in Chinese History.* Stanford: Stanford University Press, 1959.

Yü, Chün-fang. *The Renewal of Buddhism in China: Chu-hung and the Late Ming Synthesis.* New York: Columbia University Press, 1981.

POPULAR RELIGION AND RELATED TOPICS

AHERN, EMILY M. *The Cult of the Dead in a Chinese Village.* Stanford: Stanford University Press, 1973.

BODDE, DERK. *Festivals in Classical China.* Princeton: Princeton University Press, 1975.

BURKHARDT, V. R. *Chinese Creeds and Customs,* 3 vols. Hong Kong: South China Morning Post, Ltd., 1953–1958.

ELLIOT, ALAN J. A. *Chinese Spirit Medium Cults in Singapore.* London: London School of Economics and Political Science, 1955.

GROOT, J. J. M. DE. *Sectarianism and Religious Persecution in China,* 2 vols. Leiden: E. J. Brill, 1901; rpt. Taipei, 1963.

HSU, FRANCIS L. K. *Under the Ancestors' Shadow.* New York: Columbia University Press, 1948.

JORDON, DAVID K. *Gods, Ghosts, and Ancestors: The Folk Religion of a Taiwanese Village.* Berkeley: University of California Press, 1972.

OVERMYER, DANIEL L. *Folk Buddhist Religion: Dissenting Sects in Late Traditional China.* Cambridge, Mass.: Harvard University Press, 1976.

WOLF, ARTHUR P., ed. *Religion and Ritual in Chinese Society.* Stanford: Stanford University Press, 1974.

MODERN TRENDS

BUSH, RICHARD C., JR. *Religion in Communist China.* Nashville and New York: Abingdon Press, 1970.

CHAN, WING-TSIT. *Religious Trends in Modern China.* New York: Columbia University Press, 1953.

MacINNIS, DONALD E. *Religious Policy and Practice in Communist China.* New York: Macmillan, Inc., 1972.

THOMPSON, LAURENCE G.   "Notes on Religious Trends in Taiwan." *Monumenta Serica,* 23 (1964), pp. 319–349.

WELCH, HOLMES.   *The Buddhist Revival in China.* Cambridge, Mass.: Harvard University Press, 1968.

————————. *Buddhism under Mao.* Cambridge, Mass.: Harvard University Press, 1972.

Index

Shen Pu-hai (Shen Bu-hai), 37
Shen Tao (Shen Tao), 37–38
Sheng (sage), 50. See also Sages
Shih (shi: knight, scholar), 34
Shih (shi: phenomenon), 46, 50
Shih (shi: position, situation), 38
Shryock, John, 48
Shu-ching (Shu-jing). See Book of History
Shun, Emperor, 6, 26, 112–113, 116, 125–126
Silent Maiden (Lin), 151. See also Ma-tsu
Simplicity, 132
Sirén, Osvald, 98–99
Six Receptacles, 69
Sixth Patriarch Cutting Bamboo, 98 (illus.)
Sociological expression, 5, 16, 20–22, 157–181
Son of Heaven, 21, 29, 58, 62, 64–67, 91, 144, 148, 158, 160
Soul. See Hun and p'o
Specifically religious groups, 41, 162–163
Spirit, 69
Spirit medium. See shamans and spirit mediums
Spirits of Land and Grain, 29, 146–147
Spiritual dimension, 3, 5–6, 10, 17
Spontaneity, 132
Spring and Autumn Annals, 33, 36, 64–65
Spring Planting Ceremony, 40
Spring Silk Cultivation Ceremony, 40
Ssu-ma Ch'ien (Si-ma Qian), 61
Sui Dynasty, 44–49
Sullivan, Michael, 96–97
Sun Wu-k'ung. See Monkey
Sung (Song), ancient state, 120, 122
Sung (Song) Dynasty, 7, 24, 49–52, 119
Sung T'ai-tsu (Song Tai-zu), Emperor, 115
Supreme One, 38
Supremely Exalted Lord Lao, 116. See also Lao Tzu
Supreme Ultimate, diagram of, 19 (illus.)
Suzuki, D. T., 97

TABLETS, ANCESTRAL AND COMMEMORATIVE, 48–49, 159, 167–168, 171, 173–174, 180
Ta-hsueh (Da-xue). See Great Learning
T'ai-chi (Tai-ji). See Supreme Ultimate
T'ai-hsu (Tai-xu), 54
Taiping Rebellion, 55, 60
T'ai-tsung (Tai-zong), Emperor, 48–49, 52, 102
Taiwan, 57–58, 70, 119, 139, 142, 150–156, 184–186
T'ai-yi (Tai-yi). See Supreme One
T'ai-yi sect. See Taoism
Tales of the World, 72
Tamer of Oxen. See Fu Hsi
T'ang Dynasty, 44–49, 102, 115
T'ang San-tsang (Tang San-zang). See Hsuan-tsang
Tao (Dao: way), 8, 103, 114, 118, 123–124, 127–134
Taoism
  brief overview, 8–10
  Ch'üan-chen (Quan-zhen) sect, 53

Taoism (continued)
  history, 36, 40–42, 44, 47, 52–53, 57–58, 60, 68–76
  immortality, 9, 47, 68–71, 73, 75–76
  Ling Pao (Ling Bao) sect, 42, 73, 116
  liturgical dimension, 9–10, 42, 53
  Mao Shan sect, 42, 47, 73, 116
  meditation, 9, 36–37, 71, 76, 133
  mystical dimension, 9–10, 42, 53, 71, 75–76, 133
  priests, 9, 15, 20, 73, 78, 118, 140, 142–143, 168
  rituals, 9–10, 20, 42, 47, 70, 142–143
  scriptures. See Taoist Canon
  T'ai-yi (Tai-yi) sect, 53
  Way of Celestial Masters sect, 42, 53, 117
Taoist Canon, 115–117
Tao-te-ching (Dao-de-jing), 8, 47, 114, 116–117, 127–134
Tao-t'ung (dao-tong). See Transmission of the true Way
Ta-t'ung (da-tong). See Grand Unity
Te (De: virtue), 8, 122, 126, 128
Temple of Agriculture, 148
Temple of Confucius, 3, 48–49, 79 (illus.), 159
Temples, 2 (illus.), 3, 49, 79, 86 (illus.), 100 (illus.), 160–161, 175–177, 182–183. See also Architecture; Palace of Audience; Temple of Agriculture; Temple of Confucius
Theoretical expression, 5, 16–19, 110–134
Theravāda. See Buddhism: Hinayāna
Thompson, Laurence, 117, 168
Thousand-league Eyes, 155
Three Fields (alchemical), 69–71
Three Heavens, 69
Three Jewels, 174, 176
Three Kingdoms Period, 13
Three Palaces, 69–70
Three Sovereigns, 24, 26, 117
Three Teachings, 5, 15–16, 20, 22, 44, 114, 117, 186
Three Teachings Religion, 52
Three Vermin, 69–71
T'ien (Tian). See Heaven
T'ien-li (Tian-li). See Heavenly Principle
T'ien-shih (Tian-shi). See Celestial Master
T'ien-t'ai. See Buddhism
Ti-tsang. See Bodhisattva
Tradition, great and little, 5, 15 (illus.), 19, 42, 110
Transcendence, 40–41, 68, 83
Transmission of Dharma, or of mind, 46, 49
Transmission of political rule, 49
Transmission of the true Way, 49
Treatise of the Most Exalted One on Moral Retribution, The, 56
"Treatise on Why Buddhist Clerics Need Not Pay Obeisance to Kings," 84
Trigrams, Eight, 33
Trinity (of Heaven, Earth, and Man), 66
Tripitaka, 102–103, 105–109, 115–116
Tsao Chün (Zao Jun). See Lord of the Stove
Tseng Tzu (Zeng Zi), 80
Tso-chuan (Zuo-zhuan). See Commentary of Tso